RACIAL ALTERITY, WIXARIKA YOUTH ACTIVISM, AND THE RIGHT TO THE MEXICAN CITY

DIANA NEGRÍN

RACIAL ALTERITY, WIXARIKA YOUTH ACTIVISM, AND THE RIGHT TO THE MEXICAN CITY

THE UNIVERSITY OF
ARIZONA PRESS
TUCSON

The University of Arizona Press
www.uapress.arizona.edu

We respectfully acknowledge the University of Arizona is on the land and territories of Indigenous peoples. Today, Arizona is home to twenty-two federally recognized tribes, with Tucson being home to the O'odham and the Yaqui. Committed to diversity and inclusion, the University strives to build sustainable relationships with sovereign Native Nations and Indigenous communities through education offerings, partnerships, and community service.

© 2019 by The Arizona Board of Regents
All rights reserved. Published 2019
First paperback edition published 2024

ISBN-13: 978-0-8165-4001-3 (cloth)
ISBN-13: 978-0-8165-5530-7 (paper)
ISBN-13: 978-0-8165-4059-4 (ebook)

Cover design by Leigh McDonald

Publication of this book is made possible in part by the proceeds of a permanent endowment created with the assistance of a Challenge Grant from the National Endowment for the Humanities, a federal agency.

Library of Congress Cataloging-in-Publication Data are available at the Library of Congress.

Printed in the United States of America
♾ This paper meets the requirements of ANSI/NISO Z39.48-1992 (Permanence of Paper).

For Juan and Yvonne Negrín for setting me on this journey.

Para ne yau Juan por enseñarme a hacer campo y a escribir.

For Plinio, Iyari, and Julián for accompanying me.

Y para los universitarios wixaritari, ¡qué sigan floreciendo!

CONTENTS

List of Illustrations   ix
Acknowledgments   xi
List of Abbreviations   xv

Introduction: Negotiating Expectations, Articulating Identities in Urban Mexico   3

1. The Long Arc of Indigenismo: Mapping Vision, Race, and Nation   22
2. Acción Indigenista and the Development of Wixarika Territory   51
3. Tepic: City of Inclusion, City of Exclusion   85
4. Guadalajara de Indias: Searching for the Right to the City   118
5. Makuyeika: She Who Walks in Many Places   150

Conclusion: Walking Together   183

Notes   191
References   201
Index   215

LIST OF ILLUSTRATIONS

1. Map of Mexico, with locations of Guadalajara, Tepic, and Mexico City 2
2. Juan Ríos Martínez, *Visions of the Blue Deer, Tamatsí Maxayuawi* 4
3. Porfirio Díaz and Venustiano Carranza pose before the Aztec Calendar stone 27
4. Various Wixarika artists, *Vochol* 80
5. Ernest Louet, *Souvenirs de la Campagne du Mexique de 1861–1867* 101
6. Yacht club billboards in Cruz de Huanacaxtle 111
7. Rebeca Iturbide and unknown models pose in Wixarika attire 115
8. *Detalle de plano de la Nueva Galicia de Hernán Martínez de la Marcha, Compostela, 1550–1551* 125
9. *La colonia*, cartoon by Pancho Madrigal 128
10. Antonio Hayuaneme García demonstrating during Guadalajara's celebration of International Indigenous Peoples' Day 146
11. Mixtec, Wixarika, and Tzeltal students at the International Day of Mother Tongues 175

ACKNOWLEDGMENTS

IN MANY ways, the present book has been incubating from the moment I gained consciousness, or at least since my earliest memories in the Wixarika community of Tuapurie, in the highlands of northern Jalisco. I must have been three years old, and in my vague recollection, we were arriving to somebody's ranch. More vivid than this visual recollection is the memory of the scent of wood burning and tortillas cooking on the traditional clay comal. A decade would pass until my return to Tuapurie alongside my father. The smell of wood and tortillas suddenly brought me back to my first years of life, when our family spent extended periods at the ranches of their Wixarika *compadres* and *comadres*. I was now fourteen, and three years had passed since my mother, my sisters, and I had moved to the San Francisco Bay Area. My father's environmental and social work in Wixarika territory had brought him a fair number of enemies, including loggers, politicians, and local caciques. By the early 1990s, the tensions that surrounded his work were intensified by his battle with epilepsy, and my mother felt it was best for the family to take a break across the northern border in her country of birth. Although my father joined us several years later, his heart never left Wixarika territory, and as I got older, I became his travel companion. These visits with Wixarika friends in Tepic, Guadalajara, and the sierras undoubtedly planted the first seeds for my research.

While an undergraduate at UC Berkeley, I spent a year studying and conducting research in Mexico under the guidance of my academic mentor,

Percy C. Hintzen. These first attempts at ethnographic and archival research centered on a series of controversial infrastructure projects in and around Wixarika territory. After a two-year stint doing social work in Los Angeles, I returned to school eager to go back to the sierras of Jalisco wearing my new hat as a geographer. But a rough year of graduate school and online conversations with Wixarika university students rerouted my focus to the western cities of Guadalajara and Tepic, where a growing number of Wixaritari were claiming their rights to higher education and professional careers. In this way, the theoretical and practical questions that I address in this book resulted from a constellation of familial and academic relations that exposed the need to speak to the current experiences and paths that young urban Wixaritari are taking in Mexico.

I am grateful to Atilano Carrillo and Kena Bautista's frank conversations, which initiated my temporary departure from the realm of political ecology and development studies. Their experiences as indigenous students in private universities demonstrated the urgency of addressing the social and economic inequalities reproduced in Mexico, from university campuses to crafts markets and public offices. Tutupika Carrillo was an early colleague in this research, connecting me with many other Wixarika students in Tepic and remaining a trusted colleague to date. Juan Aurelio Carrillo Ríos and the Ríos family opened their home and hearts to me, making Tepic a more familiar place. Beyond our family's deep friendship, Juan Aurelio has been a committed partner in this project. At the Autonomous University of Nayarit I was fortunate to count on Tukarima Carrillo, Maximino Muñoz, Tzicuritemai and Álica Rentería, Octavio Salas, Oscar Ukeme Muñoz, and several others to organize events, break bread, and critically analyze the paths that Wixarika youth are taking inside and out of their communities. In Guadalajara, much of my research was anchored to longtime friends and colleagues, but Hayuaneme and Aukwe García dramatically shifted the ground I was walking on. At any hour I could count on these brilliant siblings for critical, honest, and often emotional conversations about any number of topics, but especially about the state of race and belonging in Mexico. Anastacio Hernández, Claudio de la Rosa, Agustín Carrillo, Santos de la Cruz, Jamaima Carrillo, Lisbeth Bonilla, and all the members of Universidad Solidaria were instrumental in helping me ground my research and direct my arguments. This work is indebted to the stories that so many Wixarika youth generously shared with me over the past few years.

During the time of this research, I was a doctoral student at UC Berkeley's Geography Department, where Beatriz Manz served as my dissertation chair and emphasized the importance of holding long-term political commitment to our research projects. Richard Walker was an unexpected and irreplaceable addition to my graduate work, as he helped me navigate the fields of urban studies and economic geography. His emphasis on proper syntax and uncontrived prose was exceptional and helped foster my love for writing. Finally, I am grateful to Percy C. Hintzen, who has directed my academic work from the time I was an undergraduate student fumbling around with literature from his UC Berkeley course, the Political Economy of the Third World. When I mentor students, I always think of Percy because without his guidance, I may have never written an undergraduate thesis nor pursued a graduate degree. When I returned to Berkeley, I found his door open, and his graduate seminars became instrumental for fostering my intellectual growth and my continued engagement with black and diaspora studies.

I want to thank Guillermo de la Peña from CIESAS-Occidente for inviting me to participate and discuss my research findings with other scholars working on topics pertaining to indigenous peoples' right to the city and for serving as my host during my two-year postdoctoral tenure at CIESAS. Guillermo's pioneering work on indigeneity, citizenship, and cities is coupled with his firm commitment to applied research and broader political change. During my postdoctoral tenure at CIESAS (2015–17), I had the fortune of gaining insight from brilliant colleagues who show a simultaneous commitment to social justice. Jorge Alonso, Santiago Bastos, Renée de la Torre, Andrés Fábregas Puig, Pablo Mateos,

Francisco Talavera, and Ivette Flores are just a few colleagues who have since led me toward new research inquiries.

Research is virtually impossible without financial support, and during my graduate career I was fortunate to receive fellowships that made my work possible. The Ford Pre-Dissertation Diversity Fellowship facilitated three years of research and writing and brought me into an invaluable community of scholars who are invested in social equity and excellence in higher education. And the Bancroft Library Study Award signaled a turning point in my research by providing me with a year of access to their unique collection of works on western Mexico. The staff at the Bancroft Library, especially Susan Snyder, David Kessler, Theresa Salazar, and Diana Vergil, were fantastic in helping me locate materials and feel at home, along with my first child, in the quiet reading rooms of the library.

I am indebted to the elder generation of *huicholeros*, whom I consider my extended family and my earliest mentors. *Huicholeros* is a loving term many use for those who are not Wixarika but have worked with Wixarika communities—a term that is memorialized in Rocío Echevarría's musical composition "Huicholeros de corazón." Patricia Díaz Romo's pursuit of social and environmental justice for Wixaritari has been a constant inspiration, and I was fortunate to accompany her to Tepic on several occasions. Carlos Chávez and the staff at AJAGI (Asociación Jalisciense de Apoyo a Grupos Indígenas) gave me a place to work and exchange ideas along with young Wixarika professionals who worked or passed through the offices to hone their skills for the territorial, cultural, and ecological defense of their communities. One of the first huicholeros who heard my incipient ideas for the present project was John Lilly. Sitting in his house in Zacatecas, John became excited when he spoke to me of young Wixarika students, and he encouraged me to bring to light their stories as a matter of social justice. It would be the last conversation we would have, as he passed away a few months later in that eerily beautiful colonial city, as close to Wixarika territory as he could get.

Another spirit that has accompanied me over the past few years is that of Benito de la Cruz, whose tragic passing, far away from Tuapurie in San Antonio, Texas, reminds me of the large net that Wixarika artists cast to make a living in a world that too often devalues their work. And last, I want to thank Silviano Camberos Sánchez, who also thoughtfully discussed my research ideas in his magical home in Guadalajara. He passed away suddenly, leaving behind a legacy of medical service and knowledge that reached across geographic and disciplinary boundaries.

Finally, I would not have been able to navigate my graduate studies and postgraduate journey without an important circle of friends and peers. A very special thank you goes to Jennifer Devine and Nicole List, who became mothers at the same time as I and demonstrated that we can do field research, write dissertations, and teach all the while raising children. Other peers who have given me endless encouragement and advice include Sandra Rozental, Paulina Alcocer, Iracema Gavilán, Paul Liffman, James Battle, Lindsey Dillon, Laura-Anne Minkof-Zern, Javier Arbona, Alicia Cowart, Juan Herrera, and a great many others over the years. I am especially thankful to Rachel Brahinsky for being an unconditional colleague in critical urban geography and bringing me into the University of San Francisco community. Of course, none of this would have been possible without my immediate and extended family, who believed in this work, particularly my late father, Juan, and my mother, Yvonne. Last but not least, Plinio Alberto Hernández was a dear witness and cheerleader to this long process. *Pampariusi!*

ABBREVIATIONS

CDI	Comisión Nacional para el Desarrollo de los Pueblos Indígenas (National Commission for the Development of Indigenous Peoples)
CFE	Comisión Federal de Electricidad (Federal Commission of Electricity)
CONASUPO	Compañía Nacional de Subsistencias Populares (National Company of Popular Subsistence)
DAI	Departamento de Asuntos Indígenas (Department of Indigenous Affairs)
EZLN	Ejército Zapatista de Liberación Nacional (Zapatista Army for National Liberation)
FONART	Fondo Nacional para el Fomento de las Artesanías (National Fund for the Fomentation of Crafts)
III	Instituto Indigenista Interamericano (Interamerican Indigenist Institute)
INEGI	Instituto Nacional de Geografía y Estadística (National Institute for Geography and Statistics)
INI	Instituto Nacional Indigenista (National Indigenist Institute)
ITESO	Instituto Tecnológico y de Estudios Superiores de Occidente (Western Institute of Technology and Higher Education)

JIU	Jóvenes Indígenas Universitarios (Young Indigenous University Students)
MORENA	Movimiento Regeneración Nacional (National Regeneration Party)
PAN	Partido Acción Nacional (National Action Party)
PRD	Partido de la Revolución Democrática (Party of the Democratic Revolution)
PRI	Partido Revolucionario Institucional (Institutional Revolutionary Party)
SEP	Secretaría de Educación Pública (Ministry of Public Education)
UAN	Universidad Autónoma de Nayarit (Autonomous University of Nayarit)
UCEI	Unión de Comunidades y Ejidos Indígenas (Union of Indigenous Communities and Ejido)
UCIHJ	Unión de Comunidades Indígenas Huicholes de Jalisco (Union of Indigenous Huichol Communities of Jalisco)
UEIM	Unión de Estudiantes Indígenas para México (Union of Indigenous Students for Mexico)
UPIN	Unión de Profesionistas Indígenas de Nayarit (Union of Indigenous Professionals of Nayarit)
US	Universidad Solidaria (Solidarity University)
WAAU	Wixaritari, Artistas y Artesanos Unidos en la Zona Metropolitana de Guadalajara (United Wixaritari Artists and Artisans of the Metropolitan Area of Guadalajara)
ZMG	Zona Metropolitana de Guadalajara (Metropolitan Area of Guadalajara)

RACIAL ALTERITY, WIXARIKA YOUTH ACTIVISM, AND THE RIGHT TO THE MEXICAN CITY

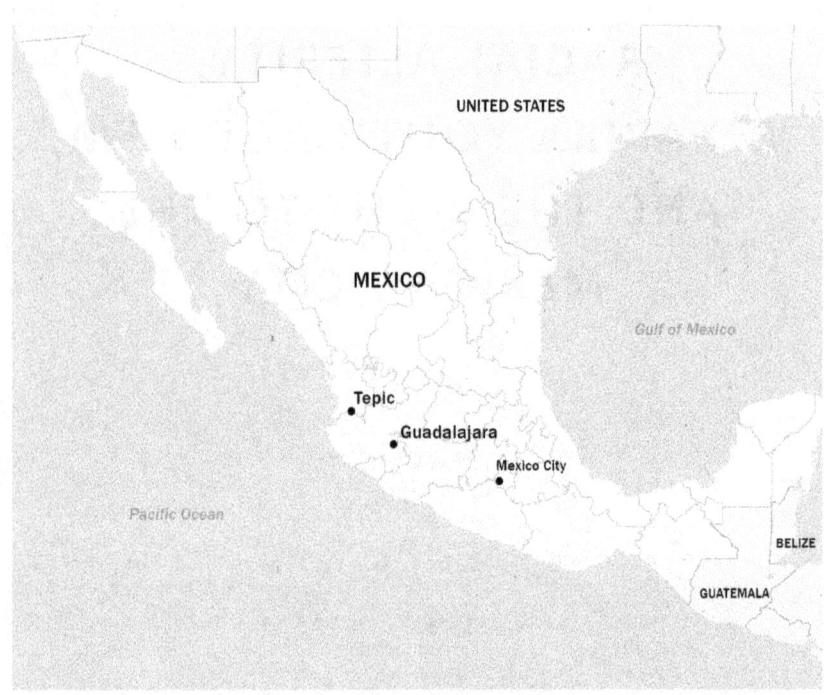

FIGURE 1 Map of Mexico, with locations of Guadalajara, Tepic, and Mexico City. Map by Darin Jensen.

INTRODUCTION

Negotiating Expectations, Articulating Identities
in Urban Mexico

I am what time, circumstance, history have made of me, certainly, but I am, also, much more than that. So are we all.
—JAMES BALDWIN, NOTES FROM A NATIVE SON

IN JUNE 2009, Juan Aurelio Carrillo Ríos wrote an email to the nonprofit organization I collaborate with, after coming across a biographical essay written about his grandfather by my father.[1] Juan Aurelio's grandfather Juan Ríos Martínez had been a good friend of my parents since the early 1970s and was one of the most renowned *xaweri* (Wixarika violin adapted from Spanish fiddle) players and yarn painters of his time. Ríos Martínez had passed away in 1996 in Compostela, Nayarit, a town christened early in the Spanish conquest of western Mexico. A native of Carretones de Cerrito in the eastern part of the state, Ríos had been forced to move to Compostela just south of Tepic as a result of family conflicts (J. Negrín 2003a, 2003b). Juan Aurelio's email stated that he had not been fortunate enough to know his grandfather but was excited at the prospect of meeting someone outside his family who had nurtured a close friendship with his legendary kin. He added that he was an undergraduate student at the Autonomous University of Nayarit (Universidad Autónoma de Nayarit, or UAN), "proudly Wixárika," and would love to find a way to reconnect the Ríos and Negrín families. This was a serendipitous moment not only because my parents had lost contact with Ríos's descendants but because I was in the first stages of conducting research on Wixarika university students in Guadalajara, Jalisco, and Tepic, Nayarit.

FIGURE 2 Juan Ríos Martínez, *Visions of the Blue Deer, Tamatsí Maxayuawi*, 1973, 4.0 × 2.6 feet, beeswax and wool yarn on wood. Courtesy of George and Laurie Howell.

In late September, I made my way to Tepic with a close family friend and pesticide activist, Patricia Díaz Romo. After a long day of visiting families poisoned by pesticides along Nayarit's coastal communities, I was able to meet my *primo* (cousin) Juan Aurelio. Not only was Juan Aurelio a Wixarika student at the UAN, he also led an association that advocated for indigenous students. I arrived at his house just as several other Wixarika and Náayeri (Cora) students were there planning for the evening's welcome dance for incoming indigenous students. It was a tearful encounter that symbolized the beginning of a new generation's friendship and collaboration. During all my subsequent visits to Tepic, I stayed with Juan Aurelio's family. And in July 2010, my mother was able to accompany me to Tepic and celebrate the birthday of Juan Aurelio's mother. Other Ríos family members traveled from Compostela to Tepic for the reunion, and together they reminisced about our families' trips in my parents' 1970 white Suburban. This included the time that Ríos Martínez visited us in Guadalajara and found a Stradivarius violin in a trash can that he then used to play his heart out.

During one of my stays in Tepic, Juan Aurelio's mother, Pablina, recounted to me how she had become a bilingual teacher in Wixarika villages. Pablina was part mestizo, part Wixarika, raised by a father who had followed his people's shamanic teachings yet who lived outside the enclosed nuclear communities of the Western Sierra Madre. As a result, he readily engaged with Mexican mestizo culture. During the 1960s and 1970s, rural schools in indigenous communities were established under the leadership of the Instituto Nacional Indigenista (National Indigenist Institute; INI). Gradually, mestizo teachers were replaced by native bilingual teachers. In fact, for several decades teaching became the emerging field of professionalization for indigenous peoples in Mexico. Although she spoke minimal Wixarika, Pablina became one of these rural teachers. Her first position was in a remote Wixarika village accessible only by foot or jet. She remembers landing on a small strip wearing a knee-length skirt, a blouse, and shoes with small heels—the casual uniform for her profession. Pablina laughed as she recalled how she had not been informed that she would need to walk several kilometers from the landing strip to the village and how authorities had not made any arrangements to have someone meet her and show her the way. Dusk was drawing near as Pablina wondered how she would make the trip with her heeled shoes and suitcase in hand. She soon met a couple headed toward the village who invited her to join them on the short but rocky journey. Pablina's recollection of this first teaching experience came as she neared retirement. Thirty years into her career as a rural teacher, Pablina had gained fluency in the Wixarika language and married a Wixarika artisan from the village of Guadalupe Ocotán, Nayarit. She spent weekdays in the villages and returned to Tepic on the weekends to join her six children, who spent varying degrees of time in Wixarika territory.

The Ríos family illustrates the heterogeneity of the Wixarika population and points to the present book's historical analysis of western Mexico's racialized urban geographies and the "unexpected" and increasingly dynamic presence of young Wixaritari in spaces of higher education. The Wixarika protagonists of this work reflect unique paths that distinguish them from the normative images of indigenous peoples as spatially conscripted to particular strata of society. In this sense, the book is about expectations and how these are defied through the everyday lived experiences of contemporary Mexicans. I use Wixarika, rather than the more common Huichol, in recognition of the appeals made by indigenous peoples to scholars and the wider public to drop the Hispanicized terms as a gesture of respect. I use the term Huichol only when referring to that which is linked to nonindigenous representations of Wixarika culture and people—in all other cases I use Wixarika or its plural form, Wixaritari.

My ethnographic research with Wixarika students and professionals explores how the geographic expectations of indigenous belonging are becoming increasingly untenable as the demographic realities of Mexico continue to shift and as indigenous peoples push for recognition as citizens within a heterogeneous national community. Regina Martínez Casas and colleagues note that general demographic growth coupled with a "re-energized ethnicity" in urban communities (migrant or not) led to a population that identifies as indigenous growing from roughly 6.0 percent in 1990 to 14.8 percent in 2010 (2014, 47). Yet literature that critically analyzes Mexico's processes of urbanization remains limited, particularly regarding the presence of indigenous populations living in the nation's cities. Moreover, research on urban indigenous peoples has yet to seriously consider the experiences and contributions of the university students and professionals who are the key actors of the present work. In this way, this book not only examines contemporary urban interracial relations but does so through the prism of an overlooked segment of the indigenous population—one that can bring new ways of understanding complex questions of identity while adding valuable content and texture to the still growing body of critical work addressing the politics of multiculturalism and race in Latin America (Nelson 1999; Povinelli 2002; Hernández Castillo, Paz, and Sierra 2004; M. E. García 2005; C. R. Hale 2006; Postero 2007; Speed 2008; de la Cadena and Starn 2009; Mora 2018). The experiences of the protagonists of this work show that Wixaritari engage and negotiate dominant notions of cultural authenticity and spatial belonging in multiple ways.

Through examining the historical development of the western cities of Tepic and Guadalajara, my research marks an important step in critical urban studies of Mexico. As I began my archival investigations, it became clear that Mexico City remained supreme in academic studies on urbanism in Mexico. Relatively little has been written about the political economic and social development of Guadalajara, and even less work has been carried out on Tepic. Furthermore, I realized that to understand the contemporary experiences of Wixaritari living in these cities, I had to appreciate how each place had developed distinct ethnic identities rooted in their respective and emplaced foundational mythologies, which represent the geographic and racial relations stemming from the long colonial encounter. The social conflict and redrawing of space that I trace in the West follows María Josefina Saldaña-Portillo's argument that Mexico's geography has been "produced, materially and representationally, through historical, social, and racial relation with indigenous subjects" (2016, 6). These subjects were never monolithic, as they represented both local and migrant indigenous populations, and with the ensuing years of colonization, they incorporated other non-European peoples grouped under the term *castas*. Furthermore, historical contingency was highly relevant in the forms of engagement among colonial subjects, rebels, and the administrative apparatus, whether this be the Spanish Crown, the Catholic Church, or republican governments. Saldaña-Portillo notes, "Just as racial geographies produced historical differences in the meanings of Indian and indio, so too they produced different modes of indigenous engagement" (15). The historically situated yet dynamic grounds on which Wixarika urban youth interpellate their political, geographic, and cultural identities is at the heart of this book. And through examining the intersection of the political, economic, and social forces that shaped the consolidation of these two cities, we can understand the conjunctures of place and identity as they manifest through the lives and agency of today's urban Wixarika citizens.

ARCHIVAL FORECLOSURES, RACIAL ALTERITY, AND INDIGENISTA PRAXIS

To grasp contemporary representations and practices that target Mexico's indigenous peoples, we must first understand the work of *indigenismo* as a central ideological force that has defined the country's racial relations over five centuries. Chapter 1 begins this effort by drawing inspiration from geographer Allan Pred's use of spatial and chronological interplay, moving back and forth between the present and the past to understand how racial stereotypes are sedimented, recirculated, and redeployed across time and space (Pred 2004, xiii). Through the action of zooming in and out of history in a spatially grounded way, we can better understand how ideas of race and racial hierarchies become part of a society's common sense and are facilitated through the use of visual and literary technologies intricately tied to state practices. Pred's analysis pushes us to consider the ways in which racial fictions are transformed into fact, and how these fictions intensify over time and are put into practice through emplaced actions that riddle the quotidian experiences of the racialized Other. Ultimately, the deployment of racial stereotypes through everyday forms of institutional and popular discrimination work to obstruct the mobility of the racialized Other in nonsanctioned spaces (84). This framework helps explain the challenges that today's Wixarika university students and professionals face in Mexico's cities, as the fictions that surround Wixarika identity prevent both the state and society from recognizing them as heterogeneous urban citizens with professional qualifications and civil rights.

Indigenismo reflects the interplay of fact and fiction, past and present, that shapes contemporary racial expectations and stereotypes of indigenous peoples in Mexico. Since the second half of the twentieth century, this concept has been widely discussed and debated by Latin Americanist scholars, who have discussed indigenismo's celebration of glorious empires past (e.g., the Aztec, Maya, and Inca empires) coupled with its paradoxical relationship to living indigenous peoples (Castellanos 2010; Martínez Novo 2006; Earle 2007; Herrasti Maciá 1988; Aguirre Beltrán 1967). Scholarship dealing with indigenismo has also critiqued the central role of mestizo anthropologists turned state bureaucrats and, as such, has examined indigenismo as an ideology and practice largely framed by postrevolutionary discourse. As a result, little is said about indigenismo as an episteme rooted in the long five hundred years of European contact with indigenous peoples, and, more precisely, with the ensuing sense of racial alterity that the colonial encounter nurtured. Luis Villoro's 1950 study *Los grandes momentos del indigenismo en México* proves an essential missing link in these debates for its poignant description of indigenismo as an epistemic system that reflects the social imaginaries and angst of distinct periods of Mexican history. Villoro's treatment of indigenismo as an episteme emerging from European and criollo projections of the indigenous Other destabilizes the hegemonic narrative that portrays indigenismo as a series of contentious discourses and practices concerned with the development and well-being of indigenous peoples in the Spanish postcolony.[2]

Villoro's argument is grounded in the writings of several key colonial and postcolonial criollo intellectual figures, whose collected work forms the archive on which the *indigenista* imaginary is drawn. But the archive hides as much as it reveals about the historical geography of race and race relations in Mexico. Save for a few examples, the archive tells us little about how indigenous peoples negotiated with the European colonial order and the subsequent construction of an independent Mexican nation-state. Conversely, much of what is revealed by archival records centers on the violence inflicted on or by indigenous peoples or, as Saidiya Hartman notes with relation to enslaved African women, "The stories that exist are not about them, but rather about the violence, excess, mendacity, and reason that seized hold of their lives, transformed them into commodities and corpses, and identified them with names tossed-off as insults and crass jokes" (2008, 2). Hartman not only points to the limits of the archive as a source of information about "subaltern peoples" beyond their position as subaltern, but it begs for new if imperfect ways of imagining the conditions and contestations that surrounded the displacements of indigenous peoples by seeking to "generate a different set of descriptions from this archive" (7). Throughout this book, I question the place of the archive as much as I draw from its multigenre fragments to understand how the Mexican West is shaped by the inscription of its peculiar racial geographies, fed by waves of economic interventions and popular contestation.

Reflective of Maylei Blackwell and colleagues' articulation for critical Latinx indigeneities based on "an interdisciplinary analytic reflecting how indigeneity is constructed across time and place, and through overlapping colonialities" (Blackwell, López, and Urrieta 2017, 126), this book analyzes the historical role of the racial imaginary to understand the selective celebration of indigenous heritage and the accompanying foreclosure of indigenous peoples from spaces discursively and practically designated for whites and mestizos. After foregrounding the racial imaginary in chapter 1, chapter 2 follows this path by exposing the ways in which indigenismo became hegemonic through the postrevolutionary model of *acción indigenista*, or indigenist action mediated by evolving anthropological perspectives and contingent political moments on the national scale. I explore acción indigenista through state and private interventions in Wixarika territory beginning in the early 1960s to understand the conditions that led many Wixaritari to relocate to the nearby cities of Tepic and Guadalajara. Migration to cities and the growth of indigenous rights movements emerged alongside the state's incorporation of *neoindigenismo*, or multicultural neoliberalism, and the radical indigenous politics most emblematically represented by the Zapatista movement. The national discursive shift that took place in the 1990s is part of the hemispheric move from class to identity politics that Shannon Speed explains as a dialogic engagement between global human rights discourses, radical grassroots propositions, and long delegitimized state actors (2008, 29). Since the 1990s, dynamic indigenous mobilizations over territorial autonomy, cultural recognition, and civil rights have remained key challenges for the Mexican state. Today, as a new presidential regime begins with high popularity among indigenous peoples and working-class Mexicans, new questions will arise pertaining to state-community relations, including the destination of resources for indigenous rural and urban communities and whether signature controversial capital projects on indigenous territory will remain, like the Mayan Train or mining in the sacred Wixarika pilgrimage site of Wirikuta.

CITIES AND THE CREATION OF RACIALIZED IDENTITY

The cities of Guadalajara and Tepic are separated by a two-hour stretch along the scenic highway that takes passengers through the beautiful winding mountains known as Plan de Barrancas, passing groves of agave and sugarcane, volcanic rock and *huizache* trees. While vastly different in size and wealth, these two cities are historically linked by their cultural, political, and economic geography. Their development into urban centers is most notable during the nineteenth century, when they transitioned from isolated mercantilist towns into incipient capitalist cities, which thrived by linking the Pacific ports with central Mexico. The often forgotten rivalry between these two strikingly different cities culminated with the separation of Tepic from the jurisdiction of the state of Jalisco in 1883 and the creation of the state of Nayarit, with Tepic as its capital. The secession of Tepic from Jalisco triggered a bitter polemic between those who termed it an abduction from Jalisco and those who argued that Guadalajara's leadership had neglected Tepic during decades of foreign and indigenous misrule (S. García 1878, 30–31).

Chapters 3 and 4 take a critical look at the ways in which Tepic and Guadalajara developed particular racialized identities, which are expressed through the present-day experiences of its young Wixarika residents. While Tepic is far from a bastion of indigenous pride, its historical role as a place of rebellion against the Spanish and, later, against the liberal status quo gives us a sense of how this city has nurtured an insurgent identity rooted in the personas of Náayeri king Nayar in the seventeenth century and rebel leader Manuel Lozada in the nineteenth century. Conversely, Guadalajara is best known for its Catholic and Hispanic character and its positioning as Mexico's second largest city, embracing its industrial and technological base and incessantly fostering a sense of independence from Mexico City. As Guadalajara shows its growing comfort with identifying as a multicultural city through new marketing techniques that increasingly utilize Wixarika culture, few if any structural changes have been made at the state level to ensure equitable policy and the respect of indigenous territorial and cultural rights. But why juxtapose these two cities? Their geographic proximity and historical connections help illustrate the different experiences of its contemporary indigenous residents. More specifically, a comparison of Wixarika experiences in Tepic and Guadalajara can only be understood through rooting them in the region's political economic and racial history—a microcosm of national and international tendencies toward inclusion and exclusion.

Each of these two chapters begins with a distinct narration of the Battle of La Mojonera, which took place on January 28 and 29, 1873, in the municipality of Zapopan, west of Guadalajara. The battle pitted rebel leader Manuel Lozada against liberal general Ramón Corona in what became a decisive moment for the territorial and political division of the Mexican West. More than an armed conflict, the Battle of La Mojonera illustrates deep racial anxieties in what historian Leticia Reina Aoyama terms "the century of indigenous rebellions" (1993, 11). While a footnote in Mexican history, this battle has largely been memorialized as the victory of the nationalist liberal against the insurgent conservative fighter—the triumph of the modernizing forces led by the liberal ethos of private property. A closer look at this battle also sheds light on a key moment in Mexico's racial formation, when the criollo liberal defeats the indigenous rebels, who sought the protection of communal landholdings in the face of massive land expropriations set forth under the Reform Laws of 1857. By gleaning the archive to uncover the confrontation between Lozada and Corona, I respond to Pred's method of collapsing fact and fiction as a way to reveal the historical and geographic entanglements found in each city. Following these accounts of the Battle of La Mojonera, I examine some defining moments of the economic, political, and ethnic identities of Guadalajara and Tepic that further solidified their respective racialized identities.

Chapters 3 and 4 overlap in the same way that these two cities share regional political and economic histories. In particular, the role of the port of San Blas during the second half of the eighteenth century through the first half of the nineteenth century highlights how Guadalajara and Tepic are fundamentally linked. The economic outgrowth of the port's activities created important demographic and cultural shifts in the West. Beyond these overlapping histories, I am also interested in uncovering these cities' unique differences. In doing so, I pay attention to the implications of each city's hegemonic narrative regarding its indigenous residents. A key aspect for understanding the problem rests on the pervasiveness of associating indigenous peoples with rural spaces or, in cities, associating the indigenous body with the informal economy and marginalization. Taking from Johannes Fabian (1983), these understandings of spatial belonging negate the coevalness of urban residents of distinct ethnic backgrounds and social strata.

Within Mexico, Guadalajara stands out as a city with strong European features. Both the urban layout and local culture identify with the European immigrant legacies that have left their mark on the physical and cultural landscape. Yet the celebration of this European heritage obscures the presence and influence of other ethnicities that helped create the traditions that sustain and give Guadalajara its present identity—including peoples of indigenous and African descent. The notion that Guadalajara is a "typically criollo" city is summarized well by Hélène Rivière d'Arc, who notes that from its aesthetic culture, architecture, and monuments, the construction of Guadalajara leaves "very little room for traits of the indigenous civilization to endure" (1973, 18). Unlike Tepic or the heavily indigenous cities of southern Mexico, in Guadalajara, one cannot as easily see women and men dressed in indigenous clothing. This matter has largely been attributed to the "reduction" of indigenous peoples in Jalisco and the geographic disassociation of the state's indigenous territories, where communities have been "recast in the mountains that are particularly difficult to access" (18).

Keeping with national migratory patterns, Guadalajara has experienced dramatic demographic growth in recent decades. Among its new residents are a heterogeneous indigenous population coming from as far as Chiapas and as near as the Western Sierra Madre of Jalisco. In chapter 4, I argue that the production of an ethnic identity rooted in Europe forecloses Guadalajara's indigenous presence. Nonetheless, Guadalajara's criollo identity, or what Manuela Camus calls Tapatío coloniality (2015), is gradually being contested by an indigenous population seeking to be recognized as a fundamental part of the city's past and present.

Beyond significant differences in size and wealth, Tepic is culturally and physically distinct from Guadalajara. As one of the smallest state capitals of the country, it goes unnoticed by most politicians, investors, scholars, and tourists. Tepic has been deeply influenced by its proximity to the Western Sierra Madre, whose native inhabitants have repeatedly challenged the regional power structure. The seemingly unending indigenous revolts from the Spanish conquest through the turn of the twentieth century have left an indelible mark on the city's cultural identity. Today, Tepic contrasts with other western Mexican cities because of its significant indigenous population, which has actively carved out a place in local schools, culture, and political chambers. Ultimately, the legacy of Nayarit's indigenous struggles has become a part of the state's official identity through the celebration of its namesake, King Nayar, and the elite's resigned acceptance of Lozada as a homegrown hero of the indigenous and rural peasantry. The use of Wixarika iconography in Nayarit's tourism advertisements—including the Riviera Nayarit—and the long established use of Wixarika- and Náayeri-inspired motifs in the dress of each year's Ms. Nayarit demonstrate the central role that ethnicity plays in Tepic's local imaginary.

Nonetheless, this celebration of indigeneity obscures simultaneous forms of racial exclusion. In chapter 3, I argue for a more textured understanding of Tepic's indigeneity by demonstrating the parallel tendencies that both include and exclude contemporary indigenous citizens. As with Guadalajara, Tepic holds to fixed imaginaries of the indigenous as characteristically rural. But unlike Guadalajara, these fixed imaginaries have become a central feature of Tepic's wider identity, where "Huichol" ethnicity is rendered hypervisible. Throughout the present work, I use hypervisibility as an analytical framework, or representational process, that creates a semblance of inclusion while hiding the uneven power relations activated with the production and circulation of said image.[3] Currently, despite holding such a central place in the imagination around indigeneity, Wixaritari experience a paradoxical relationship that hinges on folklorization and commodification on the one hand, and destruction of sacred places, communal territory, and cultural reproduction on the other. As such, Wixarika peoples must interpellate and negotiate with these expectations and narratives. Thus, indigenous peoples in Tepic are still expected to circulate within particular spaces and conform to preestablished identities.

By identifying key moments in the political economic and cultural formation of Tepic and Guadalajara, I highlight the moments of opportunity and foreclosure that exist for its Wixarika residents. In doing so, I draw from Henri Lefebvre's ([1974] 2000) emphasis on the multiple temporalities that are manifested in the social production of space. Lefebvre's underlining of spatial practice as a "dialectical interaction" that reveals the entanglements between conceptualized space and lived space reflects both structures of power and agency in each of these two cities (48). Ultimately, understanding the spatial production of Guadalajara and Tepic becomes an indispensable step toward understanding the current social struggles taking place within both cities.

SPACES FOR IDENTITY

My mother likes to remind me that up until the 1990s, Wixaritari who visited Guadalajara tended to prefer "mestizo clothes" to hide their ethnicity in the face of racist exclusions. Today, she marvels at the pride that many Wixarika youth have, including their desire to wear their traditional clothing and mark their ethnicity, even if Mexico's multicultural turn has done little to upset enduring racisms. In chapter 5, I explore the opportunities and new exclusions that have emerged since 1992, when Mexico constitutionally declared itself a "pluricultural" nation that must respect the rights and customs of its ethnically heterogeneous population. In so doing, my work comes into conversation with recent studies on the double-edged sword presented by Latin America's multicultural turn, which has presented native peoples with a new set of dilemmas pertaining to their own demands for equality and autonomy within the neoliberal nation-state.

Most scholarship dealing with contemporary indigenous peoples in Latin America continues to fix them to rural spaces linked to land-based cultural traditions. This surely is the case for academic research pertaining to the Wixarika people, particularly scholarship that reflects anthropology's long quest to uncover the production of religious rituals in indigenous territory (Fikes 2011; Furst 1972, 2003, 2006; Kindl 2003; Neurath 2002; Furst and Schaefer 1996). Meanwhile, academic studies that examine indigenous peoples in cities overlook indigenous professionals and, as a result, perpetuate understandings of indigenous peoples in cities as forced migrants steeped in marginality, illiteracy, and poverty. By focusing on the experiences of Wixarika university students and professionals in Tepic and Guadalajara, I bring a more contemporary and spatially grounded study into conversation with indigenous, critical race, and urban studies. This said, much terrain is left for the study of the conditions and experiences of indigenous peoples in cities, no matter their profession or economic status.

While my initial chapters follow the production and intersection of Mexico's racial and urban imaginaries, chapter 5 focuses on how Tepic and Guadalajara's Wixaritari interpellate the popular stereotypes that mold ideas surrounding their racial and spatial belonging. Elizabeth Povinelli's (2002) work on the conditions of state-sanctioned indigeneity in multicultural Australia led me to further consider the implications of racial expectations on the material livelihoods of the stereotyped. Povinelli's analysis is central for understanding how the multicultural state inscribes ideas of legitimate indigenous authenticity and, through this, attempts to harness demands surrounding indigenous political, economic, and cultural rights. The paradigms set to demarcate authentic indigeneity too often work to dismiss those indigenous peoples who have left their tribal lands, whether by force or by choice. In this context, the construction of a normative indigenous identity reflects the continuation of state efforts to homogenize a heterogeneous population. So while the multi- or pluricultural state recognizes past injustices by offering select privileges for indigenous peoples (land titles, scholarships, and social services), the mechanisms through which indigenous peoples must demonstrate their authenticity brings to light new forms of exclusion and dispossession. Too often this means that an urban indigenous person is automatically shut out from gaining said recognition and privileges.

Juan Castillo Cocom complements Povinelli by pointing to the continued effects of Mexico's neoindigenismo on the identities of indigenous peoples, who must learn to navigate the "map that was already previously created for them" (2005, 138). Through an autobiographical narrative, Castillo Cocom demonstrates that indigenous peoples can interpellate this preset racial map in multiple ways (132). Here, the words of Wixarika students and professionals destabilize the master narrative, by traveling off the map that binds them to rigid understandings of indigenous citizenship and belonging. James Ferguson and Akhil Gupta's (1997) discussion of *reterritorialization* is highly relevant for underlining the political, economic, and social contingencies that produce new expressions of identity and place: "Physical location and physical territory, for so long the *only* grid on which cultural difference could be mapped, need to be replaced by multiple grids that enable us to see that connection and contiguity—more generally, the representation of territory—vary considerably by factors such as class, gender, race, and sexuality and are differentially available for those in different locations of power" (50). At the same time, it is important to underline that Wixarika history demonstrates how reterritorialization has always been part of Wixarika cultural and territorial existence. Only through the impositions of colonial and modern discourse have indigenous peoples been fixed into particular territories and positionalities.

Finally, Stuart Hall's work on identity is key in framing cultural identity as a practice that is "lodged in contingency" and "sutured together" (Hall and du Gay 1996, 3). Hall notes that identity is a multisided process established through difference, exclusion, and the long history of representations that shape our understandings of the self in relation to the Other (4). Because it is set into motion through the constellation of quotidian interactions, Hall emphasizes identity's performative nature as it is expressed through acts of negotiation, accommodation, and resistance. In a similar vein, Ernesto Laclau and Chantal

Mouffe describe identity as a product of "articulatory practice," where relations and linkages between the individual and the collective, the intimate and the public, become the productive forces that shape social identification (1985, 105).

Chapter 5 brings together ethnographic research and critical scholarship in an effort to illustrate how urban Wixarika university students and professionals are negotiating citizenship in present-day Mexico. Borrowing from Philip J. Deloria, I endeavor to "reverse the geography of expectation" that is held for indigenous peoples (2004, 139). Throughout the chapter, I draw on the voices of Wixaritari to highlight key moments that have shaped their identities, directed their careers, and inspired their activism. The Wixarika term *makuyeika* refers to the individual who walks in many places, a particularly relevant concept given the Wixarika tradition of pilgrimage across distinct territorial points in the Mexican northwest. But makuyeika also speaks to the experiences of urban Wixaritari, by reflecting their engagement with personal identity, their ethnic communities, and Mexican society more generally. Most importantly, makuyeika stresses the importance of geography in the formation of individual and collective identities, in a way that disrupts entrenched narratives of indigenous immobility.

INDIGENOUS YOUTH AND HIGHER EDUCATION IN MEXICO

> *Many times we don't meet our expectations in the universities because the educational model is designed with Western culture at its base. So another challenge is presented to us as indigenous youth: how to take advantage of what we learn or unlearn in the universities to apply to our communities that are getting increasingly affected by the global capitalist system. Those of us who are on both sides, how do we get to work from both places? What I do think is that we need to weave together networks not only amongst students but also amongst graduates to share our work and collaborate together.*
>
> —LISBETH BONILLA, IN NEGRÍN ET AL., "VOCES UNIVERSITARIAS": TRAYECTORIAS, LOGROS Y RETOS EN EL OCCIDENTE MEXICANO

Education has long been a central mechanism through which the Mexican state has explicitly sought to create a coherent national body of citizens. Historically, assimilation through education largely meant teaching rural indigenous peoples Spanish-language acquisition and bringing them into a national civic and economic imagination shared by the larger Mexican society. As I describe in chapter 2, in the decades after the Mexican Revolution of 1910, education became a core instrument for nation building and for the assimilation of indigenous and peasant populations. Over the decades, the Ministry of Public Education (Secretaría de Educación Pública, or SEP) and institutions that work with indigenous peoples have occupied themselves with the task of creating and re-creating educational infrastructures for rural indigenous communities. In the Wixarika communities of Jalisco and Nayarit, this infrastructure did not begin until the late 1960s and was relatively thin and limited to elementary, or primary, schools that incorporated only some elements of Wixarika linguistic, oral, and experiential learning. Primary schools historically operated as room and board because they are located in the cabeceras, small settlements, connected to dirt roads, with some small goods stores and local medical clinics. The combination of both the geographic and epistemic distance during the first decades of indigenous schooling led to sporadic attendance and low completion rates. Not until the 1990s did a new generation of Wixarika educators and traditional authorities begin partnerships with institutes of higher education to jumpstart community-driven intercultural secondary schools in several communities. The development of the so-called intercultural model during this decade, and the strengthening of secondary and tertiary schools in particular, helped propel a new generation of Wixarika students to pursue college education.

While 72.6 percent of indigenous children (designated by whether at least one member of their family speaks a native language) ages twelve to fourteen are receiving a primary education today, only 58 percent of high school students continue their education thereafter, and despite indigenous people being approximately 10 percent of the national population, less than 3 percent of Mexico's college students are indigenous (Robles and Pérez 2017).[4] Notably, however, in addition to the larger debates for assessing indigenous identity, poor statistics are kept across accredited universities regarding the number of indigenous students admitted, which communities they come from, and their retention and graduation rates (Foro Consultivo 2018). Furthermore, attached factors in the school setting and in broader society shape whether colleges are interested in keeping such statistics and whether students are willing to identify themselves as indigenous to a discriminatory body. In 2013–14, the Jóvenes Indígenas Universitarios (JIU) project, led by Milca Mayo (Ch'ol), Isaura García (Mixtec), and Antonio García (Wixarika), set out to research these matters in several key public and private institutions of higher education in the Metropolitan Zone of Guadalajara (ZMG). While the University of Guadalajara (public) and the Instituto Tecnológico y de Estudios Superiores de Occidente, or ITESO (Jesuit), had established liaisons recruiting and tracking this population, other institutions either did not know their own statistics on or denied having enrolled indigenous students (Mayo, García, and García 2014). At one for-profit college, LAMAR, a staff member commented to these researchers that because the college offers degrees only in health-related fields, there would (naturally) not be any indigenous students. Ironically, the health field is the most popular area of study for indigenous students.

With this backdrop in mind, the present book attempts to show that despite the long-standing structural inequities and everyday discrimination that Wixarika youth experience, their organizational efforts have opened up significant new spaces for future *universitarios*. Over a span of ten years following the paths of many Wixarika professionals and universitarios, I have noted the landscape continually evolving through the research efforts of JIU and the recent agreement signed between ITESO university and Wixarika authorities for the ongoing admission of young Wixaritari. Meanwhile, Tepic has remained a relatively accessible place where indigenous youth can study, specifically serving Wixarika, Náayeri, and other indigenous students from western Mexico. At the UAN, the chancellor, through the student union, continues to host a successful program for indigenous students, while Tepic's Universidad Pedagógica enrolls a majority indigenous student body as a result of the continued popularity of education as a field of professionalization.

Over the span of my research and through my continued work and friendships, I have observed a great many protagonists of this research becoming trailblazers in their respective fields and geographic milieus, with a couple reaching international platforms through their activism protecting Wixarika territory and sacred places. As they make these moves and exit their stage as youth, Wixarika professionals continue to work with the new generations of college students. This is precisely the call to action that Lisbeth Bonilla makes in the epigraph of this section and that nourishes the ethnographic work from which this book developed.

A NOTE ON METHOD

My research emerges from my lifelong relationship with Wixarika culture, territory, and politics. My father, Juan, began working with Wixarika artists in 1970, and by the end of that decade, he found himself deep in advocacy work in the Western Sierra Madre just as major state development projects were descending on Wixarika communities. By the time I was a toddler, my mother, Yvonne, had stopped taking the family to the sierra, spending her time instead supporting the Wixarika guests who perpetually stayed at our house in Guadalajara while receiving medical services for acute illnesses or conducting bureaucratic and business transactions in the city. I was thus raised amid my family's intimate friendships with Wixarika families, and from an early age I was made aware of the acute racism that indigenous peoples face in Mexico—a racism that largely remains unaddressed through the nation's ambivalent relationship with indigeneity, race, and ethnicity. Having these experiences as the departing point for my research has gifted me with certain privileges, allowing me access to the people and spaces that inform my work. This is important at a time when Wixaritari have grown increasingly weary of decades of scientific inquiry by outsiders and a still growing number of researchers interested in their culture, territory, and livelihoods. I am certain that I would have been unable to gather the stories at hand were it not for my family's long-standing service to Wixarika communities and my intimate relationships with many of this book's protagonists. At the same time, this intimacy produces its own set of challenges and responsibilities.

Much of the impetus for covering the topic of Wixarika university students and professionals came from my discontent with seeing the continued production of academic studies almost solely portraying Wixaritari as rural, shamanic, and artisanal peoples. Though Wixarika culture undeniably offers an intriguing landscape for the study of arts and religion, a great number of ethnographic studies conducted in Wixarika territory have been riddled with inequities and pressures that outside researchers impose on their informants. At the same time, the presence of researchers has set into motion internal divisions and accusations of opportunism against those who serve as hosts and informants. These issues are inevitably a product of a two-way process in which both researchers and informants seek particular benefits from each other under the watchful eye of tight-knit rural communities. Unfortunately, this distrust is further compounded by the increasing presence of nongovernmental organizations and tourists within Wixarika territory, a matter that continues to evolve as Wixarika authorities encounter multiple threats to their territories and rights.

Having witnessed the fallout of other research projects, I consciously sought to engage urban Wixarika university students and young professionals who, during the bulk of my research, were relatively close to my age and who I could consider my peers and vice versa. In doing so, I hoped to minimize the power inequities so prevalent in ethnographic research. From the beginning I hoped to conduct as collaborative a research project as possible through models of participatory observation, service learning, and collectively organized workshops, discussion groups, and interviews. By using a dialogical approach, the Wixarika universitarios and I sought spaces in which my research questions could be developed and where their interests and concerns could be discussed beyond the constructs of what at the time was my dissertation research. Over the span of five years in both Tepic and Guadalajara, I visited, observed, and participated in several student events, meetings, and debates, the most memorable of which was the *taller de diálogo*, or dialogue workshop, that I co-organized at the UAN in April 2010. In this workshop, more than fifty Wixarika UAN students gathered for a day-long audio-recorded gathering comprising an inaugural address made by Guadalajara-based Aukwe García Míjarez, followed by several small-group discussion sessions and a plenary session at the end centered on a series of topics relating to indigenous identity, higher education, and contemporary Wixarika struggles. Over four summers and one full year of research in these two cities, I attended multiple social gatherings and academic events with Wixarika universitarios, where I was able to appreciate the importance of space in creating a sense of belonging for these young people, who had mostly migrated to the city to get a higher education. Gatherings like the dances with live *música regional wixárika* performances, popular among youth, and the monthly Universidad Solidaria meetings at ITESO provided me a unique window into the ways in which Wixarika youth articulate their cultural and spatial identities through the joy of the *bailes* and through the courage of their political organizing.[5]

During my research, I also volunteered for two nonprofits serving Wixarika communities—one established by my parents and based in Oakland, California, and the other in Guadalajara. Most notable was my work for the Wixárika Research Center archiving historical and community documents as well as conducting fundraising activities for a forestry project, scholarships, and defense activities for the sacred territory of Wirikuta. Through these varied activities, which included countless informal conversations on Wixarika culture, youth, and race in Mexico, I was able to fill several field notebooks that helped direct the content of fifteen formal interviews with university students and student leaders in Tepic and Guadalajara. Throughout the process of conducting my ethnographic research, I returned to the protagonists of my story for advice and critique. Frankness between a researcher and an informant is a tricky affair, but I believe that we tried to be honest about moments of discomfort and issues that were best not raised by a non-Wixarika like me.

After several years of ethnographic work, I realized that there was a notable gap in the literature on western Mexican history, the cities of my research, and urban indigenous studies in general. At the same time, it was clear to me that to understand the current debates around indigeneity, space, and power, I needed to have a better sense of the historical context that created landscapes of ethnic consumption and racial exclusion at once. A yearlong fellowship with UC Berkeley's Bancroft Library provided me with an opportunity to dig deeper into the historical geography of each of these cities and surrounding regions. The library's collection included rare primary and secondary sources, which helped me stitch together the urban development of Tepic and Guadalajara that I recount in chapters 3 and 4. Declarations written by nineteenth-century rebel leader Manuel Lozada, photo albums of foreigners visiting western Mexico in the early twentieth century, and classical historical indigenista writings all nourished my gradual piecing together of multiple stories to paint a bigger picture of the places that Tepic and Guadalajara have been, to better appreciate where they are today.

As I move forward, I continue to discuss and collaborate on projects with some of my Wixarika informants, aware that enduring friendships transcend academic studies. In the process of conducting research and being the subject of research, our many colors converge and diverge to produce the delicate challenges that infuse ethnographic practice. In the final analysis, I return to James Baldwin's poignant reminder that we are indeed products of "time, circumstance, history," yet we are all certainly much more than that. If anything, I hope that the present book can move readers to appreciate the fluidity of human experiences despite the historical and geographic processes that seemingly fix us to our presumed identities.

1

THE LONG ARC OF INDIGENISMO

Mapping Vision, Race, and Nation

How fiction-laden racializing images, how images of hypersexuality, the childlike, and the otherwise negatively charged, have circulated and connected up unpredictably in time and space, have traveled through shifting discursive networks, have readily flowed back and forth between "scientific," literary, political, and popular discourses, have had their meanings repeatedly recontextualized, their assumptions somewhat shifted and occasionally challenged, and yet—however complex the process(es)—have endured to this day, unevenly reactivated nationally and locally, over and over recycled, rearticulated, and re-present-ed, over and over put to new kinds of work, over and over taking on more or less reshaped forms that cannot be separated from the on-the-ground circumstances they already have helped produce.

—ALLAN PRED, THE PAST IS NOT DEAD

ON AUGUST 4, 2007, the column *Los Ojos del Güero* published an opinion piece titled "Los Huicholes Mayates" in the Tepic, Nayarit, newspaper *Matutino Gráfico*.[1] The author, who goes by the pseudonym El Güerote Chulote, roughly "The Hunky Blond," recounts an invitation he received to act as a judge for the beauty contest at the Xalisco Fair, just south of Tepic. As it turned out, El Güerote Chulote was far more intrigued by the Wixarika musical contingent he repeatedly calls "Huicholes mayates," who "just the same will fornicate with a cow, a woman, or a man," because they are, thanks to their ingestion of peyote, "simply beasts of having sex." The entire column was peppered with assertions that Wixaritari are not only sex-hungry savages, but sex-hungry savages who lack musical talent and spend the little money they have on extravagant "uniforms," leaving society to foot the bill for their other needs.

Within days, the Union of Indigenous Professionals of Nayarit sent an open letter to the newspaper's editor citing national and international agreements that legally protect indigenous peoples from discrimination and demanded that an immediate apology be published in the *Matutino Gráfico*. The young Wixarika professionals who drafted the letter stated, "For too long we have silenced the humiliation, the racism and the indifference of those people who call themselves civilized or educated, and from this we have been denied the right to a dignified life. There are sectors of society who to this day maintain racist and exclusionary attitudes against our indigenous brothers and sisters, but there are sectors that have become conscious of our position and have allied themselves with our just and legitimate demands" (letter to the editor, *Matutino Gráfico*, August 20, 2007). It took several letters, phone calls, and threats of protest for El Güerote Chulote and the *Matutino Gráfico* to publish a reluctant apology. For Tepic's Wixarika residents, the absurdly cheap words of this newspaper columnist made palpably clear that, despite constitutional protections and decades of purportedly proindigenous legislation, racism and its dismissal by a large portion of Mexican society continued alive and well in the twenty-first century. The interaction also confirmed that denigrating textual and visual representations of the indigenous continue to be tolerated and disregarded by the Mexican public at the cost of indigenous citizens, who experience the material consequences of these depictions.

From the Spanish conquest to the present, the Mexican Indian's image has been endlessly reworked and reimagined by the nonindigenous. Generation after generation of European, criollo, and mestizo scholars, politicians, and artists have deployed particular representations of indigenous peoples that while at times contradictory, more often than not share common racial and spatial depictions that abstract the geographic and cultural heterogeneity of Mexico's aboriginal inhabitants, past and present. While always problematic, the image of indigenous peoples was never wholly monolithic. María Josefina Saldaña-Portillo notes that there have been "multiple generic 'Indians' and 'Indios' deployed over time," from the colonial period onward as "mapped phenomena that appear, disappear, and reappear at strategic moments" (2016, 8). Centuries of representations of the Indian have led to a series of what geographer Allan Pred terms "fiFcAtCiTonS" or the "(con)fusions of fact and fiction through which racializing stereotypes are perpetuated and reenacted at dispersed sites" (2004, xi). While the horrendous depictions of bestiality and savagery that were used to "justify" the murder and enslavement of native populations throughout the Americas were eventually replaced by more subtle representations of indigenous inferiority or, conversely, glorious indigenous civilization and stoic resistance, the primordial image that has stuck to this day continues to be that of the Indian as utterly different from whites and mestizos.

Visual and literary representations of indigenous peoples have a long and diverse history in Mexico, ranging from nationalist histories and monuments to advertisements for the tourism industry. Notable examples include the pictorial, cartographic, and descriptive narratives commissioned by the Spanish Crown; the casta paintings of the seventeenth and eighteenth centuries; the nineteenth-century nationalist histories; and the much-celebrated muralist movement of the twentieth century. Artist and scholar Coco Fusco argues that old and new forms of deploying racial imagery through education, film, music, and political propaganda demonstrate a society's individual and collective fascination with consuming race (Fusco and Wallis 2003). Taking from Roland Barthes's theorization of mythical speech, Fusco affirms that the racial imagination of a nation is deeply sedimented in a preexisting set of signs and images consumed through everyday practices. The form in which these images are thus consumed and interpreted can bring a society's racial attitudes to the surface. Fusco writes of the United States, "Where and when Americans have expected or wanted to see race, as well as where and when we don't want to see it, tells us a great deal about how we negotiate our ambivalent relation to the historical legacy of racialization" (47).[2] Likewise, the invitation of Wixarika musicians to the Xalisco Fair by municipal authorities and El Güerote Chulote's opinion piece reflect Mexican society's own long-standing and competing desires to view and discuss race.

Edward Said's study of Orientalism takes this analysis a step further by pointing to the articulation between representation and power, via the imperial forces that mobilize literary and pictorial representations of the Other to justify territorial, political, and economic conquest: "Taking the late eighteenth century as a very roughly defined starting point[,] Orientalism can be discussed and analyzed as the corporate institution for dealing with the Orient—dealing with it by making statements about it, authorizing views of it, describing it, by teaching it, settling it, ruling over it: in short, Orientalism as a Western style for dominating, restructuring, and having authority over the Orient" (Said [1978] 1994, 3).

In this way, seemingly innocent and apolitical representations of particular peoples and geographies move from the sphere of discourse to that of practice through the activation of policies geared toward dominating othered subjects. Using a Gramscian understanding of hegemony, Said explains how Orientalism persists over time as a result of cultural hegemony, when society has largely bought into and accepted a hierarchical organization of culture that affirms the authority of colonial offices, the museum, the academy, and the sciences ([1978] 1994, 7).[3] Most importantly, what Said's study uncovers is the dialectic among the individual, the text, and the collective in the formation of narratives and practices that work to normalize and sustain relations of power over particular bodies and places.

This chapter analyzes *indigenismo* as the mobilizing ideology through which white and mestizo intellectuals frame their perceptions of the place of indigenous peoples within the past, present, and future of the liberal nation-state. This includes analyzing forms of visual representation and iconography widely used by the colonial and postcolonial state and civil society to portray ideals of Mexicanness and indigeneity that often stand in tense relation with each other. I argue that ideas of indigenismo and *mestizaje* emerged as a response partly to the Black Legend—the widespread anti-Hispanic sentiment that emerged during and after the colonial period—and partly to liberal and conservative desires to form a nation that rejected the dominance of Hispanic or indigenous heritages, seeking instead a hybrid rooted in the glorified and static Mexica (Aztec) Kingdom. But, following Luis Villoro's chronology of indigenismo, I suggest that perhaps the central subject of this ideological current is the nonindigenous citizen whose sense of self is developed in juxtaposition to the sacrificed indigenous Other. Finally, I begin to shift attention toward western Mexico, where I examine a few instances of the indigenous uprisings that carried over from the colonial period to postindependence, further ignited by the onslaught of liberal reforms that destabilized indigenous territorial and cultural coherence. While materially unsuccessful, these moments of indigenous rebellion did indeed feed into the popular and academic imaginary, eventually leading to the postrevolutionary movement of applied indigenismo, as well as to its relatively slow progression in the Wixarika homeland territory of the Western Sierra Madre highlands.

In Mexico, the theories and practices that have come to be known as indigenismo can be seen as a consolidation of the long legacy of often contradictory representations of the indigenous by the nonindigenous, which are then mobilized into political and civic action. Indigenismo is best understood as an intellectual, cultural, and political ideological movement, or current, in Latin America that reached its apex in the twentieth century and has fomented the study, and in many cases the defense, of indigenous peoples and cultures.[4] Indigenismo took hold throughout Latin America with varying degrees of institutional and popular support, reflecting sharp philosophical contrasts and "a variety of ideological directions" (M. E. García 2005, 63). Its most powerful manifestations occurred during the first half of the twentieth century in countries like Mexico and Peru, which recognized their sizable indigenous populations at the same time as their political leadership espoused the wonders of their most grandiose pre-Hispanic legacies—the Aztec and Inca empires (Earle 2007, 185). But as Marisol de la Cadena and Orin Starn note, it was never a singular project but one lodged in particular historical contingencies (2009, 196). To a large extent, the objective of indigenismo was to tackle the so-called Indian problem, which posed a direct challenge to a coherent nation-state by being squarely rooted in the "cultural, economic, and political legacies of conquest and colonialism" (M. E. García 2005, 63). In 1916, amid the Mexican Revolution, the preeminent indigenista anthropologist Manuel Gamio published *Forjando patria* (Forging a nation) as a call for the country to move toward a unified nation-building project. According to Gamio, Mexico's principal barrier was its geographic, cultural, and ethnic "disarticulation," which created a series of "small nations" unable to abide by larger political, economic, and cultural projects ([1916] 1960, 10–11). Along with other contemporary scholars, such as José Vasconcelos, Gamio pushed forth the idea of national unification through the process of bringing together the cultures of steel and bronze, the European and the Indian, to create ethnic, linguistic, and cultural cohesion through the celebration of the mestizo as the quintessential hybrid Mexican. The exaltation of the mestizo as the ideal revolutionary subject brought about a direct foreclosure of the indigenous as equal citizen, a matter that would lead to repeated, sustained, and diverse contestations from indigenous communities from the colonial period until the current moment.

THE RISE OF THE MEXICA—ICONOGRAPHY AND VISUAL REPRESENTATION

> *In passing from history to nature, myth creates an economy: it abolishes the complexity of human acts, gives them the simplicity of the essences, it eliminates all dialectic, any return to what is not immediately perceived, it organizes a world without contradictions because it is one without depth, a world laid out based upon evidence, it creates a cheerful clarity; things appear to have meaning by themselves.*
> —ROLAND BARTHES, *MYTHOLOGIES* (MY TRANSLATION FROM THE FRENCH)

Two juxtaposed images: Generals Porfirio Díaz and Venustiano Carranza both pose with cane in hand before the monumental Aztec calendar. While each leader now symbolizes opposing values within Mexican historiography—one authoritarian and the other revolutionary—they share the same canon that established the Mexica Empire as the founding myth of the Mexican nation. Tenochtitlán was Mexico's Rome, the country's badge of honor among the civilized nations. Although the adulation of Mexico's pre-Hispanic heritage is often associated with the grandiose efforts of the revolutionary state, the gaze of the country's political and intellectual leaders was already set on the indigenous prior to winning independence from Spain in 1821 and was well advanced during the Díaz regime (1876–1910). So with these two photographs, we have two distinct political leaderships that are nonetheless inextricably linked by the Aztec calendar's promise as a stepping stone in Mexico's path toward modern nationhood.

When Spanish Jesuit scholar Francisco Javier Clavijero wrote his epic *History of Ancient Mexico* in 1780, he set out to do so as a way to redeem the image of indigenous Mexico against what he saw as the judgmental eyes of European writers, who diligently condemned the savagery of the native inhabitants of the New World. Clavijero's self-proclaimed mission was to rewrite the history of

FIGURES 3A AND 3B Two juxtaposed images: Porfirio Díaz (*left*), 1910, and Venustiano Carranza (*right*), 1917, pose before the Aztec calendar stone. Courtesy of the Secretaría de Cultura and the Instituto Nacional de Antropología e Historia.

indigenous America in what historian Enrique Florescano calls "a manifestation of criollo consciousness" (2002, 277). In *Capítulos de historia y disertaciones*, Clavijero sternly criticizes the assumption with which his intended European readers encounter the so-called New World—namely that America was new because three centuries back it had been unknown to the European, when in reality the "New World" could boast an equally ancient history as the "Old World" (Clavijero cited in Villoro [1950] 1987, 118). Clavijero's master work, *History of Ancient Mexico*, became a classic of colonial Mexican literature, a work that rewrote the history of the Spanish conquest in a way that depicts the Mexica as a dignified and brave people with a rich history and culture, and that defies the myths written by his European contemporaries, Corneille de Pauw and Georges-Louis Leclerc, Comte de Buffon. Yet like his successors, Clavijero exalted the Mexica at the cost of other indigenous peoples like the "Caribs and Iroquois," whom he described as less apt to compete with the grandest civilizations of Europe. From architectural and engineering feats to arts and crafts, the depictions of Mexica culture by Clavijero not only disproved narratives of Aztec barbarism but sought to prove the superiority of the Mexica over most known societies, past and present (Villoro [1950] 1987, 141).

In the midst of Mexico's war for independence, Fray Servando de Mier soon followed Clavijero's exposé of Aztec glory with the 1813 publication of *History of the Revolution of New Spain*, which fomented the Black Legend by detailing Spanish despotism from the conquest onward. Florescano notes that Mier's narrative is as much an ode to Mexican independence as it is about the revindication of a destroyed continent through the renewed praise of the Mexica legacy, including the use of Nahuatl place names and the creation of "neo-Aztequist" national histories (Florescano 2002, 292–300).

Above all, the monumentality of the Mexica Empire gave the country's leadership a way of forging a unique cultural identity that they believed could challenge Europe's cultural supremacy. But as philosopher Luis Villoro poignantly notes, rather than speaking to the nation's internal realities, these efforts transpired as a self-conscious way to convince Western powers that Mexico was worthy:

> In the waiting room of its independence, America had seen the need to reflect upon herself in order to confront Europe. But if at that moment she looked to her reality, she did so always with her attention placed on the Other; she did not care so much in seeing herself as she truly was, rather, she sought to present Europe

with a distinct image of what it wanted to see. In this way, Clavijero seeks out a reality opaque for the European: the Indian. America judges herself, but her judgment is established for use by the Other, for somebody else's consumption. (Villoro [1950] 1987, 209; my translation)

Rebecca Earle's *The Return of the Native* discusses this dilemma: after achieving independence from Spain, the Latin American elite held a "double discourse," as they wrestled with the notion that they were legitimate heirs of preconquest kingdoms at the same time as they desired to hold on to elements of their Hispanic heritage (2007, 39). As with Clavijero, criollos self-consciously sought out narratives they felt could contest the circulation of imagery representing Latin America as a breeding ground for cannibalistic tendencies. Although depictions of barbarism targeted the indigenous, the African, and the mixed race, or *castas*, criollo desires for belonging to civilized societies inspired them to rerepresent their geographies. Consequently, "In defending the Aztecs and the Incas, creoles were implicitly defending themselves from European claims of degeneracy and inferiority" (28). In the context of Mexico, the nationalist texts that emerged during this period were political manifestos that "Mexicanized" the chronicles composed during the initial years of conquest by inserting the view of the conquered, even if this view was imagined and inscribed by the privileged criollo elite (Florescano 2002, 304).

According to Villoro, the challenge for these early indigenistas was to return the gaze to the Europeans by deploying American greatness and European savagery while disdaining the so-called backwardness of their darker-skinned populations. Again, the problem of criollo "double discourse" was this simultaneous praise of the grandiose pre-Hispanic and the explicit disavowal of each nation's living indigenous cultures, considered to be burdens on progress. Unlike other scholars, Villoro attributes this inconsistency of discourse not so much to a contradictory consciousness but to the elites' temporal and geographic distance from these distinct indigenous groups. In other words, the Mexica could be more easily praised and mythologized not simply because they were the imperial presence that Hernán Cortés's troops memorably confronted, nor because they left palpable material signs of a monumental civilization; the Mexica could be more easily eulogized because they no longer existed in the same time and space as these elites. Conversely, living indigenous peoples remained threatening reminders of cultural, political, and economic difference and possible enemies to the postcolonial ruling classes.

The "Caribs and Iroquois" of Clavijero would thus become the "Indian problem" that these same competing elites would break their heads to resolve through extermination, expulsion, forced labor, and miscegenation. Out of this context of postcolonial historical revisionism, indigenismo gradually arises as a powerful discursive tool for molding Mexican citizenship abroad and at home. Nineteenth-century liberals and conservatives argued over the place of indigenous peoples within a modern nation-state and promoted theories for why indigenous peoples remained segregated from the nonindigenous and how this reality could be managed by the state. While the conservatives leaned toward allowing the continuation of separate "Indian Republics" as had existed under the colonial regime, liberals increasingly called for the expropriation of communal lands as a way to expand the tenure of private property and mold the Indian into a small rural landowner. In this way, the "Indian problem" was increasingly a socioeconomic problem that interposed itself amid the battling political economic philosophies that fueled the Guerra de Reforma (Reform War) that raged between 1857 and 1861. Political and economic struggles aside, the warring factions of the Guerra de Reforma continued to produce a large body of visual and literary representations of the indigenous, in which the hypervisibility of the Mexica turned prototypical nationalist contrasted sharply with the opaque indigenous Other.

In *Mythologies*, Roland Barthes (1957) brilliantly exposes how the myth is a semiotic system that is able to reconfigure itself through time and space, creating a complex economy of meanings that, even over time, can avert being exposed in its contradictions. Mythologies live not because they are fixed or without contradictions but because they can be picked up and put to work by the individual, the collective, and the state. In this way, the images of Moctezuma and Cuauhtémoc as mythical founding fathers have been worked into the Mexican psyche to symbolize the nation's heroic difference before the world and its tragic resistance to imperial forces, then and now. Since independence, much of the nation's symbols have centered around the glory and defeat of these last Mexica emperors, inculcating a profound sense of nationalism based on a mythologized Indian past whose torch bearers are rarely the present-day indigenous communities. Notably, these representations are highly geographic and instruct the public's eye toward the monumental center: Tenochtitlán / Mexico City. These representations thus construct a racial geography that Saldaña-Portillo describes as "indexing" a "series of techniques used to produce space in racial terms" (2016, 17), where western Mexico inhabits a barbarous frontier with a rebellious and thus disposable population.

Personal memories continue to transport me to my grammar school history books, produced by the SEP. The classroom listened in awe to the teacher's story of Hernán Cortés brutally burning Cuauhtémoc alive, forcing the noble emperor to divulge the whereabouts of his peoples' treasures. The great Tenochtitlán was then buried, and a new society was erected from its ashes. Outside the classroom, these same stories were replicated on the walls of government buildings, while Mexica martyrs appeared on money, in calendars, and in children's stories. These manifestations are part of what Benedict Anderson (1991) signals as markers of an imagined national community where a common language is formed around a mythologized history and culture. In Mexico, the fall of the Aztec Empire to Spanish horses and steel, as well as the birth of the mestizo, became the ultimate embodiment of the clash of the two empires. Following Thongchai Winichakul's (1994) analysis of the colonial map, Mexico's cultural map can be understood as a projection of state desires, rather than a reflection of the country's contrasting historical and cultural realities, which sit distant from the fall of Tenochtitlán and the rise of Mexico City. Nonetheless, the narrative of the nation-state becomes hegemonic through visual technologies like the map, the mural, and the first-grade history book.

Barthes states, "Every semiotic system is a system of values; in this way the consumer of the myth takes its signification as a system of facts: the myth is read like a factual system when it is but a semiotic system" (Barthes 1957, 204). Myth making thus continues even as the nation has slowly come to replace the single narrative of the Mexica and the Spanish with notions of pluriculturalism, which aesthetically and textually recognize the nation's heterogeneity. Through the dialectic of direct encounters and multidirectional imaginaries, indigeneity has existed as permanent social, ethnic, and political alterity from the colonial encounter onward. As noted by de la Cadena and Starn, "Taking indigeneity into account requires that it be recognized as a relational field of governance, subjectivities and understandings that involve us all—indigenous and nonindigenous—in the construction and reconstruction of its structures of power and imagination" (2009, 195). In 2010, when Mexico celebrated two hundred years of independence and one hundred years since the Revolution, the government sponsored a traveling multimedia celebration called "200 Years of Being Proudly Mexican." A one-hundred-meter screen took the audience through the grandest moments of Mexican history, culminating with Pepe Aguilar's mariachi interpretation of "México lindo y querido" and accompanied by images of present-day multiculturalism: "Todos somos México," punk rockers, Indians, industrial workers, and homemakers. In late May 2010, during the unveiling of this multimedia spectacle on the UAN soccer field in Tepic, a select group of Wixarika and Náayeri students were asked to dress in their traditional attire and welcome the first lady, Margarita Zavala. The cordoned-off VIP area behind the screen appeared to be the backstage of a multicultural performance, and various attendees took photos with the indigenous guests. In the post-multicultural era, the Mexica is no longer the dominant ethnic marker of Mexico. As the multimedia presentation demonstrated, Mexico discursively imagines itself as an ethnically and culturally diverse nation, albeit one that eventually leads back to the mestizo (e.g., the mariachi) as the unifying identity of the nation.

Present models of multicultural citizenship carry equally potent forms of visual and textual representations, which continue to do the work of foreclosing indigenous heterogeneity. Racial expectations remain prevalent, as do desires to consume race in various private and public spaces. Consequently, iconography and representation continue to steer the popular imagination toward envisioning indigenous peoples in limited physical and temporal spaces, creating a situation in which indigenous peoples' recognition before state and society is contingent on this established cartography. In *The Cunning of Recognition*, Elizabeth Povinelli demonstrates that to understand the standards that have been set for recognition, one inevitably must return to "the archive," the long body of scholarly and governmental work that has come to define indigenous tradition and authenticity (2002, 230). Accordingly, the archive makes recognition contingent on internalizing and carefully performing on "the nation's and law's image of traditional cultural forms and national reconciliation and at the same time ghost this being for the nation so as not to have their desires for some economic certainty in their lives appear opportunistic" (8). Wixarika university students and professionals daily walk a careful line interpellating these expectations, choosing whether to dress up for the first lady or sit out of the performance altogether. Furthermore, as Deborah Poole notes in her study of the "visual economy" of photography in Peru, we must not forget that popular images of indigenous peoples have not occurred in the context of reciprocal and equal exchange; the targeted subject has often been mute in the exchange, though in some cases has actively consented to it (1997, 133). In this way, contemporary hypervisible representations of Wixaritari are part of the longer history of a "visual economy" that commodifies and masks subjectivity at once. The genre of casta painting helps illustrate the long arc of race and racial representation in Mexican society and more clearly connects how depictions of people and their geographies are activated at certain historical junctures, with tangible material effects experienced through the attempted forceful reorganization of peoples' relationship to territory.

TO NAME AND TO PLACE: CASTA PAINTINGS AND COLONIAL RACIAL CONSCIOUSNESS

> *The long-standing fascination in Europe with foreign lands and peoples, and Mexico's strong sense of creole identity at the beginning of the eighteenth century are some of the broader issues that need to be taken into account when examining [casta paintings]. In fact, the interest in portraying colonial life in a positive light, coupled with European's fascination with non-European cultures, lies at the core of this pictorial genre.*
> —ILONA KATZEW, *CASTA PAINTING*

I keenly remember the section in my fifth-grade history textbook that described the six principal castas of Mexico's colonial order: español, criollo, mestizo, indígena, mulatto, and zambo.[5] Within the textbook, the order and description of these six castas followed a hierarchical movement that clearly identified the indígena, mulatto, and zambo on the lower progression of society. The SEP illustrators also chose particular visual depictions. Of these, I can still clearly recall how the español wore a coat of armor and the zambo had a bare torso. The sharp contrast between the armored and nude bodies left me with an unplaceable haunting feeling. While my teacher cautioned tolerance and spoke of the castas as a long-gone phenomenon, the didactics of the textbook replicated the racial gradient on which Mexican society was still situated.

Following the first century of conquest and destruction, the Spanish colonial system became increasingly consolidated, moving toward what Margarita de Orellana terms a "new stage of alterity," which had surpassed the manifest awe and violence of contact and negotiated a future of social relations with the indigenous Other (1998, 54). This "new stage of alterity" is made visible in the casta paintings produced in colonial New Spain, which portray racial representations and racial relations in postconquest Mexico and expose a vacillation between celebratory pride in the nation's ethnic diversity and blunt efforts at containing that diversity. Analysis of these paintings' aesthetic and social content can help us understand the trajectory of representation and its codeterminate role in cementing social hierarchies, which have arguably remained quite similar across time. Ilona Katzew's formidable study of casta paintings (2004) illustrates just how important it is to bring this pictorial genre out of the shadows, not only because it can help contemporary scholars better understand the colonial social order, but because it illustrates notions of alterity and racial representation during a moment when the interest for naming, classifying, and displaying objects and peoples became an important force within European intellectual and political circles, casting important ripple effects throughout the colonized Western hemisphere.

Casta was an administrative term used during this period to designate any combination of mixed ethnic heritage and its relative position within the colonial social hierarchy. In practice, the Spanish and criollos were exempted from the casta label, which was largely used to name any person of mixed ethnic heritage. Detailing the vast ethnic miscegenation of the period, the paintings in question expose the tense interplay between the celebration of ethnic diversity of New Spain and the ways in which these racial "combinations" were subsequently laid out along the social, economic, and political hierarchy of the era. Casta paintings are thus powerful visual depictions of the racial heterogeneity and organization of the colonial era.

Did the idea of onomastics emerge in the context of New Spain? How did naming and portraying the offspring of racial miscegenation become increasingly valued for its aesthetic and social content? Katzew's study argues that this was a twofold process: On the one hand, Europeans—the Spanish Crown and Church—sought to "know" the New World by viewing it from afar. Like maps, these pictorial representations allowed the king to envision the far-off spaces of conquest that he was administering because "knowing was predicated on seeing" (Mundy 1996, 9). On the other hand, casta paintings emerged from a "strong sense of creole identity," with the descendants of Spaniards in New Spain proudly displaying the environmental and cultural wealth of their territory. European travelers exhibited similar celebration in their own writings, where the climate, customs, and inhabitants of New Spain were depicted as highly attractive to the foreign eye (Katzew 2004, 39). Orellana argues that these artistic depictions of the New World's variety largely reflected the European eye and its astonishment with the "American." In this way, images of natives were "assimilated" into already circulating medieval depictions of European pagans and infidels, while the Mexica temples resembled Roman and Egyptian ones (Orellana 1998, 52–54). These colonial cartographies and canvases were foremost what Fernando Coronil delineates as "partial perspectives" that worked in "accordance with particular standpoints and specific aims" and inevitably "apprehended" the real movement inherent within living geographies (1996, 53).

Nonetheless, emerging local writers and artists created works that proudly asserted their difference before Old Europe, emphasizing New Spain's environmental and cultural wealth. Famed poet Sor Juana Inés de la Cruz's "Villancicos" (1998) speaks of ethnic miscegenation in humorous, affectionate, and even encouraging tones, indicating how the intellectual strata of colonial society embraced ethnic diversity. As early as 1680 writer Carlos de Sigüenza y Góngora designed an arch for Mexico City that was decorated by twelve "pre-Conquest monarchs," demonstrating early signs of the coming indigenista aesthetics, which reached their height under the Porfirian and postrevolutionary regimes (Katzew 2004, 69). A look at the first wave of casta paintings indeed gives the impression of a tolerant and diverse society. For example, the 1725 *De negro e india, lobo* painting attributed to artist José Ibarra depicts a well-dressed African man and his indigenous wife and child, who similarly wear elegant huipiles, illustrating a degree of admiration for traditional indigenous dress (62).

That said, the casta paintings are an undeniable reproduction of social hierarchization obsessed with seeing and grading race. While miscegenation was tolerated and at times celebrated, it was also strongly condemned. In this way, the production of these paintings serves as a pictorial testimony to the ways in which colonial Mexico moved toward displaying and controlling ethnic difference. The 1680 *Recopilación de las leyes de los reynos de Indias* gives evidence that casta status determined tribute payments, as well as access to employment, education, and religious positions (Katzew 2004, 41). While the actual efforts to impose these laws were largely ineffective (people continued to interact and procreate across ethnic barriers), the idea of castas and their visual portrayals had material effects on those who were considered to belong to the lower rungs of the racial ladder. People of African descent were particularly targeted as carriers of "tainted blood," and colonial officials went to special ends to attempt to limit the interaction of African and indigenous peoples, seeing their offspring as the most degenerate members of society.[6] Likewise, distinctions were made between different "types" of indigenous peoples, with those thought to be descendants of nobility given a pass, as they had *calidad* (quality) and thus higher standing. Interestingly, the dichotomies drawn between good and bad Indians followed geographic lines, as the categories of *Indios bárbaros*, *Indios chichimecas*, and *Indios apaches* represented the indigenous peoples in the northern territories, where the Spanish struggled to exert their authority (Katzew 2004, 136–37). And within urban spaces, efforts were made to segregate the indigenous peoples from Africans out of fear that the two groups could mobilize against the Spanish (46).

Despite these racial hierarchies, people had the ability to better their social standing by marrying up the racial ladder, earning a reputable employment or religious position, or purchasing certificates of whiteness called "Gracias al sacar" (Thank you for removal; Katzew 2004, 49–56).[7] Notwithstanding, for Spanish colonial observers, both the casta system and its accompanying paintings indicated a degeneration of their territories and a lack of criollo control over the society they managed for the Crown. For these administrators, miscegenation was a clear indicator of criollo permissiveness that needed to be contained. Katzew points out that with the Bourbon Reforms of the second half of the eighteenth century, the Spanish strengthened their grip over New Spain, carrying out a type of "recolonization" that was in turn reflected in the casta paintings of the period, in which a heightened sense of racial hierarchization is depicted by giving each casta a specific personality and occupational trait (111–14). Consequently, the social malleability that was rightly or wrongly seen as part of the pre–Bourbon Reform period was replaced with more fixed ideas of what each racialized subject brought to society. Casta painting not only reached its apex during the second half of the eighteenth century, but did so in the context of rising European interests in naming and categorizing the world, most notably under the guidance of Carolus Linnaeus and de Buffon's "cabinets of natural history." The peoples of the New World were aligned with the worlds of flora and fauna, their depictions or actual bodies transported to Europe for the pleasure of the imperial courts and academics: "The cabinet provided the ideal forum from which colonial difference could be contained and articulated as a category of nature. Moreover, by entering the cabinet[,] casta paintings not only became part of the global categorization project fostered by eighteenth-century naturalists but were in themselves microcosms that organized nature's bounty and allocated a specific place for each element" (Katzew 2004, 160–61). As Allan Pred tells us through the story of Badin, a Caribbean man taken to the Swedish imperial court during the eighteenth century, the bodies of the stereotyped were increasingly determined and fixed by "Linnaeus' eye," the eyes of science and art, the eyes of power and discourse (2004, 30). In 1813, insurgent independence leader José María Morelos called for the abolition of casta categories in the Constitution of Apatzingán (Castelló Yturbide 1998, 73). With its independence, Mexico's political leadership sought to no longer mirror the colonial social order and made discursive strides to move toward a unified national body reigned over by the figure of the mestizo.

INDIGENISMO AND MESTIZAJE AS A MEDITATION ON MEXICAN ALTERITY

> *His life in exchange for the perpetual recognition of the other! The mestizo cannot destroy the Indian because he needs him; he needs to conserve him. The formula of this conservation will be the "transformation" of the Indian. Within it the Indian is denied in his peculiarity and autonomy, but is conserved in his existence as long as he accepts his submission to the mestizo's social, economic and cultural system.*
> —LUIS VILLORO, *LOS GRANDES MOMENTOS DEL INDIGENISMO EN MÉXICO* (MY TRANSLATION)

For the past several decades, scholars have written extensively about indigenismo and mestizaje as ideologies that heavily shaped postrevolutionary Mexican society. Much of the discussion revolves around the ways in which state and society select and assimilate certain folkloric characteristics of the nation's indigenous heritage while simultaneously deploying projects of assimilation targeted at a culturally and geographically heterogeneous indigenous population. These shifts from indigenista discourse to practice and the debates that surged within indigenista governmental and academic institutions over the "Indian problem" are further discussed in chapter 2. What is relevant for the present discussion is the failure to substantively consider indigenismo as a series of meditations on Mexican alterity that have shifted through time and space. In this light, Luis Villoro's pioneering book, *Los grandes momentos del indigenismo en México*, becomes seminal for understanding how indigenismo is not simply a product of the Mexican Revolution and the National Indigenist Institute but rather a series of philosophical quandaries that illuminate how nonindigenous peoples have sought to discover and emplace the self in relation to the country's indigenous Other. This analysis concurs with Coronil's discussion of the entangled construction of "otherness" and "selfhood," which draws on Hegelian phenomenology, whereby consciousness of the self is materialized through the recognition of the Other (Coronil 1996, 56–58). Likewise Villoro critically frames indigenismo as a problem of the mestizo consciousness and poses the question: "What of the being of the Indian is manifested in the Mexican consciousness?" (Villoro [1950] 1987, 9).

Villoro organizes his argument by looking at three "moments" in Mexico's indigenismo, beginning with the conquest and concluding with the surge of postrevolutionary institutional indigenista frameworks. Villoro uses these different moments to sustain his argument that indigenismo reflects how the racial projections of Spaniards, criollos, and mestizos are reconfigured depending on the historical context of each period. Indigenismo is thus a process whereby the Indian is "understood and judged" or "revealed" by the non-Indian, leading to material acts that define the type of "domination and exploitation" that will be used to contain the Indian ([1950] 1987, 8). More importantly, Villoro's three moments conceive of space and time as central in shaping the indigenista's philosophy and view of the indigenous in which the mestizo self is inseparable from the indigenous Other. Within this analysis, the relation between the mestizo and the indigenous subject is mediated by spatial and temporal proximity: the act of the indigenous subject being "present and close" is reflected in negative characterizations (e.g., antimodern Indian of the present moment); conversely, the indigenous subject's existence as "past and distant" allows for positive accounts of Indian glory (e.g., the imperial Mexica past). In this way, the indigenous Other is in contrapuntal relation not simply to a nonindigenous self (Coronil 1996, 73) but to distinct temporal and spatial constructions of indigenous subjectivities.

Villoro shows how each moment of indigenista thought uses a particular rationale of representation and domination and by doing so presents the indigenous as knowable and thus transparent to the European eye. Here it is worth pausing on the material effects of reason and transparency in framing racial identities. In Édouard Glissant's (1997) call for a "poetics of relation" based on the right to difference, he powerfully notes that transparency does the work of reduction and simplification through measurement. Much as Said teaches us, the deployment of reason within the context of colonial domination works to present flat and transparent representations of the Other that can be neatly ordered and categorized. Within this totalizing logic, the identities of colonized peoples are eternally opposed to those of Western peoples, creating a "limitation from the beginning," through which identity is understood as always in opposition rather than in dialectical relation (Glissant 1997, 17). For Glissant, liberation is achieved through the right to opacity, whereby people—in this case, colonized peoples—do not have to subjugate themselves to full disclosure and reduction but can choose the times and places in which they wish to reveal themselves in their difference.

Self-identification beyond that which is transparent to the colonial handbook has been inextricably tied to the power of representation and its centrality in ensuring rule, whether it be colonial, nationalist, or neoliberal. Villoro's three moments of Mexican indigenismo precisely outline the ways in which representations by the nonindigenous of the indigenous have worked, at least until the twentieth century. The first moment is that of colonial contact mediated by the writings of Hernán Cortés and Fray Bernardino de Sahagún, the conquistador and the evangelizer. At contact, the European stands in awe before an opaque Indian; the many unknowns of this new world and its people bring Cortés and his contemporaries toward the desire to know, study, and describe in order to conquer and dominate. Awe of the great city of Tenochtitlán is contrasted with a desire to expunge it. Here we have the first manifestations of the contradictory consciousness that the indigenista has toward indigenous peoples: "Naturally one will have to respect their laws and the order of their society that manifest themselves to us with beautiful colors; supernaturally one will have to destroy the idolatric stain that reveals itself perversely and demoniacally" (Villoro [1950] 1987, 65; my translation). Cortés's narratives mark the beginning of the twin indigenista tendencies of paternalism and admiration, judgment and disdain, that continue to manifest themselves today.

Sahagún's mission was not to conquer cities and empires, but to transform pagans into God-fearing Christians. From this mission, Sahagún sought to explain the origins of Indian idolatry to eliminate it through evangelization. Throughout this friar's writings, one finds ample elements of admiration for indigenous peoples' cultural values, from art and engineering to family life. Similarly to Cortés, he demonstrates appreciation and disgust at this newly encountered world. Yet in his *Historia de la conquista de México*, Sahagún includes examples of unwarranted Spanish brutality, such as Pedro de Alvarado, like an eager anthropologist, asking Moctezuma to have his people perform a ceremony to Huitzilopochtli, during which Alvarado ordered Spanish soldiers to lock all palace doors and massacre the Indians. Sahagún writes that "blood ran along the patio as water does when it rains, and the entire patio was planted with heads and arms, and guts, and bodies of dead men: in every corner the Spanish looked for living ones in order to kill them" ([1590] 1829, 27–28). His texts were subsequently placed in the Vatican Secret Archives because of his perceived sympathy for the beliefs of native peoples. One of Sahagún's principal endeavors was to comprehend the relation that indigenous peoples had with "universal history and culture" while he attempted to recognize how their beliefs could be valued on their own grounds. Notwithstanding, Villoro argues, the logic that both Cortés and Sahagún worked with reflected the understanding that the destruction of the Indian was inevitable: the Indian could only be purified through his annihilation. In this first moment of indigenismo, "destruction and rebirth mark the moment in which the Indian is expiated. And it is precisely within this purifying movement that a new nation is created. It is through the tragic renunciation of the Indian that the Mexican people are born" (Villoro [1950] 1987, 109). Saldaña-Portillo similarly notes, "The violence and suffering of indigenous people in the conquest is constantly, reiteratively affirmed and projected onto the landscape" (2016, 12). As we were told in the mythology of our Mexican textbooks, the birth of the Mexican nation and people begins at this celebrated moment of death. The original sins of Cortés and the conquistadores are cleansed by the martyred Mexica and resurrected through the mestizo.

Important parallels can be drawn between the Mexican narrative of the sacrificial Indian and anthropologist Michael Taussig's analysis of terror and healing in *Shamanism, Colonialism, and the Wild Man* (1987). The long centuries of colonial and neocolonial rule in Colombia are primarily marked by what Taussig terms the space of death "where the Indian, African, and white gave birth to a New World," and where the inequity that held these three groups together sustained colonial hegemony (1987, 5). Slowly the conqueror and the conquered become codependent—bound together through the inner workings of colonial rule, literally exemplified in the figure of the *cargador indio*, or *tameme*, in central Mexico, whose trade is to carry the white man on his back through the tortuous trails of the Andes. The white man needs the Indian to navigate the New World's territories, while the Indian needs the white man's employment to survive under the New World's economic system. In this light, torture and death as well as negotiation and submission become intrinsic ingredients of colonial hegemony:

> It was not even that this subordination of the Indian was achieved by a *blending* of force and fraud, or of arms and persuasion, or of conquest through barter and of barter through conquest. All that way of thinking is merely a truism that preserves

the separateness of the domains even while blending them; violence and ideology, power and knowledge, force and discourse, economy and superstructure. . . . But when we put the two languages together it is not the blending of force . . . that results, but a quite different conception in which the body of the Indian, in the process of its conquest, in its debt-peonage and in its being tortured, dissolves those domains so that violence and ideology, power and knowledge, become one—as with terror itself. (Taussig 1987, 29)

Cortés and Sahagún's narratives mirror this impossibility of separating admiration from contempt, where acts of reason and violence are mutually sustaining and where the death of the Indian is read as *his* and the white man's salvation.

Moreover, the indigenous subject's transformation through the space of death (whether figurative or literal) enables future acts of rebellion across indigenous territories, as well as the construction of indigenismo as a national narrative of Mexican perseverance through tragedy. The real and imagined experiences of the Indian coming close to death yet managing to survive become powerful discursive tools not only for the indigenista but for the indigenous as well. In considering the experience of the Middle Passage, Glissant similarly points to the act of death and being near death as cathartic moments that hold unknowable keys for understanding the future. Glissant signals how unaware the sufferer is of his or her foundational role in establishing the modern: "Peoples who have been to the abyss do not brag of being chosen. They do not believe that they are giving birth to any modern force. They live Relation and clear the way for it, to the extent that the oblivion of the abyss comes to them and that, consequently, their memory intensifies" (1997, 8). The act of memory—remembering the Mexica kingdom and foreclosing living historical subjects—becomes the Mexican nation's passage to the modern, a passage that rests on the back and territory of living indigenous peoples.

Villoro's second moment in Mexican indigenismo comes during the nineteenth century, as the Enlightenment and accompanying notions of universal reason take hold among the country's intellectual circles. Whereas Cortés and Sahagún's narratives are used as quintessential examples of the first moment, dominated by ideas of the supernatural and the unknown, the second moment appears through the writings of Francisco Clavijero, Fray Teresa de Mier, and Manuel Orozco y Berra, which rest on the vindication of the Mexica and on the rising interest in the classification and ordering of society through the prism of universal reason. In other words, the first moment is led by the opaque while the second is framed by conceptions of transparency, which Villoro best describes through the writings of Orozco y Berra: "Now we walk through a conglomeration of figures. All of them are there, neatly organized, polished, awaiting their turn. The inventory is perfect, nothing is missing, indigenous civilization is complete: all of their themes are laid bare, their dates, perfectly aligned ... one after the other; they sleep in their dream. It seems as if all things indigenous made it to their appointment" (Villoro [1950] 1987, 177; my translation). Accordingly, the battle between the civilized and barbarian races takes center stage in Manuel Orozco y Berra's *Historia Antigua y de la conquista de México* (1880). Most importantly, the Nahuatl people (the Mexica and other peoples of central Mexico) follow the universal law toward progress, while the Chichimecs (the indigenous peoples of the northern and western territories, such as the Wixarika) resist civilization to personal exhaustion (Villoro [1950] 1987, 181).

Villoro's critique draws interesting parallels with Dipesh Chakrabarty's (2000) conceptualization of Histories 1 and 2; the former mirrors a rationalistic European-centered ideal of historical progress, and the latter allows for alternate, nonlinear, and nonsecular models of history. In *Provincializing Europe* Chakrabarty places historicism on the table, outlining how the idea of "first in Europe, then elsewhere" falsely presupposed that all non-Western nations would eventually "produce local versions of the same narrative" already problematically imposed for determining the progression of European modernity (2000, 7). Returning to the nineteenth-century indigenista narrative, indigenous peoples, like their African and Asian counterparts, remained in the "imaginary waiting room of history," where they would need to eventually face a form of cultural obliteration to join the ranks of the modern (8). Crucially, Chakrabarty makes the "third world nationalism" emulated by the indigenista authors coresponsible with the European imperial project for their "collaborative venture and violence" in upholding the universal and the rational (42). The experiences of territorial displacement, forced acculturation, and extermination that the native peoples of the Americas witnessed during the nineteenth century manifest how this violence is both epistemic and material. In the context of Mexico, the Reform Laws dispossessed native peoples of their lands and forced them into becoming wage laborers for the hacendados (plantation owners), while the country's intellectual elite perceived the indigenous as passive objects of study that were given meaning only through the criollo and mestizo analytical eye.

As the Mexican nation-state struggled to consolidate itself amid continued foreign invasion and internal conflict between conservatives and liberals, the political and intellectual elite self-consciously debated the ways in which

Mexico could become modern. Against the backdrop of the judgmental eye of nineteenth-century academics and the literal invasions of French and U.S. military forces, the indigenous lent the discourses of Mexico's elites "specificity and consistency" that could be used to give the nation a sense of individuality and difference, which could "liberate" it from the denigrating European gaze (Villoro [1950] 1987, 209). At the same time, these elites grappled with how they would manage those indigenous peoples who coexisted with them in the same time and space. Here, Clavijero felt certain that the "inferiority" of the Indian was "purely accidental" and "dependent on historical factors," which were thus "perfectly solvable" through mechanisms of cultural, economic, and political acculturation (Clavijero cited in Villoro [1950] 1987, 136–37).

According to Villoro, Orozco y Berra heavily deploys the "scientific rational criteria" to understand the place of the indigenous subject within the modern Mexican nation-state ([1950] 1987, 187). Gathering data and subsequently classifying and analyzing it thus contributes to an idealized "objective" history of the indigenous and traces the path for establishing modes of racial relations based on segmenting the population between those deemed salvageable and those considered disposable. Drawing important parallels with the casta paintings, Villoro argues that during this second moment in indigenismo, the Indian is made "passive, inert, willing to be analyzed and classified" (181). Ironically, during the very moments in which these narratives were constructed and debated, indigenous peoples throughout the Mexican territory reacted to the political economic forces that actively worked to dispossess them from their land and culture.

REBELLION AND THE COMMODIFICATION OF LAND AND LABOR

Recuperating our indigenous connections can begin with the recuperation of their history. Recuperating our indigenous past should not be centered on the isolation and separation of the indigenous from national history. Integrating our origins must include the moments of union and separation, of confrontation and conflict that make up our present history.
—BEATRIZ ROJAS, "LOS HUICHOLES" (MY TRANSLATION)

As the Mexican nation-state consolidated, the so-called Indian problem took on cultural, economic, and political magnitude, reflected in a series of policies that attempted to harness the indigenous to the state. Throughout the nineteenth century, Mexico struggled to hold onto its independence while seeking to become a modern capitalist nation. Liberals and conservatives hotly and often violently disputed the correct ways in which these objectives should be achieved. The place of indigenous peoples within Mexico became central to these tumultuous discussions, each side blaming the other for the continued lack of incorporation of the indigenous into the social, political, and economic spheres. In short, the indigenous subject became a type of pawn within their broader discussions over property ownership, the role of the church, and institution building. Conservatives pushed for the continuation of the colonial policy of "Indian republics," which allowed for indigenous communities to retain parallel governments and engage the Mexican state only when needed. Conversely, much like Gamio would argue later, liberals believed that only through the obliteration of these republics would indigenous peoples become integrated into a more homogeneous nation-state based on the ideals of individualism, private property, and a hybridized mestizo identity. In this way, indigenous peoples continued to be an object of study, of cataloging, and of discussion, their bodies described, scrutinized, and mapped as unmoving antagonists to the troubled national project.

As Villoro so eloquently demonstrates, the indigenous subject of the nineteenth century was too temporally and spatially present for the comfort of mestizos and criollos, while the mythologized but defeated Mexica was an increasingly visible symbol of national pride. Liberals and conservatives alike replaced Spanish heroes with Mexica ones, while they drafted programs through which indigenous peoples' cultures and territories would be managed. In fact, while the colonial system exerted unimaginable violence on native peoples, many now argue that the nineteenth century brought about unprecedented dispossession by delegitimizing indigenous autonomous structures of land tenancy and governance. During this period, two contrasting faces of Indian citizenship emerged: one marked by the formidable liberal president Benito Juárez and the other by the fiercely antiliberal rebellions that spanned northern, western, and eastern Mexico, culminating in the famous Caste War of Yucatán. Covering the regions of Tepic and Guadalajara, indigenous rebellion was marked by Manuel Lozada's troops, who led a nearly two-decade uprising against land privatization. While Juárez stands today as one of Mexico's most celebrated heroes and a symbol of indigenous leadership through assimilation, the figure of Lozada (also known as El Tigre de Álica) has largely been ignored in official histories—remembered as a bandit by some and a fighter for indigenous and peasants' rights by others. The historical context in which these two contrasting figures rose is crucial for understanding how they have been differently represented and remembered: one as the symbol of the "good Indian" and the other as the "bad Indian."

The War of Reform (1857–61) split liberals and conservatives into opposing warring factions, yet recent scholarship demonstrates that the two sides shared more in common than official historiography has led us to believe (Escobar Ohmstede 2007; C. A. Hale 1989; Hernández Silva 2007). For one, both liberals and conservatives did not hold to monolithic ideologies and did indeed share beliefs in the need to establish a degree of coherence and homogeneity for Mexico to develop economically and politically. Restructuring the country's model of land tenure was central in reaching these objectives. Yet it is undeniable that liberals, influenced by the likes of Auguste Comte and Herbert Spencer, sought secular republicanism and upheld the notions of private property and individual rights as the motor for a modern society (C. A. Hale 1989). For the country's leadership, better control over the nation's territory was an essential feat that needed to be achieved to rule over such geographic and ethnic heterogeneity.

Raymond Craib's study on the state's nineteenth-century cartographic projects points to not only how map making reflected the nation's engagement with the liberal scientific models in vogue at that time, but, more importantly, how the technology of cartography afforded Mexico a sense of nation making. The *Carta General de la República Mexicana*, produced by Antonio García Cubas in 1858, mapped, measured, and standardized the land, as it also sought out and portrayed preconquest and colonial histories, indigenous languages, and archaeological sites (Craib 2004, 28). It is worth noting that García Cubas was a close colleague of Orozco y Berra and that the two of them helped reinscribe the distinction between "good" and "bad" Indians under the basis of whether a tribe was sedentary and to what degree they had "proper ruins" and thus a "history," which the national imaginary could in turn celebrate. Again, this distinction followed a geographic and cultural line, designating the indigenous peoples of the northern territories as "perfidious, traitorous and cruel," lacking the material culture that would place them in the pantheon of the civilized Mexica, Maya, and Zapotecs (Orozco y Berra quoted in Craib 2004, 36). Craib argues that the work of mapping was multifold and brought about a symbolic reconquest of the national territory, ensuring Mexico a sense of control over land that was under constant foreign invasion, developing infrastructure such as railways and roads, and opening the country's territory to foreign investment by "rendering Mexico familiar to foreign viewers" (40).

Despite much of this rhetoric being centered on the solidification and protection of the nation-state and the transformation of its citizenry into propertied individuals, land was increasingly surveyed for the benefit of a few national and nonnational elites. The collective impact of these new technologies and Juárez's Lerdo Law of 1856, which expropriated communally held lands and transformed them into individually managed plots, posed a grave threat to indigenous communities. In the final analysis, "land division became an ideological obsession, a fixation, among Mexican liberals, who saw it as the solution to a host of social, economic, and political problems" (Craib 2004, 56). For many indigenous peoples, particularly those inhabiting the northwestern part of the country, the most serious social, economic, and political problems they had faced since the initial period of conquest came about after Mexico's independence from Spain. In fact, according to historian Beatriz Rojas, Wixaritari's limited involvement in the War of Independence shifted from a brief alliance with the insurgents to supporting the Crown—this on the basis of the landholding safeguards that the colonial regime recognized (Rojas 1993, 256–57). These strategic alliances between Wixarika communities and conservatives would endure throughout the nineteenth century and continue to evolve today following specific, often highly localized political contingencies offering lesser or greater control over communal territory and access to state resources.

Nonetheless, the liberal expropriation of communally held lands under the Lerdo Law was not carried out uniformly and consistently, and while many communities escaped direct state intervention, the general frenzy and "ideological fixation" over the privatization of land created a series of informal invasions and expropriations by mestizos of their indigenous neighbors. The combination of these factors quickly led to a series of organized peasant and indigenous rebellions, mirroring Karl Polanyi's conception of a "double movement," in which "society protects itself" from a dispossessing political economic system and, more concretely, the domination of the market over the social and political: "Ultimately, that is why the control of the economic system by the market is of overwhelming consequence to the whole organization of society: it means no less than the running of society as an adjunct to the market. Instead of economy being embedded in social relations, social relations are embedded in the economic system" (Polanyi [1944] 2001, 60).

In this light, Mexico's entry into the global system of industrial capitalism shares many parallels with Polanyi's analysis of the transformations experienced by the English peasantry and proletariat during the same historical period. Similarly, under the liberal leaderships of Juárez and Porfirio Díaz, the state facilitated the privatization of agrarian lands, causing massive rural displacement toward the country's developing industrial centers.[8] Out of this context, Manuel Lozada's armed rebellion began in 1857, organizing Nayarit's countryside to take back land handed over by the state to the haciendas one year after the Lerdo expropriation law was passed (Jáuregui 1999, 259).

On the other hand, the conservative government of Maximilian I's Second Mexican Empire (1864–67) sought to establish mechanisms by which it could institutionalize and better manage land titling and allotment while protecting the communally owned property of indigenous peoples by declaring it a special classification of private property (Meyer 1993, 347). Historian Jean Meyer aptly describes these actions as "progressive liberalism," rather than a form of orthodox conservatism, because Maximilian agreed with the premise of converting communal properties into private ones, as long as speculators and large landowners did not override the land rights of indigenous communities (330).[9] Much of these actions transpired under the paternalist and racialized notion that the indigenous character was docile and needed protection from the more astute mestizo and white land grabbers (353–58). Contrary to the liberals, the imperial government correctly identified the problems behind indigenous peoples' rapid loss of land and gained popular support from indigenous and peasant citizens who found Maximilian's agrarian juntas to be efficient ways of regaining lost land and formalizing official title over the lands that were recognized as theirs under the colonial regime (356–57). While Juárez and the liberal forces continued to oppose the conservative monarchy, the Lozadistas gained support from Maximilian's government and returned the favor through continued armed rebellion against the liberals. Despite this alliance with the conservatives, Lozada's forces continued to maintain a degree of independence in their actions, ensuring that the territory around Tepic remained free of any permanent French troops, while continuing to receive economic subsidies from the empire (Jáuregui 1999, 252).

At the end, Lozada's autonomy from the empire proved an intelligent move, as it did not take long for the French to be ousted and for Maximilian to be executed, while Lozada's rebellion would continue for years to come. In 1873, after Lozada had seized Tepic and his troops had closed in on Guadalajara,

Jalisco's governor Ignacio Vallarta stated that Lozada's forces had "executed the most scandalous and arbitrary territorial expropriation" and feared that Lozada might go as far as taking over Mexico City with his "100,000 Indians" (Meyer 1989, 246). The Lozadistas were eventually defeated by the liberal army of General Ramón Corona on January 23, 1873, in the Battle of La Mojonera, on the outskirts of Guadalajara, and El Tigre de Álica was executed shortly thereafter in Tepic, a matter that foregrounds chapters 3 and 4.

Benito Juárez has left an indelible mark on Mexican history, becoming a central mythological figure within the country's imaginary. His rise to power during a period of great violence toward indigenous peoples should not be understated; at the same time, his ability to engage national political economic questions while incorporating himself into a mestizoized identity demonstrate that elites *could* accept an "assimilated" indigenous leader. The trademark image of Juárez shows him in formal statesman's attire and is stamped on the five-hundred peso bill (formerly on the widely circulating twenty-peso bill). This image has uncritically stuck in the Mexican popular imagination as an example of political, economic, and racial nation building, indisputably making him one of the most popular historical icons for monuments and murals throughout the country, even among the Mexican American population in the United States. His famous quotation, "El respeto al derecho ajeno es la paz" (Respect for the rights of others is peace), is widely circulated as a manifestation of moral lucidity and tolerance. Sadly, respect for the rights of others held only within the liberal framework of property ownership and individual progress—the displaced survivors of the liberal laws are witnesses to this irony.

By contrast, Manuel Lozada's figure is seldom seen except in a few towns of his native region of Nayarit, where his troops' descendants continue to celebrate and mythologize him for rebelling against injustices that continue to plague peasant and indigenous communities today. Lozada began his career as one of countless bandits who assaulted shipments traveling from the port of San Blas to Tepic and Guadalajara; he eventually became a type of Robin Hood figure and the leader of an "organized peasant movement with a strong leadership and a justice-laden ideology of agrarian vindication and millenarian revolution" (Rugeiro 1997, 16). Three known photographs exist of El Tigre de Álica, all taken toward the end of his life, when the traces of sickness and impending defeat were clear in his expression (Jáuregui 1999, 277). In two he poses in a simple white button-up shirt and blazer; in a third he lies dead in a Franciscan shroud. When Lozada was marched into Tepic on horseback by soldiers, he had one foot in a boot and the other in a sandal, a defeated fighter in an agrarian war that Lozada summed up as follows: "My belief is that the people should be in possession of the plots of land that justly belong to them with proper titling so that, at all times[,] this question remains clear, convincing the government and the rest of the country's people that, if a violent step was taken[,] it was not to take that which belonged to others, but to recover stolen property, in such a way that the ends justify the means" (Lozada quoted in Meyer 1997, 57; my translation).

The question is not why Manuel Lozada has not been nationally recognized or acclaimed in the same vein as Benito Juárez. After all, he was not a national leader, and he fought against established nineteenth-century patriots. As Jean Meyer notes, "Lozada left us a useless, unusable, inadmissible image that prevents official and spectacular celebration" (Meyer 1997, 60). Rather, what should be of interest to us is the juxtaposition between the good and the bad Indian, and a consideration of the images that stuck for both figures. Juárez and Lozada thus stand as symbols for the salvageable and unsalvageable indigenous subject, the assimilated and the rebellious during a key moment of nation building. In 1998, a sculptor placed Juárez and Lozada side by side in a mural at the headquarters of Nayarit's Superior Court of Justice. The former's image was accompanied by the text "Reform Laws," and the latter by "Agrarian Struggle"; despite their ideological differences, both figures stand as clear reflections of the changing social and political economic landscape of the nineteenth century (Jáuregui 1999, 282).

Over the previous pages, we have seen various examples of how indigenous alterity has been engaged, refashioned, and retooled at different historical moments. Allan Pred argues that in these reworkings of the racial imaginary, the sticking image of a distorted racialized Other is actively reinforced through everyday taken-for-granted practices. Of utmost importance is that these practices are popular and hegemonic, difficult to dispel because of their longstanding embeddedness in a political, scientific, and social logic sustained over centuries. A clear result of this is that a twenty-first century columnist can feel liberty and justification in describing indigenous peoples as less than human— literally as animals that are wrongly incorporated into civic life. El Güerote Chulote's racist outburst over "Huicholes mayates" was not only imagined by the author, but enunciated, passing the approval of the editor and meeting the eyes of local readers, among these the very Wixarika people who stood accused.

In this chapter, I have also covered Luis Villoro's moments of Mexican indigenismo, which demonstrate the fluidity between the distinct periods of discourse and practice elaborated by the nonindigenous of the indigenous. In this way, the narratives established by Cortés and Sahagún are neatly followed by those of Clavijero, Mier, and Orozco y Berra, and later, by the formidable indigenista anthropologists and bureaucrats of the twentieth century, whom I examine with more caution in the next chapter. Similarly, the vibrant casta paintings that depicted colonial Mexican society pose important questions regarding early understandings of what was considered to be inevitable and, at times, valuable racial miscegenation. Yet this apparent tolerance of miscegenation and celebration of Mexico's cultural richness carried a darker side, marked by rigid colored hierarchies. Most important for the present discussion is to understand the work that casta paintings did in classifying and naming bodies, signaling the rising acceptance of science as an "objective" instrument for racial and territorial domination.

In the nineteenth century, despite the proclaimed prohibition of racial categorization, the political and intellectual leadership of postindependence Mexico employed established racial narratives and hierarchies to implement new visions of nationhood and citizenship. The mestizo rose from the ashes of the Mexica Empire as the quintessential figure of Mexican citizenship, figuratively foreclosing the indigenous at the same time as midcentury reformers enacted policies that clamped down on the material livelihoods of indigenous communities. Regional rebellions like the one led by Manuel Lozada were the beginning of what would explode under the authoritarian regime of Porfirio Díaz, leading to a prolonged bloody and ideologically anxious revolution. With each moment of resistance, the tense interplay between the visibility and invisibility of Mexico's racial legacy becomes ever more apparent.

2

ACCIÓN INDIGENISTA AND THE DEVELOPMENT OF WIXARIKA TERRITORY

Between me and the other world there is ever an unasked question: unasked by some through feelings of delicacy; by others through the difficulty of rightly framing it. All, nevertheless, flutter round it. They approach me in a half-hesitant way, eye me curiously or compassionately, and then, instead of saying directly, How does it feel to be a problem? they say, I know an excellent colored man in my town; or, I fought at Mechanicsville; or, Do not these Southern outrages make your blood boil? At these I smile, or am interested, or reduce the boiling to a simmer, as the occasion may require. To the real question, How does it feel to be a problem? I answer seldom a word.
—W. E. B. DU BOIS, THE SOULS OF BLACK FOLK

IN THE opening chapter of *The Souls of Black Folk*, W. E. B. Du Bois begins with an exploration of how black people in the United States have come to be understood as a "problem" through everyday acts of inquiry and discourse ([1903] 1994, 1). In the context of the emancipation of enslaved blacks and the dawn of the modern industrial age, the presence of black people posed a logistical problem of labor, property, and political rights, summoning existential questions of ethics. How would a social, political, and economic body politic based on a legacy of white supremacy reconcile the presence of a free nonwhite population in the same geographic space? The black subject, rather than white supremacy, is labeled the problem; and, as Du Bois makes painfully clear, the black person, as the continued target, bears the weight of the label. From this dilemma Du Bois articulates a broader statement, pronouncing that "the problem of the twentieth century is the problem of the color-line,—the relation of the darker to the lighter races of men in Asia and Africa, in America and the islands of the sea" (9). Implicit in Du Bois's exploration is the difference between those who are considered to be the problem and those who, directly or not, activate the question from a position of power. In this way, to be considered a problem demands interpellation on an intimate individualized level; but, as Du Bois signals, to be a problem also requires a larger social response. This response becomes the dilemma of the twentieth century, one that, enmeshed in colonial relations of racial and geographic domination, transcends Du Bois's turn-of-the-century United States and takes center stage for peoples across the globe.

During the twentieth century, Latin American intellectuals increasingly debated "the Indian problem" or the "Indian issue" (*la cuestión indígena*), linking it to broader questions of political representation, class politics, and economic productivity, often centered on agrarian tenure (Mariátegui [1928] 1979). The debates taking place among Mexican scholars and politicians framed the Indian problem as direct, implicating the formation of a coherent nation-state with a more uniform cultural identity, based on the increasingly mythologized mestizo figure. As with the black man or woman of the United States, the indigenous subject in Mexico was viewed by the country's leadership as a problem because of the economic and political rights that their presence put into question, but also because of the cultural anxieties that their difference raised. The indigenous person presented the ruling classes with the "most radical of alterities" (Villoro [1950] 1987, 224). Yet, the Spanish colonial legacy of miscegenation and the exaltation of the mestizo as the prototypical Mexican led to a series of theories and practices that pushed for indigenous inclusion via acculturation, as opposed to segregation, unlike its North American counterpart. In fact, as clear in Gustavo Aguirre Beltrán's famous thesis on "regions of refuge" (1967), segregation was considered one of the strongest impediments to resolving the "Indian problem."

During and after the years of the Mexican Revolution (1910–20), the so-called Indian problem became palpably clear through the armed conflict over land and labor rights. Particularly through the forces of Emiliano Zapata in central Mexico, the struggle of peasants against the landowning oligarchy brought together the poor rural mestizo with indigenous communities, creating a sense of unified class struggle that absorbed the indigenous into the mestizo. The agrarian rights granted through the Constitution of 1917 only solidified the notion that the Indian problem was one of land tenure and, for many people, of class. In fact, the theme of class versus ethnicity and race became a mobilizing concept for many Marxist indigenistas, such as Peru's José Carlos Mariátegui and the post-1968 generation of Mexican indigenistas.[1]

Fundamentally, revolutionary state rhetoric sought to refashion the nation as a politically, economically, and culturally egalitarian society. Yet, like the discourses and practices of indigenismo of the previous centuries, revolutionary ideology manifested a series of contradictions regarding indigenous peoples: on the one hand, the state sought to bring them into the nation as acculturated citizens who had shed their ethnic difference, and on the other, indigenous visual culture and folklore was viewed as a vital signifier of Mexicanness. Anthropologist Guillermo de la Peña describes the indigenista definition of acculturation as "the gradual introduction of Western elements into the daily lives of indigenous people, supposedly in exchange for indigenous elements that enrich the national culture. This latter part tends to be simply understood as the commercialization of craftwork," or consumable folklore (2002, 101).

At the crux of the issue is the ambivalent recognition of indigenous citizenship demonstrated by the Mexican state's vacillation between eliminating the indigenous through programs of acculturation and salvaging indigenous folklore as a central piece of national identity. In this sense, Claudio Lomnitz affirms that despite broad discourses of nationhood as a "single fraternal community," practice has demonstrated a constant distinction between "full" and "part" citizens, "weak" and "strong" citizens, where women, children, and peoples of color are relegated to second and third tiers of citizenship (2001, 12). Nonetheless, this reality continued to be obfuscated by the framing of revolutionary citizenship as "a harmonious interconnection between popular classes under the protection of the revolutionary state" (74).

This chapter examines how the Mexican Revolution discursively and practically reinvigorated indigenismo by making it an applied national project, reaching Wixarika territory in the 1960s. Through the Instituto Nacional Indigenista (National Indigenist Institute, or INI), acción indigenista (indigenista action) emerged as a "hands-on" effort to bring the centralized state to indigenous communities through the building of schools, clinics, and productive projects that sought to mold indigenous peoples into ideal revolutionary and, later, multicultural citizens. Founded on the notion of resolving the Indian problem, the administrators of acción indigenista targeted indigenous territories and cultures, producing laboratories of development in various ethnic enclaves of the country. The practices of the postrevolutionary Mexican state resonate with Michel Foucault's analytic of governmentality, whereby a population is targeted and administered through an assortment of state apparatuses and knowledges that respond to a particular political economic logic—in this case, state capitalism

(2007, 108–9). Fundamental to this discussion is how indigenismo, and acción indigenista, were an outcome of hegemonic notions of the Indian problem embraced by state bureaucrats, private entrepreneurs, and popular culture.

The second part of this chapter pays special attention to the INI's projects in Wixarika territory beginning in the 1960s. Considered one of Mexico's remaining "regions of refuge," the inclusion of Wixarika communities in the INI's policies came later than that of most other indigenous communities. Wixarika resistance combined with the inefficiency of state bureaucracies led to these projects' shortcomings. The neoliberal reforms of the 1980s and of the Salinas period in particular marked a rupture with the Partido Revolucionario Institucional (Institutional Revolutionary Party, or PRI), and relations with indigenous peoples led to changes in state policy under the conservative Partido de Acción Nacional (National Action Party, or PAN). The sequence of new "pluricultural" constitutional agreements and international human rights law combined with the appearance of the Ejército Zapatista de Liberación Nacional (EZLN), and its broad national and international support, brought about new platforms through which indigenous peoples could voice their grievances and demand their rights. These shifts also brought about the replacement of government programs with ones orchestrated by nongovernmental organizations.

The chapter concludes with a brief examination of the temporary and permanent migrations of Wixaritari to mestizo-dominated cities. These migrations are presented as textured and complex movements that result from a combination of long-standing traditions linked to Wixarika territoriality, political economic transformations brought about by state and market forces, and commonly held desires to find opportunities in new places. The result is a growing heterogeneous Wixarika population in Guadalajara and Tepic, and its growing political and social power.

MANAGING HEGEMONY THROUGH ACCIÓN INDIGENISTA

The attainment of modern capitalism inevitably required a postcolonial landscape like Mexico's to shed forms of racial and cultural alterity associated with economic deficiency and backwardness. These "painful adjustments" associated with economic development and modernity would in fact become part of the post–World War II global paradigm for capitalist development (Escobar 1995,

4). Although referring to the colonial project, Ann Stoler's discussion of the European Pauperism Commission of 1901 in the Dutch-controlled Indies can help us understand Mexico's nationalist project by signaling how "clusters of people" became the subjects of the state: "Ways of living were congealed into 'problems,' subject persons were condensed into ontological categories, innocuous practices were made into subjects of analysis and rendered political things" (Stoler 2010, 30). This "sorting of people" emerged from and solidified ideas of how race "shaped distinct habits and inclinations" (30).

The practice described by Stoler was a central component of the Mexican revolutionary state's corporatist structure, which reached its zenith under the presidency of Lázaro Cárdenas. Corporatism effectively "sorted" distinct groups of people into politically activated interest groups that included indigenous communities, industrial workers, and campesinos (Joseph and Nugent 1994; Gilly 2001; Boyer 2003). According to Rhina Rhoux the key objective of this corporatist structure was to effectively govern distinct social sectors by responding to their particular interests in ways that maintained the social order while advancing the state's capitalist agenda (2005, 171–72). However Machiavellian the revolutionary state may appear to have become at this juncture, corporatism largely functioned because of the consent gained by the Revolution's popularity, particularly among those sectors of society, such as peasants, that had long struggled to see their demands recognized by the state (Boyer 2003, 217). Based on the combination of new constitutional laws and "pre-existing social forces," the Cárdenas administration successfully constructed alliances between the state and urban and rural interest groups—alliances that would rupture under subsequent administrations (Gilly 2001, 164). Through a combination of personal character and reformism, President Cárdenas established an unprecedented sense of approval among the majority of the Mexican population. Adolfo Gilly attributes this feeling of popular consent for the administration to the idea that Cárdenas "shared a territory, an imaginary, a vision of the nation and of its natural environment" (2001, 156).

On the other hand, coercion remained an integral part of rule, where membership and allegiance to state-sanctioned syndicates became the only avenue for voicing demands to the government. This was especially true for indigenous communities, in which the state instituted new leaders who did not represent the traditional governance system: "To make their reforms work, the Cardenistas and their successors reached inside the native communities, not only changing leaders but rearranging the governments, creating new offices to deal with labor and agrarian matters" (Rus 1994, 267). Jan Rus's analysis of Cárdenas's policies in the highlands of Chiapas exposes the contradictory results that Tzeltal and Tzotzil communities experienced: content with advances made with land reform while finding themselves under the direction of new caciques (local strongmen), who became their only interlocutors for addressing labor and agrarian matters (279). The displacement of traditional indigenous political voices by government-friendly indigenous representatives became a widespread problem in the second half of the twentieth century and has recently regained attention under the presidency of Andrés Manuel López Obrador.[2]

During the initial decades of the revolutionary state, popular understandings of indigenous peoples and the Indian problem became ever more solidified through the Secretaría de Educación Pública (Ministry of Public Education, or SEP), led by José Vasconcelos, and through the visual culture of the muralist movement, headed by the likes of Diego Rivera and David Alfaro Siqueiros (often sponsored by Vasconcelos). This burgeoning public art movement combined with the SEP's curriculum retold Mexican history "from below." Like their nineteenth-century predecessors, revolutionary indigenistas maintained the trope of the Black Legend and the tragic fall of the Indian redeemed through the figure of the mestizo. Reflecting the centralist notion of the state with its epicenter in Mexico City, the Mexica remained the glorious representation of indigeneity, while the image of living indigenous groups remained caught between an exotic rural past and the ambiguously tragic mestizo citizen.

From this context emerged the practices that guided acción indigenista and solidified their popular appeal. Keeping with the Gramscian concept of hegemony, the postrevolutionary Mexican state installs a "profound measure of social and moral authority" across different sectors to steer the "productive forces of development" in the interest of the ruling classes (Hall 1986, 18). In fact, Mexico's political system of the mid-twentieth century epitomized the construction of a hegemonic order based on a "historic bloc" that forged "expansive, universalizing alliances" to maintain its leadership (15). But as William Roseberry points out, "Gramsci does not assume that subaltern groups are captured and immobilized by some sort of ideological consensus," so their relation to the state remains open to possibilities that range from acceptance of governmental intervention to resistance (1994, 360). Through this, the work of governmentality remains essential, as it supports the "intersection of the public, private and voluntary, in which there is no clear sovereign authority, and in which trust conventions, networks and non-formal obligations and reciprocities figure centrally" (Watts

2003, 12). But as the Mexican state's hegemonic hold began to crumble in the late 1960s, so too did the legitimacy of indigenismo, and reformulations within anthropological thought and practice pushed for reforms within the INI that sought to give the institution a more inclusive face.

REVOLUTION, ACCULTURATION, AND THE FATHERS OF INDIGENISMO

Ac·cul·tur·a·tion: The modification of a primitive culture by contact with an advanced culture.
—THE AMERICAN HERITAGE DICTIONARY 1970

Ac·cul·tur·a·tion: 1) The modification of the culture of a group or individual as a result of contact with a different culture. 2) The process by which the culture of a particular society is instilled in a human from infancy onward.
—THE AMERICAN HERITAGE DICTIONARY 2006

After the Mexican Revolution and through much of the twentieth century, indigenismo became the official state philosophy guiding relations between nonindigenous and indigenous Mexicans, and it framed the discourse of development initiatives in and around rural indigenous communities. Doctors, environmentalists, teachers, anthropologists, seekers of shamanic spirituality, and politicians generally coalesced in seeing certain values in the country's indigenous cultures. Conversely, these same groups actively engaged in practices that sought to mold indigenous peoples to suit particular models of development and "bring them into modernity," or, in some cases, keep them frozen in mythical times and spaces. This often included reshaping indigenous agricultural methods, banning or reinventing traditional attire, marginalizing traditional authorities by supporting new leaders, and, most of all, celebrating indigenous cultures through ethnic tourism (Gamio 1948; Herrasti Maciá 1988; Rus 1994; Hernández Castillo, Paz, and Sierra, 2004; de la Peña 2002). Through these varied interventions, the practices of indigenismo have often concealed the dispossession of indigenous peoples and communities. Indigenismo has undergone discursive shifts that correspond to the larger cultural and political trends of the times—including the movement away from mestizaje and toward multiculturalism. Much like the definitions of acculturation noted in the epigraph, indigenismo's foundational preoccupation with indigenous peoples is based on a perceived socioeconomic and cultural endpoint that implies a certain abdication of indigenous traditions.

During much of the twentieth century, revolutionary ideology fostered and institutionalized indigenismo through the creation of state entities that would study and seek the assimilation of indigenous peoples into the national body. Public education and agrarian reform were two of the cornerstones of this integration. Moisés Sáenz, one of the chief architects of the public education system was guided by the philosophy that national integration required the "democratic participation" of indigenous peoples, marking the schooling system as a key vehicle for achieving this goal (Martínez Casas et al. 2014, 45). The INI as well as the schools and institutes of archaeology and anthropology founded by Alfonso Caso would serve the double purpose of creating specific projects for indigenous communities while educating the general public about Mexico's indigenous heritage. President Lázaro Cárdenas firmly believed that a revolutionary and democratic Mexico would never be complete as long as indigenous peoples remained outside the nation-state "isolated, uncultured and in misery" (Cárdenas in Gamio 1948, xiii).

A brief exploration of two of indigenismo's most influential twentieth-century proponents can better illustrate this point. Manuel Gamio, considered "the father of Mexican anthropology," accepted Lamarckian theories of racial evolution, while Gonzalo Aguirre Beltrán's creation of the centros coordinadores (which became the essence of acción indigenista) strove to put an end to what he deemed Mexico's uneven economic geography, which kept indigenous people oppressed. The differences and similarities that marked the work of these anthropologists illustrate the ongoing search for national identity as it negotiated the racial, cultural, and spatial alterity presented by the presence of indigenous peoples and articulated through the evolving discipline of anthropology.

EL INDIO TRISTE AND THE NOBLE INDIGENISTA

Naturally that civilizing bath did not go beyond the epidermis, leaving the body and the soul of the Indian as they were before, pre-Hispanic. In order to incorporate the Indian let us not pretend to "europeanize" him with one brushstroke; on the contrary, let us "Indianize" ourselves a little, in order to present him our civili-

> *zation diluted with his, which he will then no longer find exotic, cruel, bitter and incomprehensible. Naturally let us not exaggerate to a ridiculous extreme this rapprochement to the Indian.*
> —MANUEL GAMIO, *FORJANDO PATRIA*
> (MY TRANSLATION)

On April 19, 1942, as director of the Instituto Indigenista Interamericano (III), Manuel Gamio gave a radio address for "The Day of the Indian," titled "Racism and the Indigenous Population," detailing the disregard and racism experienced by indigenous people at the hands of the Mexican nation: "Slavery and misery, perennial spiritual and material defeat, would be all that the sad eyes of the Indian could discern around himself, growing and mastering in his aching soul forever the complex of inferiority, timidity and fatalism that were born from the swords of the Conquista, the *encomiendas* of the Colonia and even the prolonged oblivion of the republican governments" (quoted in Gamio 1948, 36–37). Gamio continued by stating that the continent's aboriginal groups now lived in a state of unconsciousness about themselves and their fellow Indian communities, who share the same histories of oppression. Lifting their spirits could be accomplished by teaching them that "they are the true discoverers of the continent" (37). As the "Father of Interamerican Indigenismo," Gamio directed the III for eighteen years, helping establish several indigenista institutions throughout Latin America. Nonetheless, his primary focus was on his native Mexico, where his preoccupation with Indian misery blended with social Darwinist notions of the "inferior evolutionary stage" of native peoples (2).

In the early stages of these newly formed indigenista institutions, methodologies were created to help anthropologists and indigenista workers distinguish which populations needed improvement. In this light, Gamio pointed out that an indigenous person like Benito Juárez would never have needed assistance, as his characteristics were no longer "of indigenous build." (1948, 2) To facilitate this process, Gamio and his colleagues created a table that would be used to designate which indigenous would need "indigenista attention," laying out several domestic and work items, each of which was assigned a "utilitarian classification," marking those that were considered "deficient" (the traditional grinding stone, or metate, corn tortillas, and traditional sandals, or huaraches), "detrimental" (liquor, gambling games, and marijuana), and "efficient" (traditional indigenous dress, decorated vases, and European items like the phonograph and saddle; 1948, 8).[3]

Peter Wade notes that Gamio worked within a functionalist framework based on the study of so-called traditional folk communities popular in the 1930s and 1940s. As noted with Gamio's "utilitarian" table, this framework attributed indigenous marginalization and underdevelopment to geographic isolation and deficient technology (Wade 1997, 42–43). In Gamio's magnum opus, *Forjando patria* (1916), he affirms that the Indian can be as "capable" as the white man but must first shake off the colonial legacy, which oppressed him, to receive a proper education, which will help him "seek broader horizons" and "assimilate European culture" (22–24). Meanwhile, nonindigenous Mexicans were encouraged to "indianize" themselves through the careful selection of positive indigenous cultural traits, as taken up by the muralist movement (96).

Anthropologist Ricardo Pozas also discusses the functionalist orientation of indigenismo by emphasizing the INI's focus on taking the "benefits of the revolution" to Indian communities to attack the root problem: that of being Indian and not Mexican (1988, 237). For many anthropologists and public officials of the time, the "Indian problem" was understood through the lens of the Revolution, whose rhetoric enabled discussions of indigenous marginalization and mistreatment, particularly with respect to land tenancy, labor rights, and education. Undoubtedly many indigenistas shared a true concern for the conditions in which many indigenous communities lived and worked. This is particularly evident during the Cárdenas period, when concerted efforts were made to meet the social pact established by the Constitution of 1917. Essential for this revolutionary task was the transformation of indigenous citizenship through a process of acculturation and development that would allow them to share the benefits of revolutionary reforms. Specifically, acculturation would be met through programs of *mexicanización* and *castellanización* (adoption of the Spanish language), which would help indigenous people properly take advantage of the Revolution.

Mestizaje was perhaps the most vocal manifestation of Mexico's attempt to build a coherent Mexican citizen. In the prologue of José Vasconcelos's *La raza cósmica*, the author states that mestizaje would eliminate racial discrimination and bring about an inevitable sense of equality among humans (Vasconcelos [1948] 2007, xv). Seemingly, mestizaje would be the antidote to racism. Yet Vasconcelos's own theorization of mestizaje was indisputably embedded in notions of racial hierarchy, as he was certain that not all racial miscegenation paved the way toward superior civilizations. Additionally, Vasconcelos firmly believed that spirituality could resolve even the most "contradictory of mestizajes," as one needed only to look at the ways in which the Christian faith had been able to "advance American Indians, within a few centuries, from cannibalism to a state of relative civilization" (xvii). At the end of the day, mestizaje was viewed by Vasconcelos as a noble sacrifice that whites would need to make for the *patria*:

> By completing their destiny of mechanizing the world, [racially pure whites] have unknowingly placed the stones for a new era, an era of fusion and mixture of all peoples. The Indian does not have any other door toward the future but the door of modern culture, nor another path than the path already cleared by Latin civilization. The white man also will have to leave aside his pride, and will seek progress and posterior redemption in the soul of his brothers of other castes, and he will confuse and perfect himself in each one of the superior varieties of the species. (Vasconcelos [1948] 2007, 13; my translation)

It is worth underlining how within Vasconcelos' redemptive mestizaje lies a discussion of indigenous acculturation as a manifestation of white man's burden. Like his liberal predecessors of the nineteenth century, Vasconcelos believed that Latin American nations could not get around their racial reality. Grudgingly or not, a country like Mexico would need to take it on itself to devise programs that would incorporate the Indian, if only for the sake of securing a modern nation-state. Mestizaje thus operated as a dialectic whereby the dysfunctional traits of indigenous peoples were resolved through the transformative incorporation of whiteness, while the identities of whites could become reterritorialized through the selective absorption of native traditions.

It is worth pausing here to consider how racism is put into conversation with mestizaje, when the latter is seen as inherently antiracist or, at the very least, racially neutral. In a brief biographical essay on Manuel Gamio, Ángeles González Gamio (his granddaughter) references a polemical debate in 1974 that ensued when anthropologist Arturo Warman critiqued Gamio's racially problematic tendencies and his service to the state over indigenous communities (González Gamio 1987, 449–50). According to González Gamio, Warman's accusation of Gamio's racism was impossible simply because Gamio was a supporter of mestizaje. González Gamio found a "patent contradiction" in Warman's assertion that Gamio was both racist and pro–racial miscegenation. While Gamio critiqued Mexicans' contempt toward indigenous populations and the nasty paternalism that indigenista practices brought to light, he repeatedly stated his belief that indigenous peoples were "biologically deficient" and as a result carried corresponding cultural and economic deficiencies, which could be remedied through development programs (Gamio 1948, 9). As the first remains of postrevolutionary indigenismo surfaced, new paradigms would emerge in an attempt to smooth out growing discursive and practical paradoxes.

ACCIÓN INDÍGENA AND APPLIED ANTHROPOLOGY

Indigenismo is in many ways a theory of practice rooted in the logic of modern developmentalism. From its inception, musings on the condition of *el indio triste* were complemented with ideas of governmental action. Nowhere is this clearer than under the presidency of Lázaro Cárdenas, who on January 1, 1936, created the Department of Indigenous Affairs (Departamento de Asuntos Indígenas, DAI; Aguirre Beltrán 1988, 12). Land redistribution through the ejido system was a first step, but it needed to be complemented with concerted efforts to tackle a series of other ingrained inequities, including improving the labor conditions in henequen fields in Yucatán and on coffee plantations in Chiapas, as well as eliminating intermediaries who prevented indigenous peoples from getting a fair price on their goods and impeded electoral participation.

In anthropologist Gonzalo Aguirre Beltrán's influential book *Regiones de refugio* (1967), he establishes the thesis that the "dominical," or feudal, process in Latin America created "regions of refuge": underdeveloped and isolated areas where the "structure inherited from the colonial period . . . found cover against the buffets of modern civilization" (1967, xv, 1). In these "regions of refuge," the caste system inherited from the colonial era continued to mediate social, economic, and political relations. A native of Veracruz and an understudy of Boasian anthropology at Southwestern University, Aguirre Beltrán conducted his first ethnographic studies in Mexican communities of African descent and became increasingly concerned with the exploitation and second-class citizenship of black and indigenous Mexicans. He saw this problem as the manifestation of the "coexistence of two societies": the modern urban society defined by the governing white elite; and the traditional and archaic rural society made up of indigenous peoples and peasants (xi). Aguirre Beltrán criticized this "dual economy," stating that economists had opted for the development of the elite, ignoring the much larger sectors of society that carried some of the economic and cultural philosophies espoused by the Revolution, such as cooperatism.

Acción indigenista was the response elaborated in different stages by the likes of Gamio and Aguirre Beltrán—a praxis intricately tied to the construction of postrevolutionary Mexican nationalism and based on the premises of agrarianism and indigenismo. Efforts would begin with ethnographic investigations of designated indigenous cultures, followed by the elaboration of projects that used "non-coercive methods" for bringing indigenous peoples—including conservative traditional authorities—into the "process of acculturation" (de la Peña 1988, 362). For Aguirre Beltrán, the intention of acción indigenista was to incorporate indigenous peoples into modernity without the loss of their ethnic identity. This could be accomplished through careful anthropological studies that designated the appropriate bridges between Western and Mesoamerican cultural traditions.

Yet good intentions did not prevent these ideas from falling into the traps of essentialism and the cultural naiveté that the indigenistas took to the field. Discussing acción indigenista a couple of decades after its inception, Aguirre Beltrán points to the paradox posed by competing images of indigeneity that informed the national imaginary and practice:

> Nationalism founded its ideology on the American past; revalorized the Indian and the pre-Columbian Indian and took his image as a paradigm. The former explains the paradoxical coexistence, in Mestizo America, of two contradictory images of the Indian; the dirty image created by ladino ideology, that persists without alteration in the regions of refuge, and the idealized image of the Indian that forms part of the official ideology and is the starting point for the implementation of a political mandate of national unity and homogenization. (Aguirre Beltrán 1967, 240; my translation)

Aguirre Beltrán showed an unusual sensitivity toward the problematic racial imaginary of indigenous peoples. In the same light as his fellow Marxist indigenistas of the time, he took particular care to point the finger at the feudal qualities of Latin American capitalism. As such, Aguirre Beltrán credited himself and a few other fellow anthropologists for the formation of "political indigenista anthropology," which analyzed "the changes generated by the capitalist world," especially the ongoing primitive accumulation taking place throughout Mexico's "regions of refuge" (Aguirre Beltrán 1988, 21).

By 1951, a focus on applied political anthropology took Aguirre Beltrán to Chiapas, where he was given the task of forming the INI's first centro coordinador indigenista Tzeltal-Tzotzil in Chamula. These "indigenista coordinating centers" were established by presidential decree to more effectively carry out the INI's programs, by having a permanent outpost in the so-called regions of refuge (Aguirre Beltrán 1967, 247–49). The centros' formidable objectives ranged from advocating for indigenous migrant workers, building schools and health clinics, and constructing roads that would link isolated communities to mestizo towns. What this indigenista anthropologist soon discovered was that indigenous communities were not wholly receptive to the new governmental presence and that the regional mestizo political and economic oligarchy was more than willing to use violence to prevent idealist public officials from enacting any changes in the local power hierarchies. As the first director of the centro coordinador in Chamula, Aguirre Beltrán witnessed the inherent violence of mestizo-indigenous relations and was accused by the governor of being a communist agitator (Aguirre Beltrán 1988, 18). These local realities quickly eclipsed the indigenista idealism generated from the nation's capital.[4]

INDIGENISTA CRITICS AND INDIGENOUS ACTIVISM

By 1968, the revolutionary rhetoric of the Mexican state had clearly ruptured. At the same time, growing discussions had ensued among anthropologists around the problematic practices of indigenismo. A new school of critical anthropologists, including Arturo Warman and Guillermo Bonfil Batalla, surfaced and took Aguirre Beltrán's Marxist analysis further by making class a central category of analysis. In 1970, several authors (including Warman and Bonfil Batalla) published *De eso que llaman antropología mexicana* (Warman et al. 1970), denouncing previous manifestations of indigenismo as bourgeois and neocolonial (de la Peña 1988, 369). Bonfil Batalla mocked Gamio's and his contemporaries' calls for mestizaje based on a blend of the best of the West and the indigenous by stating that all it did was create a cocktail made of "*pulque* and champagne," the former a Mesoamerican alcoholic beverage made from fermented corn (Bonfil Batalla 1988, 127). While some of these young scholars spoke of an "Indian class," others designated indigenous peoples a "subproletariat" that would need to "detribalize" to enter the arena of class struggle (de la Peña 1988, 371). Simultaneously, Aguirre Beltrán replied that these new theorizations were nothing more than "eurocentrism of the left" (1988, 375).

At the national scale, through the 1970s, indigenistas and critical anthropologists alike faced a changing political and cultural landscape, which was increasingly repressive toward oppositional movements. The success of the Cuban Revolution in 1959 and the global rise of radical anticapitalist movements across the third world similarly influenced the Mexican Left to consider new paradigms for political economic development in indigenous territories. Ironically, the presidency of Luis Echeverría (1970–76) showed particular interest in the "indigenous cause" and pushed a series of new development initiatives, including massive road construction, the creation of worker and consumer cooperatives, and the introduction of Green Revolution agricultural technologies (detailed in projects like the Plan Huicot, discussed below).[5] Echeverría's funding and support of policies in indigenous regions signaled the terrible contradictions within indigenismo, detailed by his government's repression of leftist indigenous movements that were part of the Dirty War, which functioned in conjunction with the United States' efforts to counter leftist movements south of the border.

In an essay commemorating the INI's fortieth anniversary, Miguel Limón Rojas, director of the institution from 1983 to 1988, acknowledges that substantial changes were occurring within indigenista thought, largely as a result of the increasing presence of indigenous movements (1988, 81). For too long, indigenismo held on to notions of indigenous backwardness and passivity, explicitly or implicitly placing Western political, economic, and cultural constructs as superior. According to Limón Rojas, nowhere was this more clear than in the endless indigenista debates centered around creating a more "productive" and "efficient" indigenous farmer: "It is inherent of colonial mentality to think of the indigenous countryside as unproductive by definition. . . . It is incorrect to think that indigenous peoples are opposed to innovations, what is widely demonstrated is the inconvenience of imposing projects upon them" (95). The notion of imposing projects on indigenous communities had clearly reached its discursive and practical end. Although Gamio had sought to create projects that did not appear coercive, they were, by their nature, conceived and implemented by the urban nonindigenous indigenistas, who devalued or lacked knowledge of native worldviews and models of sustenance and development.

As director of the INI, Limón Rojas attempted to place indigenous participants at all levels of project development, keeping in mind that not all indigenous regions faced similar challenges or required the same levels of governmental assistance. Furthermore, economics was a key factor in the allocation of resources, as the INI had been severely defunded in the aftermath of the debt crisis and the government's ushering in of neoliberal policies (Miguel Limón Rojas, interview by author, May 5, 2010). Fundamentally, Limón Rojas claims that he no longer wished to support the tendency of placing "the professionals of indigenismo" as the primary creators and facilitators of failed policies. The aforementioned intellectual debates among indigenistas and the institutional changes within the INI indicate that the promoters of indigenismo sought ways to respond to the problems presented by indigenista praxis. At the same time, the failure of the assimilationist model of development provided a platform through which the INI would later rearticulate its institutional identity through multicultural neoliberalism.

Guillermo de la Peña's delineation of three distinct models followed by the INI from 1948 to 2001 demonstrates some of the shifts that occurred alongside the larger discursive trends: (1) the *coordinating model*, based on anthropological investigation as the guiding factor for each of the INI's centros coordinadores; (2) the *sectarian model*, which shifted the INI's role from coordinating to actually executing policy (this came as a result of the state's centralization of the institution); and (3) the *self-determination model*, which upholds multiculturalism and supports projects based on each community's needs and desires—here the INI's role is to lend out human and material resources (de la Peña 2002, 98–99). As noted by Limón Rojas, the last model was a product of decreasing state revenue and the failure of past INI initiatives designed by nonindigenous anthropologists turned bureaucrats.

During the presidency of Carlos Salinas de Gortari (1988–94), the government enacted programs that claimed to be "alternative" and "participatory," while still seeking the indigenista objectives of acculturation and development of previous periods (Pérez Ruiz 2001).[6] Yet the INI's attempt to restructure and refocus its efforts did little in the face of mounting accusations of the institution's inefficiency, corruption, and even aiding and abetting of violence against indigenous peoples (Limón Rojas 1988; Pérez Ruiz 2001). In light of these problems, the Zapatista rebellion in 1994 came as no surprise. Not only did the Zapatistas significantly shift the spotlight away from the indigenistas, but they permanently altered the debate on the "Indian problem." Throughout the 1990s indigenous organizations did, indeed, begin to call for the termination of the INI and indigenismo itself (Pérez Ruiz 2001).

Little has changed in the politics of poverty and development, as the expansion of citizen consumers through "transformative" administrative practices remains a central tenet of state policy toward indigenous peoples. Although the INI was replaced in 2001 with the Comisión Nacional para el Desarrollo de los Pueblos Indígenas (CDI), much of the discourses and practices of the previous era persist. The fact that indigenismo is replaced with a focus on *desarrollo* (development) or that multiculturalism has substituted mestizo nationalism does not indicate a renewed vision for the place of indigenous peoples within the Mexican nation-state. Most importantly, these institutional changes fail to account for the active role that indigenous peoples have played all along in mobilizing for their political, economic, territorial, and cultural rights. In late 2018, Andrés Manuel López Obrador's administration replaced the CDI with the Instituto Nacional de los Pueblos Indígenas, placing as its first director the moderate progressive Mixe Adelfo Regino Montes and relaunching a variant of the centro coordinador model, yet questions abound about whether this latest institutional shift will signify greater rights for indigenous peoples.

Before discussing development initiatives in Wixarika territory, it is worth noting the ascension in the 1960s of Wixarika ceremonial and aesthetic culture as an object of admiration and exploitation by Mexican and foreign parties. A lengthy topic in and of itself, it is crucial to keep in mind that as the indigenista machine penetrated Wixarika territory, a growing number of people approached Wixarika culture with vastly divergent aims and outcomes. This growing interest in Wixarika culture has been largely attributed to followers of the psychedelic movement, who were attracted to this indigenous peoples' sacramental use of the peyote cactus. Fascination over Mexican indigenous spiritual culture only increased with the circulation of Carlos Castaneda's narratives, whose protagonist, a Yaqui medicine man, was loosely based on the real-life persona of Wixarika yarn painter Ramón Medina Silva (Fikes 1993). According to anthropologist Jay Fikes, the convergence of Castaneda's narratives and the psychedelic movement led to a series of unethical appropriations of Wixarika culture (144). Furthermore, Fikes notes how those who engage in marketing "Huichol shamans" as an object of consumption have largely turned a blind eye on the "real life problems" that affect Wixarika communities.[7] The hypervisibility of Wixarika imagery in the last four decades has brought about an increased presence of investigators and tourists seeking to access Wixarika land and culture (Negrín da Silva 2015; Arriaga and Negrín 2018). Explicitly or not, these actors have fed into narratives of indigenous development and citizenship that ultimately have material consequences for Wixaritari in both the country and the city.

DEVELOPING WIXARIKA TERRITORY

> *The theory is that only when the Huichol no longer has to constantly preoccupy himself with simple subsistence, he will have*

> *time to think of other things, such as education for himself and his children, and only then will he have funds and time to carefully look for correct medical care in the city in place of solely trying to cure himself or trust in the magic cures or in plants within the Sierra.*
> —KAREN REED, *EL INI Y LOS HUICHOLES*

On July 8, 1960, the Centro Coordinador Indigenista Cora-Huichol was established based on the argument that Wixarika (Huichol) and Náayeri (Cora) communities presented "sensibly low standards of living, a precarious economy, great isolation and unhealthy living conditions" (Reed 1972, 54). Following indigenismo's model of acculturation, the centro coordinador would spearhead several projects focused on education, health, and economic productivity. Mirroring the analytic of governmentality, the principal tenet of the centro coordinador's programming was to guide the conduct of indigenous peoples through cultural and economic reform. According to Karen Reed's 1972 study on the INI in Wixarika territory, the centro coordinador sought to build the buying power of indigenous peoples so that they may have a "larger participation in the national economy" (80).[8] The apparently benign gesture of improving regional health, education, and economics was accompanied by dangerous shifts in the internal affairs of Wixarika communities. By examining these programs of development and the series of administrative entities that accompanied them, one can best observe how consent for social "improvement" programs are met with political coercion that strikes at the core of Wixarika autonomy.[9]

The construction of schools was a top priority, as young people were believed to be more receptive to cultural change and as such were considered vehicles through which modernity and economic buying power could enter the most remote communities (Reed 1972, 101–3). When the centro coordinador was founded, the few existing schools in the region were managed and taught by Franciscan nuns and priests. But under the INI, education would be secular, and the teachers would be mestizo and, later, bilingual natives of each community. Reed explains how in order to have a more objective stance, the INI searched for teachers who were "ethnically similar" yet stood apart from the community, asserting that teachers were not to involve themselves in political issues, much less become elected officials (103–4). Teachers were labeled *promotores* (promoters), a term that implies their role in promoting national (read mestizo) cultural, political, and economic values. As time wore on, claims of teacher neutrality in communal politics encountered the fact that teaching positions were springboards for obtaining newly created governmental posts in Wixarika communities. The Mexican government's offer of administrative positions for many bilingual teachers was the beginning of separating those who were elected by Wixarika communities for traditional political posts from those who were selected by the state to make wider regional decisions, consistently ignoring the positions of the traditional representatives (Torres Contreras 2000, 193).

The first INI schools were established in 1963 in Tuxpan de Bolaños and Ocota de la Sierra, and in 1964 in San Andrés Cohamiata (de la Peña 2002, 100). The failure of these schools became apparent as early as 1967, when high desertion rates led to the creation of boarding schools. Nonetheless, enrollment rates remained low because of the SEP curriculum's inability to accommodate the Wixarika agricultural and ceremonial cycles, in which children are active participants.[10] These interruptions to the academic calendar were compounded by the belief, from families and communal authorities, that the education administered by the government was leading young people to disassociate themselves from Wixarika tradition and internalize notions of racial and cultural inferiority (Torres Contreras 2000, 190–93).

Despite the problems raised by both the Franciscan and the government primary schools, Wixaritari have been active in seeking ways to improve their children's education. By the early 1990s, Wixarika communities began to mobilize for better schooling, including the creation of secondary schools, as well as the implementation of more culturally relevant curriculum. Tatutsí Maxakuaxí middle school (*secundaria*), which began operating in San Miguel Huaixtita (part of the community of Tateikié, or San Andrés Cohamiata) in 1995, is particularly important as its foundational philosophies manifested Wixarika discontent with the legacy of Franciscan and government-operated schools. Paul Liffman (2011) notes that Tatutsí Maxakuaxí is especially interesting as it was founded in a highly acculturated Wixarika locality that sought to strengthen its cultural and territorial autonomy by centering the Wixarika language and worldview in its curriculum. Rocío de Aguinaga, a mestizo professor from Guadalajara who was central in the school's creation, notes that Tatutsí Maxakuaxí was the result of Cárdenas-era efforts to train indigenous teachers, eventually leading to the autonomous schools that are often associated with the Zapatista movement (Rocío de Aguinaga, interview by author, May 31, 2010). Liffman complements this idea by demonstrating how this school's philosophy was created at the interface of global indigenous rights discourses brought about by an assisting nongovernmental organization and the local desire for cultural revitalization (2011, 143). Since 1995, several other intercultural secundarias and *preparatorias* (high schools) have been established in Wixarika communities. In the early 2010s, a Wixarika graduate from Guadalajara's ITESO university created an autonomous high school in Tuapurie (Santa Catarina Cuexcomatitlán), Tamatsi Páritsika. Throughout 2018, Wixarika authorities pressured both the Nayarit and Jalisco state governments to better resource their schools, with press conferences and protests even leading to an eventual electoral abstention in the community of Wautia (San Sebastián Teponohuaxtlan) during the 2018 national elections.

Simultaneous to the establishment of schools, the INI began other interventions, such as constructing landing strips to facilitate the coming and going of government bureaucrats working in the region. Following Gamio's model, state employees were to facilitate the execution of "selective acculturization," choosing which aspects of Wixarika culture would be preserved and which ones would be discarded and replaced (Reed 1972, 93). This led to the introduction of the hand mill for corn, radios, agrochemicals, and other items as well as the replacement of native animals with high-grade cattle. Although several of these introductions have been welcomed by the communities, others, namely agrochemicals, caused negative short- and long-term effects (Díaz Romo 1994).[11] The INI also introduced seeds that would produce higher yields and that purportedly had a higher nutritional value than the native crops. At the same time, the INI established the first CONASUPO (Compañía Nacional de Subsistencias Populares, or National Company for Popular Subsistence) stores, which, along with basic food staples, sold higher-yielding seeds with their accompanying fertilizers and pesticides. CONASUPO also helped commercialize Wixarika craftwork. Tied to these initiatives was the authorization of agricultural credit by Banrural (the state-operated rural credit union) under the condition that Wixaritari create individual land parcels divided by barbed-wire fences supplied by the government (Torres Contreras 2009, 342).

Healthcare was another central element of the Centro Coordinador Indigenista Cora-Huichol's efforts to bring governmental assistance to Wixarika communities. Despite these efforts, health clinics continue to be few and far between, forcing many sick to continue to travel to nearby mestizo towns and cities to treat more serious illnesses.

Over the decades the government has created various political councils to serve as intermediaries between the traditional Wixarika authorities and the municipal, state, and federal governments. The extant traditional religious cargo system has thus been intervened by new, changing entities, which may or may not reflect the mandate of the religious authorities and council of elders. For instance, the three main councils created from the 1960s to the 1990s were the Consejo de Bienes Comunales (Council of Communal Goods), the Consejo Supremo Huichol (Supreme Huichol Council), and the Unión de Comunidades Indígenas Huicholes de Jalisco (Union of Indigenous Huichol Communities of Jalisco), which supplanted the Consejo Supremo Huichol in 1990. These political entities have been a mixed blessing for Wixarika communities: at times they have presented a legitimate and unified Wixarika opinion before the state, while at other moments, they have usurped the powers of the traditional governors, creating conflict within the communities over who the legitimate representatives are. Liffman (2011) describes how the *kawiterutsixi* (principal elders) lament the erosion of their authority in recent decades through the replacement of their leadership with new representatives who do not reflect legitimate religious communal authority and increasingly exercise "greater territorial-administrative control" (149).

Created in the 1960s, the Consejo de Bienes Comunales has for the most part been an effective tool for mediation between the distinct communities and the Mexican government, often mirroring and siding with the kawiterutsixi against projects promoted by the state. To some extent, this council has maintained dialogue with the Mexican government while allowing for the traditional governors to have their say, thus attempting to strike a balance between Mexican and Wixarika models of governance (Juan and Yvonne Negrín, interview by author, March 2, 2004). While there is one Consejo de Bienes Comunales for each community, the Consejo Supremo Huichol (established in the 1970s) designated one INI-elected Wixarika representative to speak for all the communities. The first Consejo Supremo Huichol representative was Pedro de Haro from Wautia. De Haro was a mestizo who became fully incorporated into Wixarika tradition and was one of the most effective agrarian leaders of the region. Under his leadership, Wautia regained some of the land it had lost to mestizo encroachment since the colonial period. Conversely, de Haro's successor, Maurilio de la Cruz Ávila, brought about corruption and conflict within Wixarika communities. Under de la Cruz Ávila's leadership, mestizo land encroachment increased, and logging and drug plantations became a serious problem for the territorial, political, and economic integrity of the region. In 1990, the Consejo Supremo Huichol was terminated by popular demand as a result of de la Cruz Ávila's undemocratic and corrupt presidency.

Thereafter, Unión de Comunidades Indígenas Huicholas de Jalisco (UCIHJ) was formed to replace the Consejo Supremo Huichol, giving leadership to the president of Bienes Comunales, who is considered to be most knowledgeable and capable of working across these divergent systems of governance.[12] The elected president, whose term lasted one year, not only made political and economic decisions for the three nuclear communities of Jalisco but also received and administered development funds for the region. Like its predecessor, the UCIHJ confronted the problem of choosing people who legitimately served the interests of the communities. Yet, as with the teacher-promotores, the UCIHJ's leadership comprised "new elite groups" (Liffman 2011, 33). Although the UCIHJ accepted various development projects without properly evaluating them and without discussing them with the Wixarika council of elders, it also eventually banded up with nongovernmental organizations imbued with Zapatista discourses of cultural revival and autonomy (216). The UCIHJ was terminated in 2000 when the CDI replaced the INI and implanted a decentralized model. Since then, the Consejo Regional Wixárika para la Defensa de Wirikuta and the Unión Wixárika de Centros Ceremoniales de Nayarit y Jalisco have emerged as the new intercommunal political bodies, albeit questions of legitimacy and leadership remain central to both.

Today, Wixarika civil leadership continues to be a critical issue as state and private development projects are proposed in and around Wixarika communal territory, as well as in more distant sacred areas, including the eastern pilgrimage route of Wirikuta in the state of San Luis Potosí and Haramara in the state of Nayarit. Whether the issue at hand is the penetration of new roads in the sierra or mineral extraction in Wirikuta, state entities and nongovernmental agencies of all ideological walks easily misinterpret the complex system of religious and civil cargos in Wixarika communities. Furthermore, these various changes in civil leadership structures are complicated by intercommunal disputes over land and development initiatives. Indeed, current disputes are reflections of past state and private development projects, which left bitter tastes in the mouths of some and inspired thirst in others. In the following pages, I briefly explore a few of these projects, which are credited with influencing regional migration.

PLAN HUICOT

Named after the geographic region of the Sierra Madre highlands, which comprises the Huichol (Wixarika), Cora (Náayeri), and Tepehuan (O'dam) communities and partly funded by the United States' Alliance for Progress, Plan Huicot was part of the larger Plan Lerma regional development initiative, which spanned the 1960s and 1970s (Torres Contreras 2000, 200). Specifically, Plan Huicot set out to promote the development of these three indigenous groups as well as some peripheral mestizo communities that "have remained at the margins of all human progress, and live at primitive levels" (Estados Unidos Mexicanos 1966, 9). The documents that outline the plan begin with an overview of the region's geography and demography based on studies prepared by the INI, the Franciscan religious order, and a survey carried out by the National Commission for the Eradication of Malaria. These documents repeatedly speak of the Huicot region as being backward as a result of its inhabitants' passivity toward global economic and cultural transformations: "Here, like in many other aspects, *everything is yet to be done*; as observed in the area of nutrition, housing, dress, health, culture, etc." (Estados Unidos Mexicanos 1966, 14; emphasis mine).

Displaying the classic paternalism of revolutionary indigenismo, Plan Huicot placed the state as the protector of indigenous peoples, who were seen as easy targets for more astute mestizos, particularly regarding territorial boundaries and disputes:

> Formerly the Huichol area was much larger, but the creation of some mestizo ejidos has come to lesion indigenous patrimony, reducing their land, a reality that the ignorance and ingenuousness of the Indian cannot comprehend; the segregated parts [of the sierra] are territories inherited from their grandparents, and they continue to occupy them[,] believing themselves to be the proprietors, with the firm hope that they will receive justice, have their rights met. (Estados Unidos Mexicanos 1966, 78; my translation)

Mirroring the words of Gamio fifty years earlier, this document depicts indigenous peoples as naïve and passive subjects who harbor an anachronistic conception of land tenure.[13] With the discovery of the Huicot region's rich timber, mineral, and water resources, the Wixaritari's use of land became subject to criticism and was one of Plan Huicot's focal points:

> For lack of infrastructure, the forests have not been industrially taken advantage of; forests that, because of ignorance, the Huichol has come to destroy, be it by irrational logging, or be it by fires that he deliberately provokes year after year before the beginning of the rains. In the mind of the indigenous person, these

fires can primordially obey the following reasons: (1) Form clouds, which produce smoke, and with them propel the rain. (2) Burn the dry brush to prepare the new harvests. (3) Destroy the grazing land to drive away the mestizos and their cattle. (Estados Unidos Mexicanos 1966, 88; my translation)

Ironically, major problems with logging appeared in the early 1970s with the first government-built roads. As these roads were being built into Wixarika territory, trees were inevitably cut down, while logging was occurring well beyond the roads' delineation, and timber companies quickly took advantage of the roads to clear-cut the forests (Juan and Yvonne Negrín interview).

Under Plan Huicot, military officials and tourists also took advantage of the landing strips and roads to enter the region. One member of Tuapurie described Plan Huicot's confusing fallout to anthropologist Guillermo de la Peña:

> There came soldiers to build more landing strips and there came many jets, of the government and private. They also fixed some roads. Those of the Plan built buildings for clinics and schools, and gave money to the parents so that they could send their children off to school. The people were scared of the soldiers . . . and the coming of tourists and mirones [voyeurs] . . . it was something very bothersome. (de la Peña 2002, 102–3; my translation)

De la Peña also mentions the general competition between different governmental agencies over Wixarika territory, resulting in the waste of economic resources through corruption and abandoned or deficient projects. The influx of soft money that came into the hands of intermediaries and businessmen, specifically new elites and caciques who gained significant power under the government's projects, gradually led to the usurpation of power from elected Wixarika officials and kawiterutsixi. Although Plan Huicot stopped functioning by the mid-1970s, it left long-term consequences, particularly because it was a period that disenfranchised Wixarika communities from land and resources (Torres Contreras 2000, 35).

THE AGUAMILPA HYDROELECTRIC DAM

Roughly a decade after Plan Huicot was terminated, the construction of the Aguamilpa hydroelectric dam began in the state of Nayarit. Located where Wixarika, Náayeri, and mestizo territories converge at the foot of the Western

Sierra Madre, the Aguamilpa Dam sits where the Chapalagana, Huaynamota, and Santiago Rivers meet. Under the Salinas administration, there was a resurgence of interest in hydroelectric power. The Aguamilpa Dam, financed by the Comisión Federal de Electricidad (Federal Commission of Electricity, or CFE), World Bank loans, and the private construction firm Grupo ICA, became part of a global initiative to take advantage of the Santiago River (Torres Contreras 2000, 21). Although its preliminary planning began in 1954, engineering studies for the dam were not carried out until 1980, and construction did not begin until 1989 (Ignorosa Mijangos 1994, 74–79). The CFE and Grupo ICA placed the dam's capacity at one million cubic meters of water, inundating a surface of thirteen thousand hectares that belonged to twenty-two ejidos, three communities, and three properties of the municipalities of El Nayar, Tepic, and Santa María del Oro (120). Of the affected communities, 61 percent were Wixarika, and the rest were mestizo. According to the CFE, the principal objectives of the dam were electricity generation for urban centers, local fishing industry development, infrastructure construction in the area, irrigation to boost crop production, and flood control (77).

Much like other governmental initiatives in the region, state authorities entered the communities offering little forthright information about the costs and benefits of the dam. According to a study by Luis Eloy Rodríguez, the majority of Wixaritari were unclear about the consequences they would face with the construction of the dam—79.1 percent stated that they did not understand the project. Furthermore, the project was discussed only once in Spanish, with no visual aids. Many of the inhabitants, especially women, speak only Wixarika, and 93.4 percent would have preferred an explanation in their own language (Eloy Rodríguez 1994, 109). Consequently, 62.0 percent of the Wixarika population polled did not believe that all their land was properly indemnified, and 87.2 percent believe that the indemnified land was not properly compensated (112). Although indemnification money was intended for the economic reestablishment of the displaced communities, Eloy Rodríguez's study found that money distributed to the affected inhabitants was largely spent on immediate necessities, such as clothes and household goods. As a result, few people invested their money in long-term productive needs. Over the years of my personal travels to Tepic, I have met several families who were displaced by the construction of the Aguamilpa Dam. Because the land given to them by the government was so poor, many eventually moved to the city to make a living selling artwork or by entering the urban labor force.

The Plan Huicot, Aguamilpa Dam, and INI initiatives discussed here are only some examples of the Mexican state's interventions in and around Wixarika communities. Besides the inherent racial and developmentalist notions that embody these strategies, the projects' lack of continuity is a fundamental problem. As a longtime activist in the region, Yvonne Negrín points out that whenever an INI program was introduced, the end of the six-year presidential administration (*sexenio*) would come, and the programs of the outgoing administration would be dismantled, producing a tremendous waste of resources: "They [the government] would spend all this time, money, and energy building up an infrastructure, and then the *sexenio* changes, the new guy comes in, and there is no continuation of the programs that might be 80 percent finished. And that's it; the new guy comes in, and he's got his own ideas and *his* new programs!" (Yvonne Negrín, interview by author, March 2, 2004). The government's inefficiency has subsequently led to stronger local support for nongovernmental organizations (NGOs) operating in the region. Beginning in the 1980s and intensifying through the 1990s, support for NGOs converged with international trends toward economic liberalization and decentralization that pushed for governmental withdrawal from providing social services. This led to the rising presence of private entities engaged in economic development, health, and education projects, as well as mediating land disputes.

The past few decades of government development projects in Wixarika territory demonstrate how the legacies of the "Indian problem" and acción indigenista are more reflective of Mexico's problematic racial imaginary and race relations than of the perceived socioeconomic and cultural deficiencies of indigenous peoples. Rather, the Indian problem reflects on the cultural and political economic endpoint that the state has desired indigenous peoples to reach. Following Arturo Escobar's analysis, acción indigenista is a clear illustration of development as a "regime of representation" that is mediated by a Western episteme and historicity (Escobar 1995, 6). Yet for all the failures of applied indigenismo, the policies of the Mexican state did powerfully shape relations of governance between indigenous peoples and the state, carving the way for subsequent forms of decentralized multicultural governance. The intricacies of contemporary indigenous struggles over citizenship and national belonging can be further understood through an examination of the diverse migratory experiences of Wixaritari living in the city.

BEADS, WAGE LABOR, AND THE PROMISE OF THE CITY

> *It is difficult not to project onto the Huichol romantic concepts of the "noble savage," if he is not given the focus of a "marginal being submerged in ignorance" or a "Don Juan: sage of the peyote."*
> —JUAN NEGRÍN, ACERCAMIENTO SUBJETIVO E HISTÓRICO AL HUICHOL (MY TRANSLATION)

For thousands of years Wixaritari have moved across a large segment of the Mexican territory, with the Western Sierra Madre becoming a permanent stronghold only during Spanish colonial domination. Not to be confused with nomadism, this mobility has largely resulted from the Wixaritari's seasonal trekking across different pilgrimage routes, which take them to five cardinal points: to the north in Durango; the south in the area of Chapala, in central Jalisco; the west near San Blas, in Nayarit; the east at Wirikuta, in the desert plateaus of San Luis Potosí; and the center, Teakata, located in the community of Tuapurie, in northern Jalisco. As Liffman (2011) notes in his study on Wixarika territoriality, these geographic practices disrupt simplistic conceptions of indigenous cultural and spatial stagnation:

> Popular images of Huichol territory as geographically isolated and perpetually sacred give the impression that the resilient but hard-pressed mountain people who inhabit it are like a natural feature of the landscape. However, Huichols themselves—in exchanges with their divine ancestors and with the Mexican state—deploy flexible social and territorial relationships to relocate boundaries and sacred points of that landscape, which they then anchor historically in ritual. (Liffman 2011, 59)

This mobility has allowed Wixaritari to actively engage with different ethnic groups through distinct historical moments, often in the form of strategic efforts to retain their cultural and territorial integrity. As one example, José de Jesús Torres Contreras details how Wixarika communities agreed to submit themselves to the colonial order in exchange for being granted a degree of autonomy by accepting the title of Indian militias (Torres Contreras 2009, 56). While the neighboring Náayeri fiercely fought off the Spaniards, Wixaritari seemingly acquiesced to the invading forces, sparing themselves from the violent oppression laid on their Náayeri neighbors, who were forced into pueblos where the missionaries and soldiers endeavored to make them assimilate to the Hispanic order (63).

Despite this history of strategic negotiation, the expansion of the market in rural Wixarika communities has led to migrations to towns and cities. Torres Contreras (2009) affirms that this "exodus" to large cities occurred as a result of development programs, like Plan Huicot, which create new economic necessities and expectations that cannot be met by remaining within their home communities (90). For the most part, migrations in and out of the sierra communities do not summon ideas of forced displacement but are a result of incremental relocations largely tied to economic necessity—a more subtle yet real form of dislocation. As is the case with other ethnic and racial groups, an element of voluntary migration is also driven by curiosity and desire to live in a new place. In the following pages, I briefly discuss how seasonal labor migrations to the coast and the market in Huichol crafts have propelled the establishment of Wixarika individuals and families in Tepic and Guadalajara. As for so many millions of other Mexicans, these cities present promises of economic stability, including educational opportunities for Wixarika children.

THE ARTESANÍA CIRCUIT

In the years before the INI introduced the Centro Coordinador Indigenista Cora-Huichol, Franciscans initiated what would become a growing focus on Wixarika arts and crafts, largely revolving around the medium of the yarn painting—wooden boards covered with beeswax and emblazoned with colorful wool yarn. Although Wixarika sacred offerings and textiles had already won the attention of anthropologists and folk art enthusiasts, the yarn painting presented a contemporary expression geared toward a nonindigenous market.[14] Notable among these early efforts was Father Ernesto Loera's promotion of Wixarika arts and crafts sold in the vicinity of the Basílica de Zapopan in Guadalajara, where Wixarika artisans continue to gravitate to sell their work today. The INI soon replaced the Church as the promoter of "artesanía Huichol" through the National Fund for the Fomentation of Crafts (Fondo Nacional para el Fomento de las Artesanías, or FONART), which sold crafts at designated government stores.

In the 1950s, with the backing of the Museo de Artes Populares (Museum of Folk Arts) and Jalisco governor Agustín Yáñez (1953–59), Mexican museographer

Alfonso Soto Soria began commissioning yarn paintings, often providing the materials and encouraging the use of thinner plywood boards, which could be more easily hung on walls (MacLean 2012, 70–72). Interest in the yarn-painting medium and its cultural and religious symbolism exploded internationally in the late 1960s as a result of these incipient efforts (Arriaga and Negrín 2018). American filmmaker John Lilly's acquisition of works by Santos de la Torre were soon followed by UCLA anthropologist Peter T. Furst's promotion of the yarn paintings of Ramón Medina Silva alongside tales of the artist's shamanic abilities.[15] Furst's intervention, in particular, brought about the idea of the "shaman-artist," which resonated with the counterculture movement of the United States and elsewhere. Particularly in Tepic, mestizo shop owners began to sell these paintings alongside Wixarika textiles and beadwork, fueling the burgeoning market for Wixarika-produced goods and making this city the capital for these crafts.

Yet the exposure that Wixarika culture gained through artwork remained limited to the objectifying lens of Mexican indigenismo and international psychedelic enthusiasts. In a retrospective analysis of the more than fifty-year-old market in Wixarika arts and crafts, Séverine Durin notes, "The Baroque face of the Huichol artisan is the daughter of indigenismo and the policies to foment crafts" that gained particular traction under the auspice of the presidency of Luis Echeverría (2008, 335, 344). In 1976, Mexican writer and activist Juan Negrín described how the appreciation of commercial Wixarika crafts stood in sharp contrast to the general disrespect and racism that Wixarika artists continued to face: "At present, Huichol culture is viewed with greater appreciation in the industrialized world partly because of the crisis in values and confidence that modern capitalism is undergoing" (1976, 2). Yet Negrín cautioned that the commercialization of folkloric crafts missing deeper religious or aesthetic context risked making Wixarika arts and crafts into a "spectacle" that contributed to the public's view of the indigenous as materially and philosophically deficient peoples. From this focus, in the early 1970s, Negrín began a series of long-standing collaborations with a select group of Wixarika yarn painters, whose work would be exhibited in contemporary art museums across Europe, the United States, and eventually at the Museum of Modern Art in Mexico City.[16]

As Wixarika arts and crafts became popularized, an increasing number of Wixaritari approached government stores in sierra communities or made periodic trips to the cities of Tepic, Zacatecas, Guadalajara, and Mexico City to sell their work. Many artisans and artists confronted the double standard Negrín witnessed—the increased consumption of Wixarika arts and crafts accompanied by its simultaneous cheapening in the market, which denied Wixarika artists proper recognition and remuneration. To date, indigenous artists continue to face marginalization within contemporary art institutions while being lumped together with artisans under the umbrella of *arte popular*, or folk art. In February 2010, the son of the owner of a Tepic store that had sold Wixarika arts and crafts for several decades lamented the disappearing role of mestizo intermediaries, like him and his father, now that Wixarika artists and artisans sold their work directly to the consumer (personal commentary to author, February 2010). While dealing directly with the market presents new opportunities for Wixarika artisans and eliminates the exploitation they often experienced at the hands of government and independent intermediaries, it also poses new challenges and forms of exploitation.

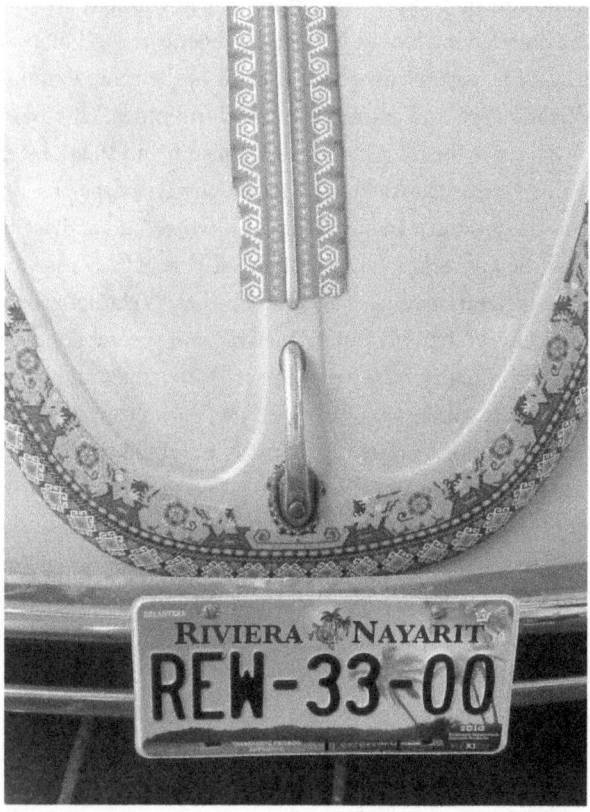

FIGURE 4 Various Wixarika artists, *Vochol*, 2010, a Volkswagen Beetle covered in glass beads on adhesive. Photo by author.

Durin claims that unlike other indigenous peoples, who often find their niche in domestic labor, the economic insertion of Wixaritari in the city has come exclusively through the marketing of their arts and crafts, which in turn has provided them with a degree of cultural prestige (2008, 337). Nonetheless, over the past two decades, indigenous artists and artisans (including Wixaritari) have faced repeated challenges to their vending in public spaces. This, combined with the sheer number of Wixarika arts and crafts on the market, has placed artisans and their families in a precarious economic situation. Because more families, in both the country and the city, rely on the sale of what are now mostly beaded crafts, their access to suitable spaces for the sale of their goods has become increasingly important for their livelihoods. These conditions have fueled several initiatives by the artisans to gain vending spaces, a topic I return to in subsequent chapters.

FIELDS OF LABOR

The seasonal migration of Wixaritari to work in the tobacco plantations along the coast of Nayarit is part of a contemporary manifestation of a long existing tradition of travel to the lowlands and the coast to leave offerings to Tatéi Haramara, Our Mother Ocean. Tatéi Haramara "is the primordial source of all water from where some of the waves emanate that are then transported by Támatsi Eakatéiwari, Our Elder Brother Wind Neighbor, later to be transformed into clouds over different cardinal points and the center" (J. Negrín 2006, 2). Pilgrimages to the coast coincide with the dry season, when families cease agricultural labor in the sierra and seek temporary employment outside their communities. In 1829, John Pringle Brodie, a Scottish merchant who did business along the coast of Nayarit, noted how the indigenous people purchased salt at the Zapotillo "Saltworks" near the port of San Blas, giving some indication of Wixarika participation in the monetized economy (Brodie, December 12, 1829, n.p.)

Anthropologist Francisco Talavera Durón estimates that Wixarika labor in agricultural fields began in the 1930s, initially in bean and corn cultivations, and within a couple of decades moved into the tobacco harvests (Talavera Durón 2003, 16).[17] Talavera Durón's study exposes the complex geographic, cultural, and economic relationship that Wixarika migration has with seasonal work on tobacco plantations. He locates distinct *jornaleros*, or day laborers, whose work at the plantations responds to communal or familial needs (e.g., paying for traditional ceremonies in the community or accruing money to get their families through the dry season; 2003, 19). Additionally, Talavera Durón notes that some jornaleros are also artisans and use their travel to the coast as only one of several destinations. As such, migration to the coast encompasses various familial, economic, and religious needs:

> Wixaritari can migrate in order to take care of their parcel of land during the rainy season, to take their children to school or to a clinic, to deposit offerings at their sacred places, to work seasonally at the tobacco plantations, and in that way face their multiple ceremonies and the hostile dry season. To migrate has been an important situation for Wixaritari; the majority of their mythical narrations make reference to this process, the process of health-sickness, their conception of sacrifice, [which] are tended to through temporary distance from the home community. (Talavera Durón 2003, 17; my translation)

Wixaritari who work in the agricultural fields of Nayarit face particularly poor working and living conditions. Patricia Díaz Romo has led the documentation of these conditions, particularly the indiscriminate use of pesticides, many of which are designated for restricted or prohibited use (Díaz Romo and Salinas Álvarez 2002, 3). According to Díaz Romo's studies, tobacco, cotton, and tomato crops not only bring in large profits per hectare, but also require the heaviest application of pesticides, bringing about dangerous health risks for the workers and local residents. These precarious conditions only worsened as agricultural practices in the region industrialized and became managed by large companies, such as British American Tobacco and Philip Morris International (2–3). Díaz and Salinas's 2002 study found that tobacco cultivations have provided an important economic motor for the state of Nayarit and consequently face little to no regulation, permitting environmental and human health concerns to fall by the wayside (4). Negligence is exacerbated because of the prevalent racism found in the large plantations, where the majority of workers are indigenous (primarily Wixarika, Náayeri, and O'dam). Talavera Durón describes how the cultural wealth that Wixarika migrations to the coast reveal is rendered invisible by enduring racial attitudes that qualify the Indian as "ignorant, dirty, drunk, resistant to workdays of more than eighteen hours" (Talavera Durón 2003, 97). The fact that tobacco cultivation has drastically diminished in Nayarit has not signified that Wixarika laborers have ended their seasonal migration for work. The need to find seasonal work outside the sierra communities has only increased with the penetration of market forces and the casting of wider migratory networks, where people search for work in areas of the country (or abroad) that do not hold sacramental meaning for Wixarika culture.[18]

HIGHER EDUCATION

Wixarika students who are enrolled in universities are most often the sons and daughters of artisans or bilingual teachers—some of them once accompanied their families to the tobacco fields of Nayarit, where they remember sleeping in the open fields. These activities have brought many families to urban centers on a temporary or, in many cases, a permanent basis. Many of the youth who grew up in these settings have sought university degrees that can help them reside in the city or provide important resources for their communities of origin (Bonilla et al. 2017). The recent boom in Wixarika university students and professionals in Guadalajara's and Tepic's universities is also the product of the government's construction of schools in Wixarika communities. Despite the shortcomings of many INI and SEP educational efforts, the training of bilingual teachers undoubtedly brought about an increased sense that schooling was an important community asset and led to the perception that professionalization could help with Wixarika struggles for political, economic, and cultural sovereignty, as seen with the autonomous schools that have been created in the last twenty years.

Gabriel Pacheco, a Wixarika poet and linguistics professor at the University of Guadalajara, obtained his bachelor's and master's degrees at this institution but holds lukewarm enthusiasm for the coming generations of graduates (personal commentary to author, October 2009). Although Pacheco presents a "success story," his weariness reflects personal experiences of discrimination in Guadalajara and in his home community of Guadalupe Ocotán. His doubts are also a response to the many Wixarika students he has taught and who have been unable to find work in their professions. Pacheco noted that too many Wixarika students were gravitating toward medicine and law, careers that offer them few employment prospects within or outside their communities. Consequently, many of Pacheco's former students find employment as mechanics and construction workers in small and medium-sized towns.

The role of higher education for indigenous youth presents important opportunities and challenges that I discuss further in chapter 5. What several years of ethnographic research have left clear is that the experiences of students and professionals are highly contingent on the city in which they are studying or working. Gisela Carlos Fragoso and Fortino Domínguez's analysis of embedded racism in the Mexican educational system notes not only that a series of regional articulations of racism affects the learning environment, but also that the presumption of a colorblind curriculum prevents any serious discussion of antiracism within the classroom (2018, 26). This begs for a critical discussion of the ways in which Tepic and Guadalajara have developed specific urban narratives with ingrained understandings of ethnic identity that make their way into classrooms and public spaces. The following two chapters examine key moments in the development of each of these cities, paying attention to the presence of indigenous peoples in the discursive and material formation of a racialized urban imaginary, which then shapes the experiences of Wixarika residents as well as the diverging political agendas of their respective organizations.

3

TEPIC

City of Inclusion, City of Exclusion

INTERLOCKING STORIES of colliding cultures, territorial dispossessions and repossessions, and astute indigenous negotiation and resistance have marked the development of Tepic. Today it is a city intensely shaped by the ebbs and flows of its indigenous presence. Ethnicity makes its way into the political chambers, where mestizo authorities sport Náayeri or Wixarika bags, and creeps into business plans that look to revitalize the regional economy on the backs of its indigenous heritage. Seldom inscribed in the city's landscape are the legacies of the African presence during the early colonial era or the foreign capitalists of later years—these contributions are best left to historians, forgotten by the popular imagination. These cues seem to demonstrate that five hundred years after the arrival of Europeans, the "Indian" still reigns over Tepic.

Despite having the bulk of their tribal territories in Jalisco, Wixaritari are often thought of as the prototypical indigenous culture of Nayarit. Even in Jalisco, Wixaritari are often believed to be from Nayarit. On the other hand, Náayeri, or Cora, culture, which is fundamentally Nayaritan, is given the short shrift in the state's tourism-oriented identity. Despite this, Nayarit's general population has long interchangeably used the diminutive and hispanized terms Coritas and Huicholitos to designate any indigenous peoples in the state. The ambiguous relationship that the nonindigenous population has developed with indigenous peoples is played out in everyday interactions in Tepic's public spaces. Much of these relations are based on fixed notions of how indigenous people ought to look, the spaces they are presupposed to inhabit, and the limited occupations they are generally believed to hold. But Wixaritari are not just craftspeople; they are taxi drivers, receptionists, lawyers, and teachers. Their visual markers as indigenous are sometimes revealed but often go concealed as they move through city spaces of work and leisure. Because in Mexico, skin tone and phenotype are not the sole indicators of race and ethnicity, it is not until Wixaritari are dressed in traditional attire or heard speaking their native language that they encounter direct forms of exclusion or inclusion (Martínez Casas et al. 2014, 53).

The present chapter offers a historical geography of Tepic and the broader Nayarit region, gleaned from various sources to interrogate how its identity has been shaped over time, creating past and present-day forms of inclusion and exclusion. This and the following chapter both begin with narratives that contrast the Battle of La Mojonera as a constitutive moment in the construction of the Mexican West's racial imaginary. I then present a broader historical overview, offering regional context for understanding the key moments that have created the structural and experiential conditions for present-day struggles over the city space by indigenous residents, particularly the younger generations. This chapter in particular contributes a rare historical geography of a city and region that not only is absent from urban studies, but even fails to appear on the radar of most scholarship on race and indigeneity in Mexico.

THE FALL OF THE TIGER

> *Lozada continues to be a fanatical cacique, sold to foreigners; of the defense of the people it is better not to utter a word. When ditches are opened to install pipelines in the streets of Tepic, treasure seekers believe to have found those belonging to Lozada all over the place. The descendants of Ramón Corona have inherited the lands of Lozada's town, San Luis, today San Luis of Lozada, but they do not risk visiting them, because "the Indians of San Luis" continue their dispute.*
> —JÁUREGUI AND MEYER, *EL TIGRE DE ÁLICA*
> (MY TRANSLATION)

On September 16, 1870, on the sixtieth anniversary of Mexico's independence, Manuel Lozada's followers issued an invitation to the Mexican people to join his cause, creating a more just nation that vindicates the rights of indigenous peoples, peasants, and the urban proletariat, who had been politically and economically disenfranchised by liberal reforms. The declaration was signed by 468 residents of distinct parts of what is today the state of Nayarit. Its contents were not as radical as the country's staunch liberals expected, for the movement's goal was not to eliminate the wealthy class but to level out the playing field, allowing the people of Mexico "what is necessary for subsistence" (cited in Aldana Rendón 1983, 86). Having established himself as the leader of a successful armed movement, Lozada's words in this declaration seemed conciliatory, reassuring the wealthy that the eradication of hunger among the poor would not mean that the rich would have a less sumptuous table; that the people's ability to dress decently would not impede the rich from wearing their luxurious clothes. Most importantly, the declaration stated that the Mexican people's right to own land that could be passed down to their progeny did not imply that the landed class would be left without sufficient property to maintain their economic interests.

Manuel Lozada was born in 1828 in the town of San Luis, just east of Tepic. In 1883, Mexican politician, doctor, and lawyer Salvador Quevedo y Zubieta described Lozada as a "small man part Indian, part European, part Mulatto, because his copper colored face had it all, with a flattened forehead and sharp cheekbones, accented by a coarse beard that showed the predominance of a race distinct from the indigenous. It is said, that he was born to a Spanish man and a Mulatto woman; but having been born in an Indian region, he acquired from these his habits, inclinations, and character" (quoted in Jáuregui and Meyer 1997, 92). Lozada was raised in the context of the region's heavily monopolized land tenure system, where the same four families had owned large ranching and agricultural plantations since the days of Nuño Beltrán de Guzmán's vicious sixteenth-century colonization (López González 1984, 31). During the same period, the region was shaped by the circulation of imported goods, which traveled from the port of San Blas, east to Guadalajara, to the Mexican northwest and California. Much of this commerce was controlled by British merchants, who simultaneously encouraged a vibrant contraband market that evaded Spanish and, later, Mexican taxation and regulation. Centuries of indigenous unrest and a heavy foreign presence made the region surrounding Tepic known for its lawlessness, offering the perfect soil for the birth of a complex and misunderstood rebel leader. Legend has it that Lozada became an outlaw after kidnapping an indigenous woman and subsequently fleeing with her to the mountains, abandoning his years as a hacienda laborer. He would soon become one of many bandits who assaulted shipments carried from the port of San Blas to Tepic and Guadalajara.

Yet the peasant turned bandit proved to be a strategic alliance builder and soon discovered his ability to leverage power through his dealings with the powerful commercial house Barron, Forbes and Company. Although he is considered a fervent ally of the conservative cause, he astutely played the liberals off the conservatives to secure his leadership over Tepic and its surroundings. His allies benefited from their relationship with Lozada because they could more freely operate in the rebellious canton of Tepic. But Lozada's early years as a hacienda peon, coupled with his subsequent experiences with the regional business and political classes, led to his politicization and eventual position as an agrarian leader fighting for the underdogs of the nineteenth-century Mexican countryside. A close look at Lozada's trajectory shows that he experienced "qualitative ideological jumps that took him from being a common bandit to the precursor of agrarian struggle in Mexico" (Aldana Rendón 1983, 106).[1] By 1857, the *lozadeños* had begun invading and redistributing land to the indigenous communities of the Western Sierra Madre, accelerating activities in 1868, as the movement expanded through the states of Jalisco and Zacatecas (Meyer 1969, 536–38). In a December 28, 1868, letter addressing the agrarian conflicts in eastern Nayarit, the "communist outlaw" called for a generalized and speedy expropriation of large landholdings, underlining that territorial delimitations should revert to the way they were "prior to when the pueblos were enslaved by the tyranny of governments and the rich" (537).[2] According to Lozada, if these actions appeared harsh, they were only in response to a justice system that had shown itself to be both "worn and ephemeral" for the people of the countryside (537). The Tigre de Álica's fifteen years of rule over Tepic and influence over a large swath of the western region emboldened him to seek the larger goal of promoting a national movement to vindicate the landless. The taking of Guadalajara would be the first and definitive step in this journey.

The faceoff at La Mojonera came soon after the death of Benito Juárez, who had maintained a polite enmity with Lozada and was weary of an all-out war against the indigenous communities of the seventh canton of Jalisco (Aldana Rendón 1983, 106; Jáuregui and Meyer 1997, 27).[3] Juárez's presidential successor, Sebastián Lerdo de Tejada, quickly ended this respite and joined forces with Jalisco's liberals under the intense lobbying of General Ramón Corona. On

December 2, 1872, Lerdo de Tejada disregarded the Comité de Estudio y Deslindes (Committee for Study and Demarcation), established by Lozada to deal with land redistributions; in addition, the president ordered troops to Tepic and had the 14th and 21st Battalions travel from the state of San Luis Potosí to Jalisco (Meyer 1969, 541–42).[4] This declaration of war by the federal government led Lozada to call on his bases to converge and announce the Plan Libertador (Liberatory Plan) on January 17, 1873. The plan stated that the people had "awakened from their lethargy" and now stood arms in hand under the principle that "the people govern for the people" (543).[5] Jalisco governor Ignacio Vallarta claimed that the Plan Libertador sought a widespread caste war and the "most scandalous territorial execution" seen in modern history—an ironic statement coming from someone who enthusiastically contributed to the "golden age of the hacienda" in Jalisco (544). As a lawyer who in 1856 was named administrator of indigenous affairs, Vallarta called for the expropriation of indigenous landholdings, arguing that these actions would benefit the "disgraced race" by forcing them to become modern liberal citizens (González Navarro 1994, 26, 31). For liberals like Vallarta, Lozada's movement into new territories ignited a deep fear of agrarian revolution dressed in the language of racial warfare.

The fast march to Guadalajara of Lozada's and Plácido Vega's mostly Wixarika troops would be the first time Lozada fought outside his territory (Meyer 1969, 545).[6] It was also the first time since the 1541 Mixtón War that indigenous rebels directly targeted the city. To this, the sensationalist newspaper *Juan Panadero* noted that the "the beasts of the Sierra of Álica have left their caves" and called on Guadalajara's population to "defend property, the honor of our families, the dignity of the State" (545). The 14th and 21st Battalions led by Corona soon met Lozada at a property called La Mojonera, located in the municipality of Zapopan. The quick defeat of Lozada's forces lent Corona a victory that would launch the general toward his political career. Yet testimonies abound that the Tigre de Álica's defeat had little to do with Corona's military prowess and more to do with the betrayal of Lozada's most trusted military companions.[7] From La Mojonera onward, Lozada experienced a series of seditions leading to military defeats and many desertions, the most painful of which was the betrayal of Domingo Nava, the "faithful executor of [Lozada's] agrarian policy" (552). Nava not only handed Lozada's arms to federal forces but helped them penetrate the terrain that Lozada had held undefeated for nearly twenty years. Treason was the ultimate instrument used to squash the rebellious population of these western mountains.

On July 19, 1873, Lozada was executed for the crimes of banditry and kidnapping at the Loma de los Metates outside Tepic (Meyer 1969, 535). Jean Meyer's study of Lozada's fall argues that the movement's composition as a "great western confederation" of indigenous peoples was a key element for both its success and its downfall, as it rested on a long history of ethnic division extant prior to the arrival of the Spaniards (562). The Tigre de Álica's leadership had been the "confederation's" unifying force. Upon Lozada's gradually weakening health and retreat from Guadalajara, these preexisting divisions were used by the enemy to sink the movement's momentum. His attempt to transcend geographic and ethnic boundaries for the larger cause of social justice and land redistribution collapsed. On the other hand, the failure of social revolution was turned into profit for Tepic's bourgeoisie, who, ten years later, gained independence from the state of Jalisco and became the Free and Sovereign State of Nayarit (568).[8] For the rural mestizo and indigenous communities of the West, the defeat at La Mojonera and Lozada's execution signified the continued loss of land, compounded by additional territorial disputes stemming from the newly created state boundaries between Nayarit and Jalisco, which cut through Wixarika communities (Rojas 1993, 259–60).

To date, Lozada's figure remains controversial, as scholars and politicians argue over his place in regional history.[9] Nonetheless, Lozada's centrality during the events that marked the second half of the nineteenth century has been ambiguously accepted. Was he a bandit? An opportunist who lent his services to British merchants and French imperialists? Or a revolutionary whose efforts at returning land to indigenous communities endures as a specter for the region's oligarchy? A mural in the State Congress building depicting Nayarit's heroes includes such controversial characters as Nuño Beltrán de Guzmán and King Nayar but excludes Lozada (Jáuregui and Meyer 1997, 26). Even so, the Tigre de Álica is alive and well for many Nayaritans: while he may not appear in officially sanctioned monuments, Jáuregui and Meyer note that the ancient fig tree where Lozada was executed is the scene of anonymous offerings on the yearly anniversary of his death and on the Day of the Dead (29). One of the most notable homages to Lozada was the sign in front of the church in the Náayeri village of Jesús María, Nayarit, that in 1940 read: "Long live the most excellent sir General of Division Don Manuel Lozada, viceroy of the Coras and Huichols" (15). With this sign and countless mythologies, the Tiger attains his historic place among the descendants of his indigenous supporters in the Sierra of Álica, where a mixture of fact and fiction have kept him alive.

NAYARIT'S IMPOSSIBLE CONQUEST

> *Her mountains were the nest of rebellious Indians who lived freely, jealously protecting their pagan customs, rites and ceremonies and inebriating themselves with peyote; a constant source of rebellions and refuge of all evildoers and Indian apostates, who maintained the surrounding Spanish population and the High Court of Nueva Galicia in a continuous state of alert.*
> —SALVADOR REYNOSO, AUTOS HECHOS POR EL CAPITÁN DON JUAN FLORES DE SAN PEDRO (MY TRANSLATION)

When Nuño Beltrán de Guzmán made his trek west in search of treasure and lands to settle in the name of the king of Spain, he quickly made a distinction between "indios amigos" and "indios de guerra" (Razo Zaragoza 1970, 26). The friendly Indians were those who accompanied him along his notoriously murderous journey, or who put up little or no resistance against his colonizing forces. His brief stay in Tonallán (today Tonalá, part of the Metropolitan Zone of Guadalajara) provided an exemplary manifestation of "friendly Indians," who lavishly served the conqueror. The brief battle that led to Tonallán's submission to Spanish rule was a small headache in comparison to what Guzmán's forces would face as they made their way northwest. It was here that the "Indians of war" shaped what seemed to be an impossible conquest. For three more centuries, the Western Sierra Madre and the area surrounding Tepic would remain beyond the grasp of the Crown and, later, Mexico City's leadership.

The lands that led to Tepic were sumptuous. In every direction, fertile valleys and water could be found. Here thrived the Great Dominion of Xalisco in the Valley of Matatipac. On July 8, 1530, Guzmán laid claim to the region of Xalisco and Tepic: "Two crosses were placed in Xalisco and another two in Tepiq, which is a temperate place, with many springs and very mild, a good river passes through it, it is a place with a lot of sown land and cotton fields, of all kinds of food and orchards; lodging has been left for Spaniards that stop here" (Guzmán quoted in Razo Zaragoza 1963, 53; my translation). The Sangangüey volcano, which resembles a gigantic mortar and pestle, stood watch over a promising countryside nestled between the Western Sierra Madre and the Pacific Ocean. For the pious Catholics, this land was a manifestation of the Garden of Eden and a prize to be won. Under the orders of Guzmán, the Spaniards were searching for the ideal location to settle the administrative headquarters of Nueva Galicia. It seemed he had found the place in Tepique, named after a fast-growing corn that can be cultivated in fifty days—a reflection of the region's abundance. In a letter to King Charles V, seeking approval to establish the capital in this location, Guzmán described the "docility" of the more than two million "souls" and asked permission to enslave them, as the area provided few "beasts of burden" (37).[10] The Spaniards carried on marking their territory with crosses and the blood of the indigenous peoples who fought them with arrows. Many native people fled to the mountains to escape persecution. According to an account written by Juan de Samano on January 20, 1530, when the chiefs of Xalisco were summoned to meet with the conquerors and failed to appear, Guzmán ordered that Xalisco be invaded and burned, and that those who escaped death be rounded up and enslaved (135). Samano narrates how two individuals believed to be indigenous leaders were ordered to have their hands cut off and necks slashed. Although Pedro de Carranza, another member of Guzmán's party, stated that Tepique was found in peace, orders were given to burn, kill, rape, and enslave the natives.

Yet Guzmán's people were not the first Spaniards to attempt a conquest of the area; in 1527 Hernán Cortés's brother Francisco Cortés de Buenaventura had tried colonizing this western territory (Santana 1930, 33). The matter would pit the Cortés brothers against Guzmán and reach the Spanish Crown's tribunals in 1531. In the trial, several Spaniards who participated in the westward expeditions testified before the president and judges of the Royal Court (Real Audiencia), describing gross cases of murder at the hands of Guzmán's troops; these testimonies also provided descriptions of a plush geography (Guzmán [1531] 1937). The feud between the conquistadores made clear how much this region was coveted for its rich resources and moderate climate. In a testimony by Gregorio Saldana and Francisco Verdugo, extending the territories held by the conquerors offered a promising "remedy for many Spaniards that are lost and poor and do not have anything to eat" (366). With great expectations, the city of Santiago de Compostela de Nueva Galicia, today Tepic, was founded on July 25, 1532 (López González 1984, 18). But the arrogance and violence that Guzmán brought would make the conquest of the region a seemingly impossible feat, as wave after wave of indigenous rebellions would push the capital of Nueva Galicia to the less hostile region of the Valley of Atemajac, sinking prospects for fully colonizing this Garden of Eden of the Indies. In 1540, the New Galician headquarters were moved south to Coactlán (presently the town of Compostela), leaving the Spanish colonies in Xalisco-Tepic with a small and destitute population.

In 1541, a decade and a half worth of Spanish brutality led to an all-out war against the Spaniards in the territories that had been christened Nueva Galicia. Although brief, the one-year Mixtón War (1541–42), which spanned from Culiacán to Guadalajara, set an important precedent for the rebellions to come. Written testimonies from this period draw a grim picture of both Spanish and indigenous struggles with disease and lack of food. The few Spanish colonizers in the area barely eked out a living and spent much of their time defending themselves from the area's native populations. Friar and historian Antonio Tello gives a clear indication of Spanish desperation in a letter he wrote to the king of Spain in 1543, which tells of the "continual war" with the natives and demands for more *vecinos* (neighbors), or Spanish immigrants, to help fight off the rebels and ensure the colonization of this western territory (Calvo 1990, 60).[11] Throughout these first years of attempted conquest, a small segment of the indigenous population of the West did become integrated in the besieged Spanish system, either through religious conversion or as laborers and assistants. Nevertheless, the bulk of the surviving native population kept the pressure on the Spaniards. Some attacks against the foreigners, such as the 1585 murder of Franciscans in Huaynamota, would then be followed by increasingly violent Spanish reprisals (89–92).

The legendary indigenous leader of this period was King Nayar, who was said to have founded the Kingdom of Xecora (or Xícora) during the final years of the fifteenth century; in 1500 he became the appointed leader, or king, of the Náayeri people who lived in adjacent territory to the Wixarika (Gutiérrez Contreras 1974, 53).[12] Today, the king is the namesake of the state of Nayarit, and homage is paid to him through a monument one sees upon entering Tepic. His leadership brought together the various Náayeri communities under one government, facilitating their territorial domination from the Pacific Coast to Mazapil in the present-day state of Zacatecas (53). A fierce enemy of surrounding indigenous populations, King Nayar is said to have helped ignite the Mixtón War, fearing that his own people could fall victim to looming Spanish brutality (78). Salvador Gutiérrez Contreras's study of Nayar draws on texts written by several of his Spanish contemporaries, showing that the Náayeri leader demonstrated some level of diplomacy with the colonizers, apparently becoming baptized in 1592 and granting some land to the Spaniards so that they could found the settlement of Guaynamota (88–89). In another indication of Nayar's collaborative spirit, Father

Uranzu named the sierra after the leader following an encounter in 1613 with an old and blind Nayar (97–98).[13] Despite King Nayar's friendly gestures toward the European colonizers, subsequent colonial leaders feared the cult surrounding him of the region's indigenous peoples. His ambiguous position as both an *indio amigo* and an *indio de guerra* endured as a threatening symbol to the colonial system. When Juan Flores de San Pedro successfully conquered much of the indigenous sierra territory in 1722, King Nayar's remains were removed from their shrine in Tzakaimuta and taken to Mexico City (195). One year after the cadaver was removed from its shrine, an auto-da-fé was proclaimed, and Nayar's remains were publicly burned in the Plazuela de San Diego, where countless other inquisition burnings had taken place (196–97).[14] Historian Luis Pérez Verdía affirms that among the accompanying objects burned with Nayar was a stone disk representing the sun, possibly the only of its kind found in New Galicia (cited in Gutiérrez Contreras 1974, 198). With these actions induced by colonial anxieties and Catholic superstitions, the Spanish authorities thought to have laid to rest their indigenous opponents in the Western Sierra Madre.

Following these first turbulent decades of conquest, mines were discovered in Nayarit. While promising to provide the Spaniards with only a fraction of the wealth generated by the mines of Zacatecas, the incipient mining activity (which was largely controlled by the clergy) was essential for the economic development of Guadalajara's seventeenth-century merchants (Calvo 1990, 126, 187). The expansion of mining and agriculture to feed the growing number of arrivals led to continued encroachment on indigenous land (Torres Contreras 2009, 154). Incessant upheaval coupled with the Spaniards' inability to navigate the sierra and conquer its inhabitants led the invaders to establish dozens of presidios along the "frontier of San Luis Colotlán" (156). Within this territory, the colonizers also sought political, economic, and geographic separation between pacified and warring Indians, the Spaniards and their descendants, enslaved Africans, and castas. The Wixaritari communities that became known as *indios fronterizos*, or frontier Indians, allied themselves with the Spaniards in their efforts to subdue their Náayeri enemies in exchange for certain privileges (168–82). As a result, Náayeri communities suffered much heavier repression, with the burning of their temples and the mass incarceration of their people. Cooperating Wixarika communities were largely left at the margins of this violence (210).[15]

In 1709, upon the discovery of mines in Chimaltitán, near Bolaños in the heart of the Western Sierra Madre, Captain Juan Flores de San Pedro sent a request to the president of the Royal Court of New Spain to "pacify" Nayarit through the "use of any means judged convenient" (Flores de San Pedro [1722] 1964, 12). On December 24, 1722, Captain Flores de San Pedro set off for the "definitive conquest of the Province of Nayarit," affirming that he would first attempt a "peaceful penetration" through evangelization and, if this failed, "reduce" the natives by armed force (12). As with his predecessors, the captain would find that he had entered a most difficult geography, which had been and would continue to be a type of fortress for its native inhabitants. He also found that "these Chichimecas" were disinterested in conversion and willing to fight any armed incursion (43). By April 17, 1722, Flores de San Pedro asked the governor of New Spain for military backup, as the indigenous believed the Spanish mission was not conversion but solely conquest for the precious metals housed in their mountains (103). With Flores's request granted, the inhabitants of the sierra were officially subjugated after fierce battles.

Throughout the unstable sixteenth century, Tepic was whittled down to a transitory town for those travelers and merchants who came and went from the coast (López González 1996, 26). The Spanish colonization of California, however, helped boost the floundering economy of the towns of Tepic, Xalisco, and Compostela. As interest for the northern territories grew, the need for carpentry, construction, ironwork, and agriculture to maintain these new arrivals increased. According to historian Pedro López González, beginning in late 1632, "the town of Tepic was not only considered a refuge along the road, but an indispensable stopping point, a place of rest, much more secure than the *tierra caliente* (the coast) which they dreaded because of its fevers, and a place of preparation to continue the journey to the center of New Spain" (28). As the decades progressed, San Blas would play an increasingly important role in the development of New Galicia's emerging cities of Tepic and Guadalajara.

SMALL PORT, BIG CAPITAL

¿Cuándo me traes a mi negra? / Que la quiero ver aquí / Con su rebozo de seda / Que le traje de Tepic

When will you bring me my Black Woman? / I want to see her here / With her silk shawl / That I brought her from Tepic
—"SON DE LA NEGRA" (POPULAR MEXICAN SONG)

Colonial Mexico was not solely composed of indigenous peoples and colonizers struggling over political, economic, and territorial power. In fact, there was a large but today much forgotten African presence in New Galicia. As the years progressed, Asian and Middle Eastern immigrants would also come to test their luck in the promised and often lawless lands of the Mexican West. Eighteenth-century Tepic had a small but increasingly heterogeneous population, with mulattoes making up the largest and fastest-growing racial group because of the need for their labor in agriculture and cattle ranching (López González 1984, 20–21). At the beginning of the nineteenth century, Scottish captain John Pringle Brodie described the region's demographic composition: "The people in the various towns and on the Haciendas are generally a well made race of people. None of them can be strictly called Indians, and the whites are very few, but you have all the different shades from the one to the other, so mixed and crossed that it is utterly impossible to make out what proportion they bear" (Brodie, June 23, 1831, n.p.). As discussed in chapter 1, the colonial casta system offers a glimpse into a hierarchical society that tolerated miscegenation. With few European women in a city like Tepic, marriages across racial lines were quite common. This heterogeneity would continue to grow once San Blas was formally established as a naval base and commercial port in 1768.

Initially, San Blas was an integral part of the Spanish empire's geopolitical project along the northern Pacific coast. At this port, boats were built and sent north to "pacify and rescue" the territories of Sonora and Alta California from incursions by Russians and the British (López González 1984, 38). While Acapulco remained the most important West Coast port in New Spain, the route between San Blas and Mexico City was far easier to travel and included the important city of Guadalajara along the way (Mayo 2006, 4). During the second half of the eighteenth century, the activity created by the port led to a series of accompanying economic developments, and the region experienced rapid demographic growth (Meyer 1990, 26). Expeditions out of New Galicia to the slowly colonizing northern territories made the region of Nayarit an obligatory stopping point, connecting central Mexico with the Pacific. The most famed of these expeditions was Father Junípero Serra's departure from San Blas in 1768 to carry out his evangelizing mission in the Californias.

In the economic sphere, San Blas became a key contributor to the commercial development of New Galicia, allowing for an increasingly independent trade network between the western territories, Asia, the Caribbean, and Europe. The growth of imports from Asia, and the galleons from the Philippines in particular, helped make Tepic an emerging merchant city. During this period, Tepic was considered relatively important because of its vibrant commerce and its well-attended marketplace (Meyer 1990, 50). The city's late colonial reputation for its bazaar can be appreciated in one line from the classic mariachi song "Son de la negra," which indelibly points to the silk shawl brought from Tepic and, as a result, the silk imports brought from Asia to Tepic via San Blas.[16] The "Son de la negra" is also a clear indicator of the abovementioned African presence in the Mexican West—a presence that was often embraced within the contradictory colonial race relations.

The activity of San Blas inevitably had a ripple effect on the surrounding countryside as rising amounts of agricultural goods were produced for the port town, for the merchant and naval fleets that came and went, and for the northbound journeys (Meyer 1990, 43). During the colonial period, Tepic's hinterland became an ideal setting for raising livestock; this was particularly true along the largely unpopulated and well-watered coastal region (López González 1984, 29). In the eighteenth century, the livestock raised here took up the bulk of the region's exports. By 1742, thirty thousand cows were sent per year from New Galicia to central Mexico's burgeoning urban centers—40 percent of these were raised in Tepic's jurisdiction (Meyer 1990, 30). According to Pedro López González, the families that controlled the livestock business were the heirs of the large haciendas acquired during the initial years of conquest and lacked an innovative spirit, preferring to live off rent (1984, 31–33). Tobacco proved to become another important crop for Tepic's landed class and for the Spanish Crown (41–43). Up until a decree in 1768 that gave preferential advantages to tobacco produced in Veracruz, Nayarit had demonstrated that its land was prime soil for this cultivation (Meyer 1990, 40). Although sales from the entity subsequently decreased, the entrepreneurial spirit of the time sought more than the exportation of the raw material and established a tobacco processing plant in Guadalajara controlled by capital in Tepic.

During the final years of the colonial period, the Napoleonic wars placed the Spanish Crown in a difficult position to assert control over its colonial territories, particularly those like New Galicia that were already isolated from the major centers of colonial authority. The disjunction of Spanish rule coupled with the Bourbon Reforms solidified the sense of growing independence among the criollos in the Spanish colonies. The reforms not only decentralized political and economic power, but they broke away from the long-established protectionism of the Spanish colonial system and ushered in free-market policies. With the establishment of a consulate in Guadalajara in 1795, the West's already extant sense of political and economic autonomy from Mexico City strengthened. In San Blas, the convergence of these factors precipitated the rising economic influence of British capital (Mayo 2006, 7–8). In the absence of Spanish colonial authority, British, Panamanian, and South American merchants who built ties at this port were able to directly connect the San Blas–Tepic–Guadalajara commercial axis with the Isthmus of Panama, South America, and the West Indies without going through the previously hegemonic Mexico City–Veracruz–Spain circuit (8).

San Blas gained significant clout during Mexico's War of Independence when insurgent leader José María Morelos held the port of Acapulco under siege—sending all naval traffic to New Galicia's coast. Between 1812 and 1817, the blockade of Acapulco created a period of unseen prosperity for Tepic and Guadalajara (Meyer 1990, 49). José María Murià notes that this period of commercial affluence continued, specifying that between 1821 and 1827, San Blas received 58 percent of the Pacific's customs transactions, compared to Acapulco's 29 percent (cited in Jáuregui 2010, 308). The new traffic of people and goods passing through San Blas and the lack of centralized authority made the West prime land for contraband and gave the region a reputation for lawlessness. This tumultuous prosperity was framed by British capital, which flooded the western commercial network. In fact, the Barron, Forbes and Company commercial house quickly emerged as the political and economic mover and shaker in the Tepic area. Through the nineteenth century, commercial houses like Barron, Forbes and Company not only profited from the sale of contraband but were directly involved in securing the movement of illicit goods throughout Mexico's West (Meyer 1990, 60). John Mayo's study on the matter estimates that between 1811 and 1814, twenty-five banned foreign ships discharged goods in San Blas that were paid for with silver and gold illicitly extracted from the Western Sierra Madre (2006, 5). Much like present-day discussions on the role of the black market, government authorities would complain about how the traffic in illicit goods was damaging the already struggling public coffers. Despite the government's concerns, the public now enjoyed access to far cheaper consumer goods than those sold legally via the Veracruz–Mexico City axis (6).

Barron, Forbes and Company held "a position of unrivalled, if often reviled, political influence and economic power" in western Mexico, and with the company's infamously "uninhibited" attitude, it would seemingly always get its way (Mayo 2006, 67). Eustace Barron was an Irishman born in Spain who used his inheritance of landed property in England to begin his career in South America, where he volunteered between 1818 and 1822 for the soon-to-be defeated Spanish Royal Army (67). He is believed to have met Scottish entrepreneur Alexander Forbes in South America, where they both followed the commercial ships northward to the promising port of San Blas. Eustace and Alexander would subsequently found their commercial house in 1823, with the former handling operations in Tepic and the latter spending the trading season in the sweltering port town of San Blas (69). Aside from their economic activities, both became consuls in Mexico—Barron served as British consul and Forbes as consul for the United States and Chile (Degollado 1857). According to Jean Meyer, foreign capitalists in Mexico often became consuls to their home countries: "The consular function provides the businesses with proved protection. All are consuls, all are cosmopolites, all do a little of everything, including contraband" (1990, 54).

Barron and Forbes would master these roles for several decades, making their fortunes from the combination of licit and illicit merchandise. The pair also became important creditors, acquiring large sums of property in exchange for unpaid debts (Plascencia Flores 1984, 34). By 1867, their company had become the largest financial institution in the country and provided loans for presidents Benito Juárez and Lerdo de Tejada (35). Forbes's *California: A History of Upper and Lower California*, written in Tepic in 1835 and published in 1839, is a testament of the capitalist's imperial dreams, whereby Mexico's debt to Britain could be used to acquire Alta California before the Yankees could get a secure foothold on the territory (Forbes [1839] 1937, 92–93). In the style of the East India Company, Forbes proposed that California be ceded to a company (xxv).[17] While Forbes's dreams of colonizing California never took hold, in 1846 his company dubiously acquired shares for the newly christened New Almaden quicksilver mine in Santa Clara County. Toward the end of his life, Alexander Forbes would face charges in U.S. courts for fraud and forgery of land titles (Herbert Ingram Priestley in Forbes [1839] 1937, xiv–xvi).

In the 1850s, Barron and Forbes linked up with a bandit who had reached a famed reputation for success in the treacherous Sierra de Álica, or Nayarit. The relationship between the British capitalists and Manuel Lozada surely came as a result of their mutual enmity toward the liberal regime. For the commercial house, hostility toward the liberals in Mexico City had local reverberations, as their major competitor in Tepic was the liberal Castaños family (Gámez 1863, 8). Years later, when Lozada turned his attention to large-scale agrarian struggle, Barron and Forbes aided in securing his defeat. During this same period,

Barron and Forbes also came under fire by Jalisco's liberal governor, Santos Degollado, who in 1855 accused the capitalists of buying off local authorities and using their position as consuls to ensure their immunity from their role in the contraband network. In an 1843 letter to the Earl of Aberdeen, Eustace Barron recounted the strength of British capital over all others, excusing its links to contraband as a direct result of the high tariffs set by Mexican customs (Meyer 1990, 57). In the letter, Barron also underlined the progress of Tepic and Guadalajara's textile industry, which was intricately woven into the network of foreign agriculture and commerce from Guayaquil to San Blas (50–51). The convergence of poor governance during Mexico's rocky path to nationhood and the geographic autonomy of western Mexico ensured that "semi-illicit international trade, originating in the factories and warehouses of Great Britain, wormed its way through Jamaica, Panama, San Blas, Tepic, and Guadalajara before finally tapping the wealth of rich silver mining towns like Zacatecas" (David Walker quoted in Mayo 2006, 29).

Once Acapulco regained its footing and other far better-equipped western ports, such as Mazatlán, began to emerge, San Blas and, by extension, Tepic began a steep economic and demographic decline. In 1831, Captain Brodie described San Blas as a town in ruins, noting the infrastructural decay of the port, which had already been in process during his previous visit in 1829. In the same trip, Brodie labeled Tepic as an increasingly "dull and solitary" city (Brodie, December 12, 1829, n.p.). These changes did not take place overnight, as Tepic continued to be considered an attractive destination during the 1830s, with a still dynamic agricultural production in its hinterlands and its important textile industry anchored in the factories of Jauja (founded in 1838 by Barron and Forbes) and Bellavista (founded in 1833 by the Castaños family; Meyer 1990, 20–21). Yet these merits could not hold for long with San Blas's poor reputation driving the port into obsolescence, bringing down with it the regional economy during the newly independent nation's longest period of political and economic instability.

Tepic's declining prosperity occurred at the height of the Mexican state's venture into land prospecting and privatization under the Leyes de Desamortización (Laws of Disentailment) of the Reforma. Specifically, the Ley de Deslinde y Colonización de Terrenos Baldíos (Law of Demarcation and Colonization of Vacant Lands) of December 15, 1883, led several of the hired survey companies to drastically reconfigure Nayarit's territorial structure (Meyer 1990, 32–33). Hiding behind the shroud of modern cartography and

FIGURE 5 Ernest Louet, *Souvenirs de la Campagne du Mexique de 1861–1867*. Tepic during the French occupation. Courtesy of Bancroft Library, University of California, Berkeley.

liberal land ownership, these companies could receive a third of the land that they disentailed in exchange for their work and subsequently sell these parcels off for profit (32–33).[18] Although this practice would later be repealed, cartographic data compiled by Francisco Díaz Covarrubias and Cossío (1911 and 1922, respectively), placed Tepic among the ten most affected entities in the country, showing a dramatic dispossession of indigenous landholdings in the sierras and along the coast (Meyer 1990, 33). The violent nature of these land surveys is evident by the military escorts that accompanied the firms as they measured and seized land in Nayarit (147). As with the fate of the Yaqui rebels of northern Mexico, families who resisted having their land expropriated were often detained and sent to Yucatán to conduct forced labor in the henequen fields (139). Despite Lozada's execution, Nayarit's rural population continued to organize against the onslaught of land privatization through the use of guerrilla tactics, including robbing local haciendas. The local elite—including Barron and Forbes—predictably responded by subsidizing the military persecution of the so-called rebel gangs (141). As the nineteenth century drew to a close, low-intensity warfare would continue to haunt Nayarit's countryside and temporarily spill over onto Tepic's streets.

Today, the small port town of San Blas shows few remnants of the glorious years it lived during the late colonial period and early years of Mexican independence. As with the textile factories of Bellavista and Jauja, San Blas's present economic relevance rests on bringing in tourists to surf its beach's waves and explore the crocodiles that wander its swamps. During the rainy season, sandflies continue to plague its dirt and cobblestone streets, a geographic malady it has been unable to shake. For Wixarika culture, San Blas remains an intrinsic location in their sacred geography and a necessary place to meet religious obligations. Wixarika families come here to leave offerings to Tatéi Haramara, Our Mother Ocean, "who is petrified in the sea of the West Coast . . . as a sacred white peak called Waxiewe . . . where Our Mothers of Rain originate and the fertile soils mingle with the essential salt for spicing meals; it is also where the dead begin their journey in the underworld, before they are released to the heavenly realm of Taheimá, where our Creator (Sun), Taweviékame, turns into quartz crystals, *teiwarixi*" (J. Negrín 2006, 1–2). Presently, Tatéi Haramara is threatened by tourism prospecting. In late 2011, two tourism enterprises announced that they had acquired the property rights of this sacred site where Waxiewe is located. They soon appeared to retreat after rapid protests by the Wixarika population and Mexican civil society, already galvanized over mining concessions in the eastern sacred pilgrimage site of Wirikuta. Nonetheless, tourism expansion across the branded Riviera Nayarit is a latent threat to this sacred place, keeping Wixarika authorities alert. After centuries, Nayarit's golden road to capitalism continues to be subject to the rebels of Álica.

A SLEEPY CITY ENTERS THE TWENTIETH CENTURY

As the nineteenth century drew to a close, San Blas and Tepic would be painfully cut off from a modernizing Mexico, with the railroad making a celebrated arrival to many other parts of Mexico, including Guadalajara (Meyer 1990, 199). Although these two places had been essential in the infrastructural development of the West, they were now largely economically and politically irrelevant

(López González 1984, 50). A sign of these changes is evident in the speech given by Juan Avina during the inauguration of Tepic's Porfirio Díaz Theatre on September 15, 1907:

> [The theater] marks an interesting stage in the material progress of Tepic, which has been achieved despite the insuperable obstacles faced under the current situation where we lack railroads, our old commercial relations have virtually disappeared, we have an absence of capital and entrepreneurial spirit, and we only can count on the fertility of its soil, with the unexploited wealth of its mines, with its coast bathed in the stormy waves of the Pacific; with the springs that overflow from the rocks of its mountains, with its wealth of creeks and rivers that encircle its plains like silver serpents, spreading its verdure and freshness everywhere, in this region that is marvelously endowed by nature. (*Adelantos y mejoras materiales* 1909, 17; my translation)

A few years before the Díaz regime was ousted from power, Tepic could only count on its countryside as a source of future development. The exploitation of its sugar and tobacco fields and the development of its water sources would be Nayarit's economic foundation for the twentieth century. Its previous incarnation as a center of attraction for foreign merchants and the transit of international commodities had now given way to an economic focus on the exploitation of the region's natural resources (López González 1999, 16, 23).

Save the labor strikes in its textile factories and occasional military battles, Tepic remained at the margins of the Mexican Revolution, which enveloped much of its neighboring states (Meyer 1990, 191–92). Perhaps the gravest effect that the years of revolution had on the region was a continuing downward economic trend. Barron and Forbes were long gone after reaping their fortunes, but other foreign capitalists had replaced them, including the German Delius and Company, which became the only source of credit for hacendados, down to the small tortilla shops (200). During this same period, the Aguirre family, of Spanish nationality, had effectively become the single most important property owner in Nayarit, controlling 2,471,054 acres of haciendas, cattle ranches, sugar mills, and factories (200). The old rival textile factories of Jauja and Bellavista were now both owned by Aguirre, as were the power plant, all water concessions, and the trade in wood, gas, and petroleum. The Aguirre monopoly even lent money to the Constitutionalists at the height of the Revolution in 1914 (200). In the 1930s, George Tays, an American carrying out a study for the U.S. Army, noted that land tenure in and around Tepic continued to belong to a small number of hacendados (1941, 4).

As in the rest of the nation, changes in the political, social, and economic landscape after the Revolution came slowly. The most significant agrarian shifts came at the hands of Guillermo Flores Muñoz's land invasions in 1933 and 1934, which largely brought the hacienda system to an end (Meyer 1990, 204). While the turmoil of the Revolution had sent many Mexicans abroad, the agrarian movement of subsequent years led foreign capitalists back to their home countries—including Delius and Aguirre (203). On a macroeconomic level, the late arrival of the railroad to Tepic in 1927 and the agrarian redistribution of the 1930s did little to change the financial landscape. The reallocation of large haciendas to Nayarit's peasants, however, provided a powerful symbol of hope in a region that had vigorously fought for a more just land tenure system. Julián Gascón Mercado, who would become governor of Nayarit from 1964 to 1969, keenly recalled the impact of agrarian reform on his family in the ejido of Aután, on the coast of the state: "It had been a short time since Lázaro Cárdenas had given us land and with it credit and a shipment of mules to trace and plough the earth" (Gascón Mercado 1975, 15; my translation). The peasant turned PRI politician and nationalist writer noted that the land his family was given had belonged to the powerful Aguirre family. With the Mexican state's embrace of agrarian reform, the struggle over land in Nayarit seemed to be turning a page.

Nevertheless, the PRI's trajectory from a revolutionary nationalist party to one that was increasingly authoritarian was evident in the state of Nayarit, which up until recently had remained a faithful bastion of this party. Julián Gascón Mercado and Gilberto Flores Muñoz (brother of Guillermo) marked the PRI's progressive nationalist tendencies while remaining weary of the radical Left opposition. Interestingly, both of these governors' brothers, Alejandro and Guillermo, stood as symbols of the agrarian radicalism that transcended the state's populist initiatives and recalled the rebellions of centuries past. Alejandro Gascón Mercado embodied the rising leftist opposition to the PRI during the presidency of Luis Echeverría, who tended toward populism, indigenismo, and a lukewarm acceptance of Marxism, all the while clamping down on radical Left movements. Alejandro Gascón Mercado ran for and was believed to have won the governorship of the state of Nayarit in 1975, under the Partido Popular Socialista (Popular Socialist Party, or PPS). But in typical PRI fashion, candidate Rogelio Flores Curiel was named the official victor of the race, leading Gascón Mercado to break with the PPS (considered too acquiescent to the PRI).[19] Gascón Mercado notes that in the 1980s, the parties of the Left in Nayarit were based on the organization of independent unions and the wave of popular land invasions initiated by peasant communities surrounding Tepic (8). Gascón Mercado's involvement in these land struggles is marked by his role in the founding of the Wixarika ejido of Salvador Allende, named after the deposed Chilean president.

Although promising, the ejido system ran into a series of contradictions before President Salinas de Gortari infamously amended the constitution, permitting land to become commodified and thus be bought, rented, and speculated on. Even prior to this hotly contested constitutional change, the ejido system had fallen into the hands of corrupt leaders willing to allow changes in land use in exchange for private financial gain. In 1975, journalist Fernando Benítez classified many ejido leaders as caciques or local strongmen, stating that "the cacique is the innate leader, the first subdivider, the first banker, the first authority," who sells land titles several times or makes sure that no land title is handed to the poor migrant who cannot always choose the conditions in which he or she lives (1975, 7; my translation). Benítez noted that "the time had come when the urban subdivision can reap more gains than cows and alfalfa fields" (11). Although the suburbanization of Tepic happened more slowly than in larger Mexican cities, the ejido system was consumed by monied interests ranging from new housing and commercial developments to agroindustry.

In a highly agrarian state like Nayarit, violations of the communal landholding system have largely returned the state to the monopolized land tenure of the past. This includes the concentration of land by transnational tobacco companies and the spread of industrial tomato farms owned by Sinaloans, which have led to a generalized decrease in the diversity of agricultural crops (Pacheco Ladrón de Guevara 1992, 12; Mackinlay 2008). The case of tobacco illustrates this trend. From the mid-nineteenth century onward, Nayarit held 80 percent of the national production of blond tobacco, used for cigarettes. The bulk of this production was managed by the state-owned Tabamex but took place on small plots of land that farmers acquired under the ejido system (Mackinlay 2008, 124). The privatization of Tabamex in 1990 shifted much of this production to middle- and large-sized plantations and processing plants owned by Carlos Slim Helú's Carso and Alfonso Romo Garza's Pulsar corporations. In 1997, both of these companies would sell the bulk of their production to British American Tobacco and Philip Morris (127, 138). Note that the labor force used in planting and harvesting tobacco is predominantly migrant based, historically drawing indigenous laborers from the Western Sierra Madre as well as, most recently, Zacatecans (127).[20] These farm workers are also hired on the state's sizable bean, chili, and tomato plantations. Another important influence on land tenure is the incessant presence of drug plantations. Nayarit's geography, which includes both a coast and a mountain range, has made it attractive ground for drug traffickers, who grow and move illicit crops through the state and to the United States, following the same commercial circuit from the San Blas boom years.

During the last eighty years, the city of Tepic experienced slow but significant changes in its landscape. Although demographic and economic growth has been incremental, the political leadership has often sought to modernize the city's identity through projects of urban revitalization. Perhaps the most contested of these efforts was carried out under the governorship of Flores Muñoz (1946–51), when a large quantity of the city's historic buildings were demolished to give way to wide streets and the construction of new, more commercially oriented buildings (López González 2000, 119; 1999, 26). In this way, many of the residential, commercial, and administrative buildings constructed at the peak of Tepic's successful San Blas years ceded to mid-twentieth-century attempts at urban modernization. Of the colonial and nineteenth-century buildings that survived, a large percentage underwent dramatic changes to suit the desires of assorted business owners. Local historian Pedro López González denominates the transformations of these historic structures as having "questionable aesthetic taste," the once elegant doorways widened and the interiors reconfigured for incoming retail shops (López González 2000, 14).

Not until 1972 would the city enact laws to curb the unrestrained alteration of its historic city center (López González 2000, 13). Yet by this point, the city was already undergoing changes that stemmed from the construction of new residential areas for the wealthy and working classes in outlying areas of the city. In 1950, Tepic's expansion outside its city center took an important step with the construction of the bridge over the Mololoa River, which connected the new working-class neighborhood of the same name with the downtown (123).[21] As with most other Mexican cities, from the 1970s onward, the urban growth of Tepic directly encroached on ejido lands (López González 1999, 28). López González notes that the "progressive exodus of the dominant class from the traditional center, with the goal of distancing itself from a zone lacking in green areas, crowded with precarious constructions and narrow streets that are currently insufficient for the road traffic, has in turned provoked the relocation of some of the city's essential functions, as is the case with the commerce of goods and services" (1999, 29).

In Nayarit, the PRI serves as a prime example of the political party at its most clientelistic, offering resources to those who promise electoral fidelity. Alejandro Gascón Mercado affirmed that the PRI's Machiavellian tendencies are manifest in the ways in which even the working-class neighborhoods of Tepic—founded through the land takeovers—look toward this governing party to receive improvements in services (cited in Pacheco Ladrón de Guevara 1992, 52). The continued concentration of land and the lack of credit opportunities for small farmers have inevitably led to the well-documented rural exodus. In turn, the migrant population in Tepic has largely found itself relocated to outlying urban neighborhoods, which are poorly equipped to meet their basic service and employment needs.

Despite its embrace of populism, Tepic's elite holds firm control over the region's agriculture, industry, and political power and has consequently placed few regulations that would otherwise protect the ecological resources of the state and the land and labor rights of rural populations. Undoubtedly Nayarit's history of rural dispossession continues to repeat itself. Today, however, this reality is accompanied by restrictions placed on the livelihoods of the urban poor, many of whom recently migrated from the countryside. Tepic has mimicked the sprawl of other cities by allowing an escalating number of strip malls occupied by national and international chain stores (including Walmart, Soriana, and Chedraui), which have changed the consumption patterns of the local population and displaced Tepic's small and medium-sized shops (López González 1999, 29):

> The traditional center, in large part created during the nineteenth century, is still relevant, and tries to compete, although at a disadvantage, with the commercial dynamics of the periphery. In this case it can be said that it boils down to a dispute between the local commercial elite, which still conserves many of its interests in the interior of the city—hotels, nightclubs and medium-sized businesses—and the national and international commercial capital that has been established on the margins of central spaces. (López González 1999, 30; my translation)

The revitalization plans for the historic downtown launched in the last decade of the twentieth century have done little to bring shoppers back to the mom-and-pop shops located around the downtown plaza or to curb the domination of commercial chains along the city's periphery. Yet, municipal plans *have* cracked down on street vendors as a means to "recover" the downtown and relaunch it as a place of leisure, where the remaining historical buildings can be admired under the shade of a handful of trees and the multiple fountains (López González 2000, 165–66). Many of these street vendors are Tepic's newest indigenous residents, displaced from their rural lands.

On a national scale, Tepic remains a small capital city that offers one of the lowest costs of living in the nation but few substantial attractions. An international airport launched in the early 2010s appears to be the wishful thinking of a state government engaging in shameless self-promotion through its control of the press and its practice of plastering the city with billboards announcing the government's latest achievements. Although the sugar mill at the southern entrance of the city remains active, the tourism industry appears to be taking up much of the government's imagination for future growth. Already in 1992, Gascón Mercado noted that, save for the tourism industry, the state's "development has practically been paralyzed" (cited in Pacheco Ladrón de Guevara 1991, 56). Since 1992, the successful albeit environmentally destructive and socially contested expansion of coastal resorts and condominiums from Puerto Vallarta up through the recently branded Riviera Nayarit has further stimulated the idea that tourism can stand as a replacement for other industries. In the following section, I examine how the emphasis on tourism in Nayarit explicitly draws on its indigenous heritage and, in the process of doing so, has led to the simultaneous creation of spaces of racial inclusion and exclusion.

IMPRINTING THE MULTICULTURAL URBAN SPACE

The public bus that takes passengers to Colonia Zitakua begins its route behind Tepic's cathedral, at one of the city's several small plazas.[22] It quickly passes through the narrow downtown streets and crosses the Mololoa River, where it enters the peripheral neighborhoods that have expanded over the last three decades. Before arriving to the end of its route in Zitakua, the bus must first wind through the working-class neighborhoods of La Esperanza (The Hope) and Venceremos (We Shall Overcome), named after the freedom struggles of the 1960s and 1970s, during Alejandro Gascón Mercado's municipal presidency (1972–75). After inching past the bumpy streets of Lucha Proletaria, República de El Salvador, and República de Vietnam, the bus finally makes its final ascent to the peak of the hill where Zitakua is located.

Colonia Zitakua was founded in 1988 from a petition made by Tepic's Wixarika residents—many of whom lived in precarious conditions after being displaced by the Aguamilpa hydroelectric dam (see chapter 2). Previously an area packed with brothels and bars, Zitakua is now an officially recognized urban Wixarika community and largely comprises Wixaritari who have emigrated from communities in the Western Sierra Madre and on the coast of Nayarit. Members of other indigenous groups and mestizos also reside in this neighborhood, whose central square houses a *tuki*, or *calihuey*, a big temple found at the center of all Wixarika ceremonial centers, or *tukite*.[23] Professor Lourdes Pacheco Ladrón de Guevara from the Autonomous University of Tepic affirms that the impetus for creating the neighborhood originated with the local Wixarika population and was embraced by state and local politicians when these two sector's interests converged (Manzanares Monter 2009, 22–23). For the Wixaritari, Colonia Zitakua became an opportunity to secure a place to live and continue their traditions outside their rural communities. For Nayarit governor Celso Delgado (1987–93), backing the creation of Colonia Zitakua emerged from his desire to improve the government's image vis-à-vis the indigenous, particularly after the displacements caused by the Aguamilpa hydroelectric dam (22–23).

Since its establishment, the neighborhood has experienced a series of makeovers that mirror its demographic growth as well as the city's attempts to incorporate it into its sightseeing itinerary. From a young age, I regularly accompanied my father to Zitakua, where he would visit celebrated Wixarika yarn painter José Benítez Sánchez, one of the principal founders of Zitakua.[24] I vividly remember the now-extinct rows of cantinas and brothels at the bottom of the hill and the difficult climb to the top when the dirt roads turned to mud during the rainy season. After two years of not visiting the neighborhood, I returned in the summer of 2007 and noticed that the dirt and cobblestone streets had been paved. I soon found out that the upgrade stemmed from the inauguration of Tepic's new tour bus, which now makes daily trips from the city's downtown plaza to Zitakua. My father and I chatted with a relative of Benítez's on the edge of Zitakua's central square, awaiting the arrival of the afternoon tour bus. A shiny red bus soon edged up the hill with a load of what appeared to be mostly Mexican summer vacationers. Thatched-roof stands had been set up for the Wixarika women selling traditional beadwork and quesadillas made with blue corn. The families descended from the bus and ran around what otherwise might be considered a poor periphery neighborhood but that now takes on a magical aura for the visitors, who are experiencing an "Indigenous place." After twenty minutes of sightseeing, the bus and its tourists departed.

The pamphlet that announces the bus tours states that riders will visit the most "relevant" historical sites of the city. Zitakua thus takes its place among the cathedral, the ruins of the Bellavista textile factory, and the convent where Friar Junípero Serra spent his last days before embarking on his eerily legendary trip to the Californias. The incorporation of Colonia Zitakua into the tour bus itinerary is significant because it reflects the state's efforts to boost Tepic as a tourist destination amid its declining agricultural sector. Located a couple of hours north of Puerto Vallarta and other popular beach towns, Tepic has little to offer the tourist gaze, with its historic city center mostly demolished and few of the cultural attractions found in highly visited Mexican cities. Consequently, the state of Nayarit has placed its indigenous cultures as one of the focal points of its tourism initiative. But unlike the southern states of Chiapas and Oaxaca, which are internationally associated with a rich indigenous past and present, Nayarit is a relatively unknown destination.

In this context, Wixarika culture comes onto center stage, becoming a vital instrument of promotion for Nayarit's struggling economy. Pacheco affirms that "the Huicholes are the peacocks of ethnology" and have been incorporated into the state's imaginary because of their lavish aesthetics (Lourdes Pacheco Ladrón de Guevara, interview by author, March 5, 2011). In recent years, Wixarika iconography has exploded in advertisements throughout Nayarit, particularly in the Puerto Vallarta area.[25] Restaurants, hotels, and spas have picked up Wixarika words and images, signaling the marketability of this culture. In 2010, the yacht club in Cruz de Huanacaxtle, on the outskirts of Puerto Vallarta, placed a series of billboards along its wharf, among them a two-billboard advertisement: one depicted a stoic Wixarika man standing before a backdrop of yachts, with the English words "To the soul of a culture," followed by an ellipsis, with the adjacent image reading, "A door opens." While it was unclear what the face of a Wixarika man had to do with the yacht club, the accompanying billboards—which also had Wixarika symbols and words—made evident that consumption of the ethnic Other is a strong selling point.

Tours taking visitors from Puerto Vallarta to real or invented Wixarika places or communities in the Western Sierra Madre draw further connections between this coastal resort region and Wixarika culture.[26] By carving itself out as a place of indigeneity, the state of Nayarit is betting on Wixarika culture to help grow

FIGURE 6 Yacht club billboards in Cruz de Huanacaxtle, Nayarit. Photo by author.

its economy. According to Pacheco, the gubernatorial administrations of Rigoberto Ochoa (1993–99) and Antonio Echevarría (1999–2005) explicitly boosted the Wixarika arts and crafts market and popularized many Wixarika names (Pacheco interview). For many Wixaritari, this spotlight is welcomed, as it has allowed many to find a niche in the tourist economy and in particular government posts. In Tepic, Colonia Zitakua has become a visible part of these efforts and demonstrates the vigor of the ethnic arts and crafts market as well as the ability of some Wixaritari to leverage regional political power. The municipal government's paving of the main road to the neighborhood and its subsidy of a large statue in honor of the now-deceased José Benítez Sánchez reflect these recent changes.[27]

But while Colonia Zitakua is boosted as a destination for the curious, municipal authorities repeatedly prohibit Wixarika vendors from selling their crafts in the downtown plaza, where they had done so for years. Today, they must request permits to set up stands within the designated Plaza de las Artesanías, on the edge of the city square, or relocate to the craft tables in Colonia Zitakua. This shift in local policy marks the contrast between the hypervisibility of Wixaritari as targets of ethnic tourism and their simultaneous restriction from spaces of quotidian visibility in areas located in and around downtown. While Wixarika vendors have continued to find ways to temporarily set up tables downtown, they now must do it under the constant threat of fines or the confiscation of their goods by the police. By no means is this phenomenon restricted to Tepic; Wixaritari in Guadalajara face far greater difficulties securing spaces for the sale of their arts and crafts. The regulation of street vendors, particularly in central city spaces, is a global problem deeply entangled with political economic factors, including the massive displacement of rural populations to cities where access to employment is confined to the informal economy and where vendors come face to face with police forces and the local mafias that control the circulation of pirated goods.

Wixarika vendors are selling ethnic crafts, often subsidized by the government, not pirated goods. In Tepic, artesanía Huichol is heavily marketed as a Nayaritan good, exported abroad and attracting tourism. Nevertheless, the centrality of "Huichol culture" for Nayarit's image is accompanied by its restriction to certain locations like Zitakua, marking an explicit spatialization of race within the urban landscape. M. Jacqui Alexander uses the term "nativization" to explain "the ongoing process through which an essential character is attributed to the indigenous—the 'native'—which derives largely from relationships to geography or to a particular territory, which in turn structures the context within which this 'native' is to be imagined and understood" (2005, 70). Within this logic, municipal authorities place Wixarika residents of Tepic in Zitakua despite this neighborhood being only one of many neighborhoods where Wixaritari live.

In Alexander's exploration of the tourism industry in the Bahamas, she notes how tourism is manufactured as a "savior" for local economies and carries a wide gamut of implications for populations whose identities become shaped by an attitude of servility and gratefulness toward the tourist, while increasing their dependence on the currency brought in from other regions of the world (2005, 53, 59). During the second half of the twentieth century, a growing number of indigenous peoples were directly and indirectly driven from their land to urban centers. For the Wixarika population, this has implied a major shift away from small-scale agriculture to the production of arts and crafts for the tourism sector. These arts and crafts have been a mixed blessing, bringing many families economic stability while promoting ethnic pride. Yet growing competition among vendors and the production of cheap replicas made elsewhere in the country or abroad have led to diminishing returns and a cycle of dependence on the market. Wixarika vendors must perform both for prospective buyers and for the state, reflecting established ideas of "Huicholness." This process proves fundamental for the state's tourism objectives as well as for the individual and family businesses that rely on the sale of their arts and crafts.

Further illustration of this phenomenon is detailed by Sara Alejandra Manzanares Monter's exploration of how "Huicholness" is deployed and appropriated in Tepic. Specifically, she examines "how the Huichol costume encodes a varied range of messages that depend not only on the actors, but also on the context of its use," and, resultingly, "how the Huichol costume becomes a carrier of meaning beyond 'Huicholness' and thus a central element in the construction of two different imaginaries of identity: one indigenous, one mestizo" (2009, 2). By putting the spotlight so heavily on Tepic's Wixaritari, the expectations placed on them become more defined. This includes how they should dress and speak, as well as the types of occupations they are believed to pursue. Manzanares Monter analyzes these expectations in relation to dress by pointing to the key role "traditional" attire, or "costume," has before the gaze of the general population, but most importantly, before tourists and government officials. Manzanares Monter states that the "Huichol costume" is used by Wixaritari for three distinct purposes: (1) during traditional celebrations, (2) while selling their crafts, and (3) when meeting with government officials (50). She borrows Tim Knab's (1981) term "the baroque Huichol" to describe the image that is expected of Wixaritari, an image that the Wixaritari may in turn desire to project in order to make economic and political gains:

> The artisans are aware that the buyers are interested not only in the object that is purchased, but also in the origin of the objects they buy: the culture behind the object. The use of the traditional costume, together with knowledge of the mythology surrounding the designs depicted in the objects, caters to this need. The costume serves as a visual representation of Huichol knowledge and culture; a visual confirmation that the object being bought is part of a greater set of beliefs. This not only increases the interest of the buyer on the object, but also gives the object a higher degree of "authenticity" and a higher symbolic value than an object bought on, for example, a mestizo store or from a mestizo-looking seller. (Manzanares Monter 2009, 54)

Performing ethnicity through the visual outliers of dress and speech consequently becomes a necessary feature of Tepic's landscape. The act of performing for recognition before a nonindigenous audience to acquire economic and political leverage is a topic I return to at length in the final chapter.

Colonia Zitakua is part of this construction embedded in representations of the self and the Other, demonstrating the political economic tendencies that favor tourism and the commercialization of ethnicity in general. What is not explored sufficiently by scholars and bureaucrats is how the state's homogenization of Wixarika culture obscures the Wixarika heterogeneity that exists in Tepic. Each of the three principal Wixarika communities located in Jalisco has a distinct form of dress as well as slight linguistic differences, which become obscured by the commoditized portraits of Wixarika people and culture. These communal differences are compounded by the cultural differences found among Wixarika enclaves in Nayarit. For instance, in the communities of Naranjito de Copal and El Roble, Wixaritari have largely shed "traditional attire" for the ranchero style of jeans and cowboy boots and hats, while children seldom grow up speaking Wixarika as their principal language (personal conversations with Wixarika university students from said communities, 2009–2010). Lastly, the Wixarika population of Tepic includes families composed of recent arrivals as well as those who have spent more than one generation in the city.

Ultimately, the Wixarika population of Tepic is far more culturally and spatially diverse than the popular imagination would like to believe and more dynamic than their depictions in public and private advertisements. The Wixarika population that lives in Colonia Zitakua and various other neighborhoods in Tepic reflects the dynamic and fluid life paths taken by indigenous peoples living outside their traditional territories. The fact that Wixarika culture stands at the center of Nayarit's current tourist propaganda should come as no surprise in a state that has evolved with a strong indigenous presence. Miss Nayarit has typically posed in Wixarika-inspired dress as an expression of regional pride.[28] The National Institute of Anthropology and History's photographic archive holds numerous examples of non-Wixaritari styled as "Huichols"—from 1950s actress Rebeca Iturbide to famed images of white couples turned indigenous models. As explored in chapter 1, the image of the indigenous as an essential but problematic component of Mexican identity dates back to the nation's colonial foundations. The appropriations of Wixarika culture by public and private entities in Nayarit, however, illuminates a dynamic in which fixed notions of "Huicholness" meet up with the everyday fluidity of indigenous residents in Tepic, leading to a delicate balance of inclusion and exclusion from everyday spaces of politics, economics, and culture.

FIGURES 7A AND 7B Rebeca Iturbide (*left*) and unknown models (*right*) pose in Wixarika attire.

TRANSCENDING MULTICULTURAL AMBIVALENCE

In *Más que un indio* (2006), anthropologist Charles R. Hale tackles questions surrounding ethnic and cultural alterity within the context of Guatemala's post–civil war turn toward multicultural neoliberalism. Hale's study is illustrative of Tepic's own hesitant celebration of indigeneity by exploring the racial ambivalence *ladinos* express in the face of deceptive Maya ascendancy in Guatemalan society.[29] His research finds that while ladinos claim to embrace notions of antiracism and multiculturalism, they maintain long-held racist views of indigenous peoples and desire to preserve their racial privileges, arguing that academic, governmental, and nongovernmental institutions favor indigenous peoples' concerns and funnel countless resources to indigenous peoples that *ladinos* do not have the opportunity to obtain. According to Hale, racial ambivalence refers to the "political sensibilities that encompass both the support for the principal of cultural equality and deep commitments to the social conditions that preserve *ladinos*' material and ideological advantage. By extension, the term applies to those who express solidarity with Indians, but as innocent victims rather than protagonists, as acts of benevolence deployed from a higher rung in the social hierarchy" (2006, 108). The concept of racial ambivalence can help us understand why so many people express compassion and respect for indigenous peoples while finding it difficult to come to terms with the idea that they can inhabit similar occupational positions as mestizos—even in apparently indigenous-friendly Tepic.

Wixarika university students and professionals in Tepic encounter a similar paradigm to the one Hale examines in Guatemala. While problematic, the state of Nayarit's embrace of indigeneity has opened important spaces of opportunity for its indigenous residents. This includes the UAN's explicit support of indigenous students through the dedication of special resources that support their admission and retention. As a result of these efforts, the university's indigenous student population has dramatically risen in the last decade, counting more than 300 in 2010 out of a total student population of 12,760 (Universidad Autónoma de Nayarit 2011). While it would be unfair to state that nonindigenous students in the university are explicitly unwelcoming of their indigenous peers, many do voice their resentment at the benefits indigenous students receive. UAN professor Lourdes Pacheco, has observed the ways in which mestizos complain of the "positive discrimination" that their indigenous peers obtain from the university. Pacheco notes that these objections are made from a historical vacuum that fails to acknowledge the ever-present inequality with which indigenous students continue to live (Pacheco interview). In the meantime, Pacheco recognizes that indigenous students have progressively appropriated spaces in the university, making it a far more welcoming place for incoming indigenous students than it was for previous generations. This is further supported by a chapter I coauthored with six Wixarika and Mixtec professionals, who note the important openings achieved in Tepic's and Guadalajara's universities as a direct effect of indigenous student organizing (Bonilla et al. 2017).

Nonetheless, these efforts come with a degree of backlash from their nonindigenous peers. In 2010, graduating Wixarika students at UAN requested permission to wear their traditional dress as a substitute for the cap and gown. Although the faculty welcomed this modification of the classic graduation garb, several of their peers vocally opposed the move, stating that it was yet another manifestation of indigenous students' unfair privileges. Characteristic of the assimilationist stance, opposing students argued that if indigenous students wanted to be treated as equals, then they should avoid accentuating their ethnic difference. For the Wixarika graduates, donning their ethnic dress during the graduation ceremony was an important symbol of pride for their attending families, many of whom feared that the process of Western-style professionalization could estrange them from their culture. The question of wearing one's indigenous dress is telling of the continuing tensions that exist in Mexico's post-multicultural society.

The significance of wearing visible markers of ethnicity goes beyond Manzanares Monter's argument of the role of Wixarika "costume" in the marketplace for ethnic crafts. When a Wixarika student leader from UAN was preparing for a public event at the university, he asked me if I thought he should wear his embroidered Wixarika outfit rather than a Western dress shirt and slacks.[30] This question made evident that the choice of wearing ethnic attire is often a conscious decision that raises particular anxieties when the individual is unsure of whether traditional attire will elicit forms of exclusion or "positive discrimination."

Everyday dilemmas of interracial relationships such as these strongly reflect Tepic's own wavering and always-in-process identity. Over the past five centuries, Tepic has undoubtedly reshaped itself under the watchful gaze of the Western Sierra Madre. At various moments in the region's recent history, the inhabitants of this geographic fortress have openly but not always successfully negotiated their political, cultural, and economic autonomy. A story like Tepic's demonstrates that a city's geography is not trivial. The coast and the mountains that enclose this small city have dynamically shaped its trajectory, from its brief splendor driven by proximity to San Blas to its recurrent association with indigenous nonconformity, exemplified by the figures of King Nayar and Manuel Lozada. From Tepic we now move two hours southeast to Guadalajara, the urban heavyweight of western Mexico and a place that—despite sharing much of the same ethnic history—shows remarkable differences.

4

GUADALAJARA DE INDIAS

Searching for the Right to the City

TO UNDERSTAND how racial conceptions are tied to urban space within the Tapatío imaginary, it is important to recount some of the central elements that make up the foundation and development of Guadalajara into the colonial regional capital of New Galicia.[1] This work is particularly important for understanding how Guadalajara came to see itself as an exceptionally criollo city, despite having a racially diverse population from its inception. This diversity has largely been forgotten through the literal and figurative process that José María Murià refers to as "blanquismo mexicano," or Mexican whitening (2004a, 19). *Blanquismo* sought for the genetic and cultural whitening of the population through racial miscegenation, even during the city's formative years, when, as colonial records show, a greater number of Africans arrived than Spaniards. Clearly, the miscegenation taking place in colonial Guadalajara was nuanced, for the city was a cauldron of ethnic heterogeneity rather than a laboratory of European reproduction.

As with other cities of New Spain, colonial Guadalajara was an ethnically heterogeneous space, having a majority population of indigenous peoples, mulattoes, and mestizos concentrated in ethnic neighborhoods, while the minority peninsular, or Spanish, population enjoyed political and economic dominance. As enslaved Africans were brought by Portuguese merchants at the end of the sixteenth century, registries also document the arrival of enslaved Asians brought by Filipino galleons (Calvo 1992, 144, 146). Birth registries from the seventeenth century show that a fourth of the population was black and majority female, while most of the Spaniards were male, a situation that led to a great deal of miscegenation (43). As I note in my discussion of the casta system in chapter 1, the ethnic diversity of Mexico's colonial cities mirrors the ever-expanding financial opportunities that these urban enclaves offered. In this context, Guadalajara was attractive for those seeking an alternative to Mexico City. The former's growing regional independence as the gateway to the Pacific made it an important place for the distribution of goods and, as a result, saw the passing of merchants, bureaucrats, servants, and bandits. Above all, Guadalajara's regional preeminence led to the influx of people from various ethnic and class backgrounds.

Manuela Camus denominates this historical tendency as "*tapatío* coloniality," or the "concept and practice of stratified and colonial social relations," which are manifest in present-day "dominations-subordinations, negotiations, resistances" (2015, 22). To better situate the contemporary activism of Guadalajara's Wixarika residents, in this chapter I analyze some of the colonial and postcolonial fabric that has shaped the city's identity over five centuries. From the Battle of La Mojonera onward, the Pearl of the West has straddled a normative identity, caught between the liberal spirit of private property, individualism, and capitalism, and the conservative comforts of religious doctrine and rigid social roles. But today, perhaps more so than at any other time, Guadalajara's heterogeneous demographics have led to a political and cultural opening that is partially a product of indigenous mobilizations for a dignified right to the city.

A CITY SAVED FROM THE SAVAGES

> *The country has not come to understand the transcendental importance of the fall of Lozada; it has seen it as a secondary episode within Jalisco's particular history, and it is wrong. Had the luck of arms been favorable to the tyrant of Nayarit, the entire country would have seen itself enveloped in a devastating war: the whites would have had to desperately fight against the copper-skinned people, that is, against three-fourths of the total population of the Republic, and God knows what would have become of our nation.*
> —JOSÉ LÓPEZ PORTILLO Y ROJAS, IN AGRAZ GARCÍA DE ALBA, *QUIENES RESISTIERON AL SANGUINARIO TIGRE DE ÁLICA* (MY TRANSLATION)

In January 1873, Guadalajara faced the imminent threat of invasion by eight thousand troops led by rebel general Manuel Lozada. Stories of Lozada's sanguinary Indian hordes could be heard throughout the small towns that separated the Pearl of the West from Lozada's stronghold of Tepic. On January 17, the "united peoples of Nayarit" proclaimed their Plan Libertador, which would once and for all do away with the liberal forces that sought to impose the rule of private property over a country where both the Catholic Church and the Indian Republics were founded on distinct forms of communal ownership. The Plan Libertador equipped three columns of soldiers: one that would reach the northern state of Sinaloa, another that would go east to Zacatecas, and the last and largest, headed by the Tigre de Álica, that would descend on Guadalajara (Agraz García de Alba 1997, 13). After more than a decade of painful defeats, liberal general Ramón Corona was prepared to defend the "civilized" people of Guadalajara from the massive rapes and decapitations that were rumored to follow Lozada's victory. Documents written several years after the conflict continued to point to the disastrous "Indian Empire" led by Lozada, when drunken thieves and murderers ran the area of Tepic into ruin (Gómez Vírgen 1878b). For Guadalajara's bourgeoisie, the ensuing battle was not simply a matter of upholding liberal ideals, but one of protecting the white race against thousands of poor mestizo and indigenous peoples, who came to vindicate their rights to land and political power.

On January 24, Lozada's forces took the nearby town of Tequila. The news reached Corona, who nervously prepared to meet his longtime enemy. Governor Ignacio Vallarta called all citizens to arms, creating a volunteer defense force that would remain in the city while Corona's forces were sent to meet the invaders to the west in Zapopan (Godoy [1954] 1992, 574). According to Bernabé Godoy's 1954 study of the Battle of La Mojonera, telegraphs from the period reveal widespread fear that Corona would be unable to stop Lozada, whose 8,000 men greatly outnumbered Corona's 2,400 soldiers (575).[2] One telegraph narrates that on the morning of January 27, the "modest General Corona . . . crossed the silent streets of the city amid the mute, but meaningful farewell of the alarmed population" (575). Could he beat the proud Tiger and his thousands of indigenous fighters? For Jalisco's liberals, defeat meant the advance of indigenous hegemony hidden behind the veil of conservative ideals. As such, Corona's victory would prove to be an essential ingredient for securing a liberal Mexico.

The peak of the two-day battle came when Lozada's army set ablaze the grass field that separated them from the liberal soldiers. Twenty-one years later, an eyewitness described for *El Heraldo de Guadalajara* how the "hooting Indians" and their fire terrified the liberal army, whose superior artillery was ultimately able to squash the fiercest of tactics (Godoy [1954] 1992, 586; Agraz García de Alba 1997, 41). In retrospect, the fire might have been a desperate attempt to win and a sign of the offensive army becoming vulnerable in Guadalajara's flat geography. According to fervent anti-Lozada historian José López Portillo y Rojas, liberals and conservatives alike had come to respect Lozada's military capabilities. But as it turned out, the Tiger's prowess would prove to be unsuccessful outside the sierras he and his people knew so well (cited in Agraz García de Alba 1997, 33). On January 29, the liberals celebrated Corona's victory and the departure of Lozada's people. They cheered for a city saved from the "hecatomb" (Godoy [1954] 1992, 583).

To date, celebrations commemorating the Battle of La Mojonera speak of the city's salvation from barbarism. On January 28, 2011, Zapopan's municipal president, Héctor Vielma Ordóñez, described the battle as the "triumph of liberty and unity in the country's west," adding that Corona fought for a "more free and just Mexico" that supported the principles of Zapopan's "great family."[3] What are the principles and freedoms that Corona's victory summons in Guadalajara's historical imaginary? Corona's personal trajectory may point us to some answers.

Ramón Corona was born in 1837 in the town of Tuxcueca, Jalisco, and at the age of fourteen accompanied his father to Tepic with the hope of making some business ventures ("Apuntes biográficos" 1885). According to an anonymous biography written in 1885, Corona's father soon set off to San Francisco, California, while his son remained in Tepic, where he would work in general goods and, later, in mining administration. Corona's business affairs in and around the Tepic area during the early years of Lozada's rising power led the young businessman to adhere to the Liberal Party and to join the military to fight against the so-called conservative reactionaries during the height of the national conflict pitting liberals against conservatives. His victory over an indomitable Lozada in the town of Acaponeta in 1859 earned him a military reputation. According to his biographer, the result was that Corona "no longer thought of anything but the destruction of the savage enemies of humanity and civilization" (Vielma Ordóñez 2011, n.p.). The French invasion and Lozada's collaboration with the second empire led by conservative Maximilian I further radicalized Corona. Years of defeats at the hands of the Tigre de Álica would finally come to a dramatic end in the memorable battle on the outskirts of

Guadalajara, ushering in Corona's political career. After completing his eleven years of diplomatic service in Madrid, Corona returned to Mexico in 1885 with grand presidential aspirations (López Almaraz 1984, 14; Peregrina 2004, 112).[4] On the thirteenth anniversary of the Battle of La Mojonera, Corona's candidacy for governor of Jalisco was announced in a local newspaper. A pamphlet supporting his candidacy celebrated Corona as a successor of Benito Juárez and a defender of Mexico's independence, democratic institutions, and liberty (Lagos de Moreno 1886). As governor of Jalisco, he helped bring about some of the modernization seen elsewhere in the country under the reign of Porfirio Díaz: the arrival of the train, the advance of agribusiness, and, in Guadalajara, the construction of a modern central market christened after the general (López Almaraz 1984, 15).[5] But Corona's rise to power was cut short by his assassination on November 10, 1889, by Nayarit native Primitivo Ron as the general turned governor walked to the theater with his wife, doña Mary McEntee. Theories surrounding the motives for the assassination range from Ron's mental illness to rumors of direct orders from Porfirio Díaz, who feared eventual electoral competition from an increasingly popular Corona (López Almaraz 1984, 93; Murià 1989, 11).

Corona's rise as a regional military and political legend and the Battle of La Mojonera illustrate aspects of Guadalajara's historical identity that I discuss throughout this chapter. The battle marks the culmination of Tepic's and Guadalajara's animosity and tellingly crystallizes race relations in the Mexican West. Gabriel Agraz García de Alba's study of the Battle of La Mojonera is rife with racial assumptions and stands as a quintessential example of the depiction of a vicious Lozada and a noble Corona. This author paints the Tigre de Álica first and foremost as guilty of causing a caste war in the West and "dragging more than one thousand Indians to their death" (1997, 32). This perspective is a contemporary iteration of Governor Vallarta's vision of the conflict, uttered a day after the battle on January 30, 1873: "The power of Lozada does not only consist in the warring elements he has been able to amass over many years of domination over the canton of Tepic but principally in the influence that he has acquired over the indigenous race with such an apparatus, perfectly disposing them for the invasion that they have carried out and which fortunately has been contained at La Mojonera by the great bravery and skill of General Corona and the forces he controls" (quoted in Agraz García de Alba 1984, 50–51; my translation). Following this same line, Agraz García de Alba reverts to the testimony of the aforementioned eyewitness, who chillingly affirms that Corona saved "the interests and honor of liberal families and institutions" and, as such, is remembered with great fondness by Guadalajara's residents (41). Homage to Corona's legend was literally set in stone in the monument unveiled in 1896, with an inscription that still reads: "He saved society from the invasion of the savages of Álica." With these words, the conflict at La Mojonera brings back memories of indigenous rebellions of centuries past. The coming of Lozada's forces injected fear into the imagination of the descendants of European immigrants who had made Guadalajara a refuge, while Corona's victory cemented the city's confidence as the capital of Mexico's northwest.

THE BIRTH OF A FRONTIER CITY

[Y] con la justicia que deste se hizo y con enbiar yo alguna gente, los pueblos que estaban levantados se pacificaron, y agora sirbe todo muy mejor que antes.

[And] with the justice upon which this was made and with my sending of some people, the towns in revolt were pacified, and now everything works much better than before.
—NUÑO BELTRÁN DE GUZMÁN, JULY 8, 1530, IN RAZO ZARAGOZA, *CRÓNICAS DE LA CONQUISTA* (MY TRANSLATION)

During the Spanish conquest, the Mexican West had the great misfortune of facing the forces of Nuño Beltrán de Guzmán, one of the most infamous Spanish conquerors, whom the Spanish Crown moved to detain, try, and sentence for excessive abuse of power. A native of Guadalajara, Spain, Guzmán has been inscribed in history as a calculating and authoritarian man who sought to bolster his positions of power by any means necessary. As the governor of the region of Pánuco in the eastern state of Veracruz, Guzmán was known for the enslavement of indigenous people destined for the Caribbean, often in exchange for cattle and horses. His contemporary Bernal Díaz del Castillo wrote that in Pánuco, "so many Indians were taken into slavery that the region was left virtually unpopulated" (quoted in Santana 1930, 5). By 1529, Guzmán's ambition for power and his rivalry with other conquerors (he had prominent disputes with Hernán Cortés) inspired him to embark on the conquest of new territories in the West, leading to his eventual position as the first governor of New Galicia. Despite his tainted record, Guzmán is recognized as one of the founding fathers of Guadalajara. Above all, the character of this ambitious conquistador and the foundation of this city sheds light on the ways in which Guadalajara de Indias would be imagined as a transplant of the Old World—a notion that would become engrained in the psyche of the city's colonial leaders.[6]

The confrontations that marked the voyage Guzmán undertook from Mexico City through the states known today as Michoacán, Jalisco, Nayarit, Zacatecas, and Sinaloa is documented both by the chroniclers of his era and by more recent historians. Even in cases of apparent cooperation, Guzmán, who at the moment enjoyed the title of president of the First Audience, opted to use violence to take land and enslave the indigenous population.[7] The brutal murder of the Purhépecha leader Caltzontzin at the end of 1529 set a precedent for what was to come, alarming the Crown and the church, and sending warnings of impending brutality throughout the northern and western territories. While many of Guzmán's contemporaries judged his actions as excessive, texts written by the captains and interpreters who accompanied him give us an idea of how the logic of the conquest and the construction of the natives as malefic beings justified the massacres and the enslavement of hundreds of thousands of people in the western territories, including the highest political leaders of the communities that the Spaniards traversed.

Guzmán's forces ultimately established present-day Guadalajara in the Valley of Atemajac, which at the time comprised several settlements, the most important of which was Tonallán (present-day Tonalá). Upon the arrival of Guzmán on March 24, 1530, Tonallán was governed by a woman, Cihuapili Tzapotzintli, who graciously received the foreigners, offering exquisite banquet and gifts (Cornejo Franco 1959, 23). Franciscan poet Francisco Parra memorializes this encounter in the fifteenth verse of his second canto of "Conquista de la Provincia de Xalisco":

> The Indians in their style arranged
> lodging for the newly arrived,
> they served them with abundant food,
> and to the Spanish troops and civilians,
> with music and songs amused them,
> each one dancing with their plumage.
> (Parra 1805–10, n.p.; my translation)

FIGURE 8 *Detalle de plano de la Nueva Galicia de Hernán Martínez de la Marcha, Compostela, 1550–1551*, 1550. Map of Nueva Galicia depicting the road taken by Nuño de Guzmán's forces. Courtesy of Archivo General de las Indias, MP-Mexico, 560.

Nonetheless, the hospitality of the Tonallán leader was not shared by her relatives, who governed the nearby towns of Tetlán and Coyula. This resulted in a challenging battle that the Spaniards won, thanks to the ardent participation of Captain Cristóbal de Oñate, who would later lead many other battles throughout the southwestern territories of what is now the United States.

Despite this victory in the Valley of Atemajac, Guzmán's forces sought to establish the capital of New Galicia elsewhere; yet a combination of indigenous hostility and unfavorable environmental conditions led the Spaniards to move the capital on several occasions, producing what Thomas Calvo describes as a "nomadic city" (1992, 1). After attempts to settle the capital in Nochistlán, Tonalá, and Tlacotlán, Guzmán suggested the area of Tepic as a new site. He wrote to Charles V of the "docility" of the more than two million natives of the region of Tepic and asked the king's permission to declare this his territory and to enslave the natives in the absence of sufficient beasts of burden (Santana 1930, 38). According to historian José Epigmenio Santana, the brutality of Guzmán's troops and the incessant resistance of the indigenous peoples led New Galicia to be conquered twice. The Mixtón War, or Caxcan Rebellion, of 1541, concentrated in the region of Zacatecas, reverberated throughout the entire western territory for decades to come. According to José María Murià, this resistance presented the possibility of the West becoming "cleansed" of Europeans:

> This was an authentic uprising derived from the cruel domination imposed on people who, while not offering great resistance when the conquerors first appeared in their territories sometime in 1530, were far from remaining truly subjugated. Upon learning of the true intentions of the intruders, while they still conserved energy fed by the accumulation of received injustices, they fought the way they could: until victory or death. The chronicles of the era affirm that their war cry was: "your death or mine." (Murià 1994a, 12; my translation)

Note that the Mixtón War was not a series of dispersed and anarchic rebellions. In fact, organized strategies were developed on repeated occasions for combating the Spaniards. Furthermore, Murià argues, the seminomadism of the indigenous peoples of the West gave them the advantage of mobility and led them to fiercely oppose the sedentarism that the colonial system sought to impose. By 1535, the capital of New Galicia was established in the village of Compostela, just south of Tepic, but continual indigenous uprisings quickly forced Guzmán to look for a new location for the capital, this time in the Valley of Atemajac, today Guadalajara, on February 14, 1542 (Murià 1994a, 21). After the unsuccessful experiences of establishing the capital in indigenous strongholds, the Valley of Atemajac offered ideal soil not only because of the quiescence of the local native peoples, but because of the valley's promising physical geography. As noted by Calvo, the combination of an almost circular valley with plentiful water sources (the Santiago, San Juan de Dios, and Atemajac Rivers), forested canyons, and a pleasant climate all pointed to "the seat of a future metropolis" (1992, 4). Contrary to other cities of New Spain (such as Mexico City, Tepic, Zacatecas, and Oaxaca), Guadalajara was not named after its indigenous place name, nor was it given a religious appellation (as was San Cristobal de las Casas); rather, it was exclusively baptized with the name of Guzmán's birthplace, a factor that reflects the Hispanicizing vision that Guzmán and future governors held for the city (González y González 1994, 100).[8]

Upon its establishment, Guadalajara progressively took on a strategic role for the Crown, becoming the launching pad for expeditions toward the so-called Chichimec border to the north, where the Spaniards imagined they would find endless treasures, including the fantastic Seven Cities of Cíbola and Quívira (Weckman 1994, 119). The discovery of silver in Zacatecas in 1546 further boosted the growth of Guadalajara as the capital of an increasingly prosperous New Galicia. Dana Velasco Murillo notes that the silver boom catalyzed northward colonization, "creating mining towns that led to the development of new industries, markets, population clusters, and frontier institutions," sustained on a diverse non-Spanish population (2016, 2). The administrative importance of Guadalajara led to a slow process of urbanization using the labor acquired under the agrarian dispossession of the *repartimiento* system, a colonial practice for conscripting labor that forced indigenous peoples to intermittently work for the Spanish for little or no pay (González y González 1994, 101). Initially, much of the indigenous labor force was made up of migrants from central Mexico (many of whom were already urban) and enslaved "Chichimec" children, who toiled in the homes of the elite and in the nearby mines and haciendas (Calvo 1992, 144, 148).

As noted by Calvo, Guadalajara was a city seemingly created from scratch: "This new world is expressed in the creation ex nihilo of a network of cities without links to the past, the introduction of completely new activities (cattle ranching, mines), and a populace that is in large part of foreign origin" (Calvo 1992, 190). While Calvo is correct in affirming that the "pioneering society" of colonial Guadalajara was not xenophobic (161), incoming populations were quickly placed on a steep socioeconomic hierarchy. People of distinct ethnic and class positions inhabited the city but usually under unequal conditions, which would help grow the political, economic, and clerical position of the criollo elite. Furthermore, there is little indication that the indigenous peoples from the region actually enjoyed any of the fruits from these transformations. As Pancho Madrigal's cartoon highlights, the sedimentation of official history has explicitly left out the presence of Guadalajara's nonwhite populations.

One interesting exception to this generalized racial stratification came with the arrival of two Japanese migrants in the seventeenth century. Under the Hispanicized names of Luis de Encío and Juan de Páez, these two figures became successful businessmen and integrated themselves into the upper classes of colonial Guadalajara. Páez held a long-term relationship with the high clergy and is considered to be one of the most wealthy and influential men of seventeenth-century Guadalajara, as well as one of the principal owners of enslaved people in the region (Falck Reyes and Palacios 2009, 59, 65, 121). The success of these non-European individuals demonstrates how financial wealth could make racial

FIGURE 9 The colonial period is depicted as a celebration of the European presence, leaving all other races on the margins of official historical narratives. The bubble captions read: "And us?" "Well . . . supposedly we didn't exist . . ." Cartoon by Pancho Madrigal

hierarchies irrelevant. For instance, Falck Reyes and Palacios's book, *The Japanese Who Conquered Guadalajara,* notes that the category "Chinese" signaled economic status rather than racial origin at the same time it was used to refer to enslaved people brought from the Philippines (51). The cases of Páez and Encío indicate that Guadalajara had become a relatively cosmopolitan city, with a growing relationship to regions outside its immediate orbit.

During the following centuries, the capital of New Galicia experienced slow but continuous development thanks to the formation of close ties between the established criollo families and the arrival of *peninsulares,* who constituted the administrative, clerical, and merchant classes of Guadalajara. According to Jaime Olveda, Guadalajara enjoyed relative political and economic autonomy that was further stimulated by the Bourbon Reforms, which promoted the emigration of peninsulares to the Americas: "Those who arrived to Guadalajara were natives of Santander, Vizcaya, Guipúzcoa, Alava and Navarra; they came inspired by a profound sense of Spanish superiority, and above all, possessed by an enormous desire to triumph and transform the American colonies into profitable and respectable possessions" (Olveda 1991, 40; my translation). By the end of the seventeenth century, the immigration of peninsulares to this city created important demographic shifts. Olveda's study indicates that, contrary to other regions of New Spain, the peninsulares and criollos of Guadalajara were willing and able to weave close ties with one another through marriage and political and commercial pacts, which facilitated the consolidation of a powerful regional oligarchy (Olveda 1991, 50–51). This Hispanic unity had important implications for indigenous communities precisely because it advanced the concentration of landholdings among few families and accelerated the rural dispossession and subsequent migration of indigenous peoples to Guadalajara, where they would confront the nascent monetized economy (87–88).

THE PEARL OF THE WEST: IMMIGRATION AND MODERNIZATION IN NINETEENTH-CENTURY GUADALAJARA

As discussed in chapter 3, the port of San Blas ushered in a period of economic and political growth for Tepic and Guadalajara. Although Mexico City would continue to be at the helm of the country's political, economic, and cultural power, the Bourbon Reforms and subsequent independence movement further solidified the West's sense of autonomy. The port's commercial activity fueled the infrastructural development of the San Blas–Tepic–Guadalajara axis at the same time that it heightened the privatization of lands for large-scale agriculture, used to feed a growing urban population (Olveda 1991, 125). Through the convergence of the port's activities, regional mining, and the cohesion of the urban oligarchy, Guadalajara's elite reached new levels of wealth.

Between 1812 and 1821, while insurgents captured the port of Acapulco, millions of pesos passed through San Blas, as did immigrants from Asia, Panama, South America, and Spain who worked for British firms (Olveda 2000, 122–23). The influx of capital and new populations fortified Guadalajara's elite and brought in promising alliances that would change how business was done in the city. It is important not to overstate the role this new wave of immigrants had on Guadalajara's development, for they encountered a city whose ruling class had already made great strides in transforming the urban landscape. As Jaime Olveda notes:

> [Guadalajara] figures among the American cities that blanketed a powerful bureaucracy and an elite conscious of its strength, and with a clear idea of the potential it had at its reach. The urban development that it obtained at the end of the eighteenth century symbolizes the force acquired by the dominant class. The

city space had acquired such complexity that it had become fractured along functional zones, each with its own significance, that accorded with the production and circulation of goods. (Olveda 2000, 15; my translation)

While Tepic's prosperity seemingly came and went, Guadalajara would continue to reap the benefits of the region's commercial, agricultural, mining, and financial activities. In fact, for years Guadalajara had been the recipient of the rural and mining elite's children, who sought to be educated in the city's notable institutions and to marry into the ruling Tapatío families. Even while San Blas's influence began to fade and political turmoil ravaged the country, Guadalajara would continue to receive waves of immigrants whose business affairs indicated their intent to stay in this Mexican capital.

With the conclusion of the War of Independence in 1821, great debates began between conservatives and liberals. Each party sought to determine Mexico's delicate economic future at a moment when global markets were dominated by the industrializing European nations. Although some politicians sought a modern industrial Mexico, the reality of the country continued to position it as an exporter of raw materials, resting on the operation of large plantations, which subjected peasants to entrenched forms of debt peonage and low wages (Olveda 2000, 206). Following the nation's independence, and as liberal reforms became implemented, both the country and the city experienced social convulsions rooted in the territorial dispossession of indigenous and mestizo rural communities, who were forced to try their luck in urban centers dominated by the same powerful classes that possessed the large rural haciendas.

Although Tepic attracted foreigners because of its proximity to San Blas, many preferred to reside in Guadalajara because of its far greater administrative and commercial capacity. One of the most significant political outgrowths of the presence of British and Panamanian capitalists was their ability to influence the ascendance of liberal thought in a conservative bastion like Guadalajara. This was a formidable transformation in a city that had largely been politically, economically, and culturally controlled by the clergy.[9] During the second half of the nineteenth century, immigrants from Europe and the United States continued to arrive and establish businesses that would further cement ideas of the free market. Because of their size and influence, the French represent the most notable of these incoming populations. The first generation of French immigrants comprised small businessmen who arrived in the 1830s, while the second came during the 1850s and 1860s, with greater capital to establish the city's first large textile factories and to sell imported apparel (Olveda 2000, 150). The French also established the first department stores, including the still popular chain Fábricas de Francia, founded in 1887. Following the national trend, the Tapatío elite eagerly embraced French immigrants along with their literary and aesthetic culture.

German, Italian, American, and British immigrants also found the city to offer promising business ventures and a welcoming environment in which to live. With the onslaught of the gold rush, western Mexico supplied agricultural and imported goods to California, much of which passed through German hands (Olveda 2000, 170). One of the most notable German immigrants was Theodor Kunhardt, who came during the second half of the nineteenth century and quickly dominated regional banking and imports, acquiring various properties throughout Guadalajara (170, 175). The Germans, with Kunhardt in the forefront, also established pharmacies as well as general goods and hardware stores. Naturally, the amount of capital these immigrants held helped them exert political influence, pushing for economic policies that would benefit their business ventures (178). In 1880, President Porfirio Díaz reinstated diplomatic relations with France and those nations that had sided with the European country during its occupation of Mexico. This move, along with Díaz's ambitious infrastructural projects, attracted many Europeans in search of new investment opportunities (Valerio Ulloa 2002, 7). While some resented the idea that European immigrants were exerting a form of imperialism by becoming rich on Mexican soil, Sergio Valerio Ulloa argues that it was far more common for these immigrants to arrive without capital, making their fortunes through "their labor and dedication" (8). This author also refutes the notion that most of these migrant businesspeople took their money back to their countries of origin, noting that a sizable number made Guadalajara their permanent home (8).

Clearly the trajectories of these immigrants were manifold. They came from different class backgrounds and inserted themselves into distinct economic niches that gave them varying levels of success. As their predecessors had done during the colonial period, many Spanish immigrants came from modest backgrounds and with little if any capital, but the most ambitious were able to make fortunes that would have been unimaginable in their homelands (Valerio Ulloa 2002, 14–15). While some stuck to their economic niche, others resembled Barron, Forbes and Company, eagerly taking any opportunity to turn a profit: "The veins of capitalist accumulation for these foreign businesspeople were diverse and equally sprung from the mercantile sphere as from industrial production, but also from the capitalist exploitation of their haciendas and ranches; from the renting of the land and single family homes, from usury and financial capital, from the exploitation of salaried and nonsalaried labor, from concessions and privileges, from monopolies and contraband, from bribery and corruption" (Valerio Ulloa 2002, 15; my translation).

The wealthiest arrivals invested in real estate, taking advantage of the housing demand fueled by the rising population. Olveda (1991, 1996, 2000) notes that this process led to the spatial reorganization of the city through the increased physical separation of places of residence, consumption, and work. The presence of these immigrants helped transform the spatial order and culture of the city with the construction of suburban neighborhoods, which were characterized by their location along the still undeveloped western periphery of the city. As the century progressed, an increasing number of large homes and chalets were built for the upper-class criollo and foreign families, while the colonial mansions in the city center became occupied by businesses and subdivided for the working class (Hernández Larrañaga 2001, 385).

How did these demographic and political economic transformations affect the racial discourse of the period? Note that in Mexico, the liberal concept of individualism explicitly sought to do away with categories denominating racial difference, such as Indian or casta, to push forth a consolidated hybrid identity. As the first constitutional governor of Jalisco, Prisciliano Sánchez ordered the substitution of indigenous and caste classifications with the unifying category of mestizo (Olveda 1996, 97). Later, when Governor Vallarta proclaimed the expropriation of communal lands, he argued that the laws would benefit indigenous peoples because they would no longer be forced to live as "civil corporations" and could consequently become free citizens who could participate within the capitalist economy (González Navarro 1994, 31). According to this line of thought, the shift in territorial laws, the advent of education, and the discipline provided by the monetized economy would give the indigenous subject the opportunity to become modern, as demonstrated by the prolific liberal figure of Benito Juárez. Or, as Antonio Escobar Ohmstede notes, "Indians could liberate themselves from their 'label' through social and geographic mobility[,] losing themselves in the demographic of ethnically undifferentiated and above all urbanized people, normally granting them greater comfort as mestizos" (Escobar Ohmstede 2007, 17–18). As Guadalajara's indigenous inhabitants entered the twentieth century, they would continue to find refuge under the neutralizing mestizo category, all the while being relegated to the city's stark class geography. More than ever, unregulated real estate speculation had led to a polarized city, where the poor lived in the old city and east of the San Juan de Dios River, and where the wealthy marked their territory westward through the construction of housing, parks, and boulevards (Jiménez Pelayo, Olveda, and Núñez Miranda 1995, 188).

Photographs of Guadalajara from the nineteenth and early twentieth centuries show a city in transition. Animal-drawn carriages lined the streets alongside tightly packed food stands; men went about their business under the shade of the era's prototypically large sombreros; young *aguadores* busily hustled water, while others gathered the good at the central Pila Roja fountain. The images of darker-toned women covered by shawls, milling through the city's downtown, juxtapose with the light-skinned women posing at Lake Chapala, a historical place of leisure for Guadalajara's upper classes and a present-day retirement haven for Canadians and Americans. The cultural hybridity of the city is palpably visible in these photos: German pharmacies, French department stores, older women selling medicinal herbs in the arched walkways, and men selling the tropical *tuba* drink from calabash gourds. Humble adobe constructions contrast with the elegant doorways that beckon the French trends of the time. Many of these buildings no longer exist, having given way to large open squares, pedestrian walkways, or broader streets. By the turn of the last century, the push to modernize Guadalajara led to the destruction of some of the older marketplaces frequented by the working classes. The *portales*, or arched passageways used by vendors, became a target of the period's urban renewal. The portales of San Agustín, located next to the elegant Teatro Degollado, are a notable case, as they were mysteriously set on fire to eliminate the presence of peasant vendors from the sight of upper-class theater attendees (Galindo Gaitán 2002, 66).

Finally, Guadalajara had cemented its fame as the Pearl of the West among travelers, who marveled at its luxurious accommodations, pleasant climate, and hospitality. Already in 1826, French traveler George F. Lyon made a note of the excellent quarters where he was hosted and the families who preoccupied themselves with sporting the latest French and British fashion trends. Lyon added that he would have thought he was in his homeland were it not for the women who smoked in public and the inability of theater audiences to remain quiet (cited in Muriá 2004a, 47–48). Almost seventy years later, Eduardo Gibbon wrote the following description of Guadalajara: "That city of fantastic aspect with its domes, its towers, its country houses and gardens like a big complex with its unified details forming harmony and spectacle. That city like a Sultana of the West laid out over cushions and divans dreaming satisfied in the middle of the reality of Oriental magnificence" (Gibbon 1893, iii–iv; my translation). This reputation for magnificence went so far as to reflect the notion that if one were poor in Mexico, it was best to live in Guadalajara, where even paupers were well off (Torres Sánchez 2001, 64).

URBAN EXPANSION AND NEIGHBORHOOD STRUGGLES

During the regime of Porfirio Díaz and the years of the Mexican Revolution, Guadalajara's population grew significantly, leading city authorities to become preoccupied by the growing number of "lepers and *pelados*" (Olveda 1996, 334).[10] The liberal Reform Laws led to an unprecedented concentration of land, which drove the displacement of the rural population to the cities. This crisis in land tenancy was only deepened under the Díaz regime, whose legacy of inflicting violence on the urban and rural working classes has been widely studied (Turner 1910; Womack 1969; Gilly 1971; Gilly et al. 1979; Knight 1986; Katz 1998). This reality sharply contrasted with the financial success that the upper classes experienced during this same period and is made visible in the urban changes that distanced the wealthy from the central neighborhoods now inhabited by the poor. This marked class segregation sustained a clear ethnic line, and in Guadalajara, it was the old criollo oligarchy and the foreign businesspeople who sustained a Europeanized vision for the city. Nicknames for the city, such as the Andalusia of Mexico, the Mexican Florence, and the City of Lights, exalted the identity that the local elite sought to promote on both a national and an international scale (Torres Sánchez 2001, 18). During the years of the Revolution, Guadalajara's political class continued to bet the city's political, economic, and cultural development on the influx of certain immigrants by selectively sending pamphlets to the United States, Europe, Latin America, and certain regions of Mexico (261). At the height of the armed conflict, the Tapatío press spoke of the city's continued prosperity, even though the majority of the population experienced economic hardship (175).

Following the Constitutionalist lead, between 1914 and 1919, Governor Manuel M. Diéguez engaged in a "regulatory fever," which included renaming and restructuring the city's streets, parks, and plazas; imposing laws related to loitering and the use of public spaces; reforming education, and reorganizing judicial and policing powers (Torres Sánchez 2001, 178). All this led to what Rafael Torres Sánchez describes as the rise of "modernity as a regulatory and arbitrary state practice," this time in the name of the poor (195). The populism of the new revolutionary government continued the path toward regulation by inserting itself into the everyday lives of urban residents. This included taking the country out of the city through the prohibition of chicken coops in private residences, the cleaning of public markets, and the conscription of residents to clean and repair public spaces as a part of their revolutionary duties (210–50). Needless to say, these policies were an ironic sequel to the Porfirian slogan of "order and progress."

The violence that the Revolution inflicted on the countryside led to the rapid rise of regional immigrants in Guadalajara. In the state of Jalisco in particular, armed conflict continued through the 1920s and 1930s as a result of the Cristiada, an armed movement that sparked in reaction to the state's secularization laws, which, under President Plutarco Elías Calles, led to the dramatic closure of churches. The intersection of the arrival of immigrants affiliated with the Cristeros from the northeastern region of Jalisco and the onset of "popular urbanization" organized by neighborhood parishes resulted in bustling neighborhoods like Santa Teresita (de la Peña and Martínez Casas 2004). In the absence of municipal action toward such basic infrastructural needs as potable water and street maintenance, de la Peña argues, the ecclesiastical neighborhood organization Acción Católica garnered political and cultural power over the lives of these new city residents. As more working-class neighborhoods were established during the 1940s and 1950s, conservative religious organizations secured a narrative for an ideal society rooted in the Hispanic legacy:

> The discursive content was consistent and convergent: the central point being the supremacy of the Catholic Church over any other power and the obligation governments had to honor it; the importance in Mexican history of the evangelization brought by the Spaniards—and as such the great debt Mexico had to Spain—and the apparition of the Virgin of Guadalupe; the great betrayal of the liberal governments and masons during the nineteenth and twentieth centuries because of their decreeing and sustaining the separation of church and state, and for their persecution of the Church; and the obligation that Catholics have to reject atheism and communism, and to sit watch over the integrity of the family and the purity of customs. (de la Peña and Martínez Casas 2004, 102–3; my translation)

De la Peña emphasizes that the consolidation of Acción Católica within the everyday lives of the residents of Santa Teresita models a "moral community," which facilitated migrants from rural Jalisco to come and reside in a city that was growing exponentially without the municipal government's ability to meet the basic needs of these new residents.

From 1940 through 1950, Guadalajara doubled its area from 2,620 to 4,180 hectares, attracting investors and immigrants in search of opportunities in the industrial and commercial sectors (Jiménez Pelayo, Olveda, and Núñez Miranda 1995, 227, 256). The city center was modified through the erection of modern buildings dedicated to commerce and the construction of central thoroughfares that underlined the division between the working classes located to the east of Calzada Independencia, which covers the San Juan de Dios River, and the middle and upper classes located to the west of this boulevard. Much of Guadalajara's spatial expansion came in the 1960s, as the federal government stimulated the upsurge of maquila industries away from the U.S. border region. By the late 1980s and through the 1990s, Guadalajara had earned a reputation as the national headquarters for the information technology (IT) industry and was christened the Silicon Valley of Mexico. Kevin Gallagher and Lyuba Zarsky (2007) reveal that this transpired through a combination of the relative ease of moving products from Guadalajara to California, NAFTA legislation, the city's good infrastructure and comfortable lifestyle (including its trade shows), low wages and weak labor unions, and finally, Jalisco's Economic Promotion Law, which eliminated most or all state and municipal taxes on foreign investors (2007, 130). While the IT and electronics industries continue to be a key economic engine in Guadalajara, the same factors that attracted foreign firms to the city have led to the industry's partial collapse, namely, the lack of government oversight, which allowed foreign companies to wipe out local firms rather than foment partnerships (7). Once China joined the World Trade Organization, Guadalajara lost several multinational corporations to this Asian country, demonstrating that the push toward complete liberalization had failed to sustain the city's famed IT boom (9).

Meanwhile, along the peripheral areas of the city, new residential neighborhoods popped up with little or no regulation, a trend that has only increased to the detriment of green areas and ejido lands. During the 1970s, real estate speculation accelerated with the arrival of one million new inhabitants, many of whom could not afford to pay to live in "regularized" areas. Consequently, many began living in the informal developments managed by corrupt entities, which, through the dispossession of ejido lands, were able to profit from a vulnerable incoming population (CDI 2005; Jiménez Pelayo, Olveda, and Núñez Miranda 1995, 263). Valentina Napolitano notes that unlike Monterrey and Mexico City, where land invasions have been a popular form of settling new neighborhoods, in Guadalajara, the *fraccionador*, or subdivider, purchases and services the land (Napolitano 2002, 20, 29). These subdividers beckon the caciques described by Fernando Benítez in chapter 3, as they control negotiations between the city and the residents of the new suburban neighborhoods that have contributed to the city's urban sprawl, devastating the remaining forests and water sources along the Metropolitan Area of Guadalajara (Zona Metropolitana de Guadalajara, or ZMG).

By the 1970s, these "popular," or working-class, neighborhoods along the city's periphery witnessed the presence of indigenous peoples from different parts of the country, who formed networks linking their communities of origin with their new urban homes. As a result, the old indigenous barrios of Mexicaltzingo and Mezquitán, located in the city center, no longer housed the bulk of Guadalajara's indigenous population. This new influx gave way to an indigenous population that was far more heterogeneous in its cultural and employment practices and that lived dispersed in different parts of the ZMG. The ethnic groups with the largest numbers are Purhépechas from Michoacán, Nahuas from various states, Mixtecs from Oaxaca, and Otomís from central Mexico. Each one of these groups has taken advantage of distinct economic niches, including carpentry, domestic labor, gardening, and the sale of street food (CDI 2005). Data from the National Institute for Geography and Statistics (Instituto Nacional de Geografía y Estadística, or INEGI) shows the presence of sixty different indigenous languages and ethnic groups in the ZMG (INEGI 2005). On a national level, the economic decline experienced by small and medium farmers as a result of the Green Revolution and the economic crises of the late 1970s and early 1980s caused an exodus from the countryside to Mexico's cities and to the United States. Indigenous peoples were not exempt from these movements; in fact, they lived these crises in a far more violent manner, being the victims of civil rights violations and territorial dispossession fueled by constitutional amendments and private land grabs exacerbated under the regime of Salinas de Gortari.[11]

Despite this changing reality, indigenista policies continue to focus on rural communities and, as a result, fail to design programs that meet the needs of urban indigenous peoples (CDI 2005). Anthropologist Regina Martínez Casas conducted ethnographic research with Otomí immigrants from the community of Santiago Mexquititlán, in the central Mexican state of Querétaro. The model of the youngest son inheriting land as well as the agricultural crisis are the two principal motifs that caused emigration from this community to large urban areas like Mexico City, Monterrey, and Guadalajara (de la Peña and Martínez

Casas 2004, 110). Martínez Casas found that while many Otomí families maintain strong links to Santiago Mexquititlán (marked by their participation in communal festivities and the conservation of traditional social relations in the city), many prefer to conceal their ethnic identity in public spaces, opting instead to identify themselves as *fuereños*, or outsiders: "The reluctance of many Otomís—which equally occurs in Santiago, but is intensified in the city—refers to the particularly tense and asymmetrical experience of interethnic relations: they know that if they are labeled as members of an indigenous group, the type of interaction will for better or for worse irrevocably remain marked by this label" (119; my translation). Martínez Casas observes that Otomís frequently prefer to present themselves before urban authorities as "poor" rather than indigenous, under the belief that they will receive better treatment. Finally, she argues that the rejection Otomí youth experience has serious implications in their schooling: one school where 50 percent of the total first- and second-grade population was indigenous experienced a decrease to only 17 percent indigenous by the sixth grade. The study indicates that the high desertion rates are related to indigenous students' alienation from the school environment, in addition to the domestic and employment responsibilities they must assume (126).

The Otomí experience undoubtedly shares some parallels with other indigenous groups living in the ZMG. Different patterns of migration, residence, employment, and education, however, demonstrate that we must observe these differences to avoid the tendency to homogenize the urban indigenous population. This is especially important in light of a study carried out by the National Commission for the Development of Indigenous Peoples (Comisión Nacional para el Desarrollo de los Pueblos Indígenas, or CDI) that found that Guadalajara, Monterrey, and Cancún share the fastest-growing indigenous populations in the country (Durin 2008, 13). The presence of indigenous peoples in spaces historically occupied by whites and mestizos undeniably has awakened racism among those who resent the thought of sharing the city with ethnic groups they consider undesirable. The CDI's Program for the Development of Indigenous Peoples (Programara para el Desarrollo de los Pueblos Indígenas, PDPI), 2009–12, recognizes that racism is the "fundamental cause" of the "profound socioeconomic delays" that many indigenous peoples experience. Additionally, the PDPI cites a government poll that found that 42.9 percent of nonindigenous Mexicans think that indigenous peoples "will always have social limitations" because of their "racial characteristics." Within the urban context, 39.5 percent of the sample population affirms that they would be willing to "organize" to impede indigenous families from living close to their neighborhood (CDI 2010, 22). Another study carried out by the CDI confirms these discriminatory attitudes by showing that although nine out of ten people say they would not mind having an indigenous neighbor, during the qualitative phase of the study, the possibility of holding close quarters with indigenous peoples became clearer with comments such as "I imagine my pretty house and next door a shack with dirt," or "It wouldn't happen, not because I am elitist, but because it isn't ad-hoc, it isn't normal." Other more ambivalent but equally prejudiced comments also emerged: "I would be delighted, it makes no difference to me ... if they move in next door and they are clean, that would be awesome" (CDI 2006, 40).

One event that has left a deep mark on Guadalajara's indigenous population and that highlights the city's interracial relations occurred in 2003, when residents of the upper-middle-class neighborhood of Providencia organized against the use of the local Rubén Darío park by indigenous peoples. For more than a decade, this park had become a Sunday meeting place for young Nahuas, many of whom worked as domestic servants and restaurant workers in Providencia. The neighborhood housewives soon became upset that their local park was becoming a place of leisure for poor Indians, accusing them of conducting lewd acts and "obstructing peace." The neighborhood's residential organization went as far as purchasing five squad cars to police the area, leading to indigenous peoples becoming the subjects of random searches. By October 2003, the police had detained more than forty-four Nahua men and women accused by neighborhood residents of consuming alcoholic beverages, fighting, and committing "moral offenses," none of which could be corroborated (Melgoza 2005).

Santos de la Cruz, a Wixarika lawyer who resides in Guadalajara, cites this affair as emblematic of the city's unchecked racism and classism. He recalls how, in solidarity with the alarmist housewives, the Oxxo minimart chain across from the park stopped selling goods to indigenous customers (Santos de la Cruz, interview by author, June 24, 2010). Other testimonies state that the local residential association asked Oxxo management to use separate cash registers, one for those believed to be from Providencia and another for indigenous customers. Although this case fizzled from the limited media and juridical attention it had gained, the harassment forced many indigenous peoples to stop using the park. Above all, this situation demonstrates how indigenous citizens are unwelcome to use public spaces in the very neighborhoods where they are welcomed as poorly paid workers.

This type of racial prejudice converges with a deep sense of classism reflected in the spatial organization of the city and the effects of these divisions on how the urban space is experienced from different social standings. As such, Guadalajara exemplifies the ways in which social stratification is transformed into spatial and political organization, led by the conservative inclinations of the business and political classes, whose preferred representatives have been the Catholic Church and the National Action Party (Partido Acción Nacional, or PAN), which dominated the state's politics from 1995 until the mid-2000s. This reality is further driven by the existence of conservative organizations whose principal focus rests on the preservation of "good customs" and the reinsertion of the Catholic Church into politics and the daily lives of Tapatíos (de la Torre and Ramírez Sáiz 2001, 196). As was the case in the Rubén Darío park affair, upper-middle-class women have taken prominent roles in these organizations as the self-appointed guides for rescuing the city and nation from nihilism.

Deep-seated Tapatío social conservatism has direct implications for indigenous citizens who do not neatly fit into the Catholic, Hispanic, and neoliberal ideal espoused by these sociopolitical forces. Through public campaigns, conferences, and propaganda, right-wing organizations like Opus Dei and the Sinarquistas push for free-market policies, celebrate the dominance of private property, and seek to erect barriers separating the spaces in which they live (be they homes, schools, or commercial centers) from the spaces in which the "undesirable classes" live (Guzmán Pérez Pelaez 2001, 170).[12] In Manuela Camus's study on Guadalajara's gated periurban communities, she argues that much of this population's status is derived from "social positions based on acquired privileges" (2015, 21). Camus further qualifies the ideological makeup of Guadalajara's elites as a "palimpsest" of ideals that straddle liberal and conservative economic and social impulses. In this manner, today's Tapatío oligarchy conserves the pragmatic posture of earlier years: liberal on economic policy and conservative on social and political matters. This reality presents an important challenge for a city with a spatially and ethnically heterogeneous history. In the following section, I examine Wixarika experiences in the ZMG as a case in point.

CHALLENGING THE MULTICULTURAL CITY

On April 28, 2010, an event titled "The Interpellation of Differences: In Search of Intercultural Dialogue" took place at Guadalajara's Jesuit university, ITESO. Several weeks prior to the event, the student organizers from the Department of

Philosophy extended an invitation to ITESO's indigenous students to come and share some elements of their ethnic traditions with the university's student body. The invitation was evaluated during a meeting held by Universidad Solidaria (Solidarity University, or US), an organization that provides a space for dialogue and support for indigenous and working-class students enrolled at ITESO. It was clear to the members of US that both the invitation and the accompanying agenda for this event predetermined the type of participation that they were to have: it was foremost a call for them to act like Indians, an invitation to present indigenous folklore and linguistic heritage, but not a serious conversation about the "interpellation of differences" and so-called intercultural dialogue. After much discussion, the students of US decided to participate in the event hoping to challenge the expectations of the organizers.

The finalized agenda for the event placed the indigenous and nonindigenous students on different panels. As if this separation was not enough to put into question the event's intercultural approach, students from US shared their panel with two ex-gang members, who owed their departure from *la vida loca* (the crazy life) to the gospel. Each indigenous participant donned ethnic attire and shared greetings in their native language, as well as poems and mythological stories. Correspondingly, the ex-gang members exhibited their salutations and disclosed the rites of initiation for getting jumped into the gang. The subsequent panel comprised blond students wearing sunglasses. They read poems and recounted their crosscultural experiences of exotic trips to Tijuana, Versailles, the Brazilian Amazon, Thailand, and Chenalhó, Chiapas. They spoke of their bisexual lovers in France, the experience of buying condoms in Bangkok, and the revelation that the world was unequal after an exchange with "marginalized" indigenous peoples in the mountains of Chiapas. The sharp edge of otherness could not have been better underscored with these two juxtaposed panel discussions. Why not place the impassioned poem of the Ch'ol student in the same space as the dramatic blond's tale of struggle with multiple personalities? If the event sought a dialogue around the interpellation of differences, why the crude separation?

This college event is one of many examples of everyday interactions that reveal the enduring expectations the mestizo population continues to foster toward fellow indigenous citizens, expectations that take on a particularly coarse character within the urban context. Especially troubling are the ways in which indigenous cultures are consumed within the present-day multicultural imaginary, where aboriginal culture and language is commoditized. Cultural elements are displaced, reduced, and distorted across space and scale, often in the name of indigenous peoples' well-being (Negrín da Silva 2015). Events like the one that took place at ITESO demonstrate the racial ambivalence that is so pervasive in Mexican society. While state and private enterprises participate in the discursive and practical reproduction of "the Indigenous," everyday citizens do their part in replicating and sustaining what Allan Pred calls "enduring stereotypes." The imaginary of the universal Indian thus rules over particular interactions on the ground. In other words, stereotypes, which stem from generalized notions of race and ethnicity, become concrete through everyday practices that renew the dominant social order and its accompanying taken-for-granted imaginary (Pred 2004). The aforementioned CDI surveys show the spectrum of sentiments that Mexican society continues to hold toward indigenous peoples. These feelings range from outright rejection, to pity and paternalism, ambivalence, or celebration and friendship. Pred emphasizes that the anxieties and fantasies that the dominant classes hold toward subaltern peoples rest on the "already existing and variously constructed popular racist imagination," which is intensified through the everyday application of universal images onto particular situations (177). From this imagination stems the idea that the innate home of an indigenous person is a shack made from dirt (even in the city), or that being indigenous precludes cosmopolitanism. Findings from Princeton University's Project on Ethnicity and Race in Latin America show that most Mexicans identify mestizo as their normative ethnic grouping all while "embrac[ing] a white identity," which remains tied to understandings of social mobility, particularly for those in the lower middle classes (Telles 2014, 37, 58).

Closely tied to this popular racist imagination is the idea that indigenous peoples require the assistance of mestizos to overcome the notorious stigmas of poverty, marginalization, illiteracy, and discrimination. For Wixarika student activist Antonio Hayuaneme García, cross-racial alliances are important for addressing these problems but are better orchestrated by indigenous peoples who propose and carry out their own project initiatives: "I believe it is very important that these projects come from the people themselves. I say this not just as an indigenous person, but this is something that often occurs in our state and in our country as a whole: many of us become the group of people who always need to be helped, who always need to be told how, and it is never considered that we have our own instruments, that we are thinking beings even if we consider things differently" (Antonio Hayuaneme García, interview by author, July 20, 2010). Within the current context of massive movements of people across regional, national, and international borders, Guillermo de la Peña suggests that we rethink traditional perspectives on citizenship and territory, which have become unsustainable under globalization. De la Peña argues that there should be a "construction of alternative visions of territory and nationhood by those actors who demand a differentiated participation in national life: I will call this type of participation *ethnic citizenship*" (de la Peña 1999, 3). This reconsideration of civic belonging includes the abandonment of static identity categories and the adoption of more fluid notions of identification that reflect actual social and spatial relationships, as is the case with indigenous immigrants who live in cities: "The Otomís of Guadalajara never declare that they live in this city but rather in Santiago Mexquititlán, even if they only go to the village a few days out of the year. Other indigenous peoples who feel a deeper rootedness in the urban world equally resist defining this world as one that is exclusively mestizo and homogenizing, and may even consider themselves to be fully urban and fully Huichol, or Mixtec, or Purhépecha" (de la Peña 1999, 9; my translation). From these dynamic identities emerge important initiatives, new proposed platforms from which to think of public, educational, labor, and domestic spaces. De la Peña's suggestion of "ethnic citizenship" compliments Stuart Hall's (1996) discussion of identities as "points of suture" and Ferguson and Gupta's (1997) reterritorialization of belonging, matters that I return to in the following chapter. But first, I describe two projects that have sought to change interracial relations in Guadalajara, all the while nurturing indigenous identities within the city.

WIXARITARI, ARTISTS, AND ARTISANS UNITED OF THE METROPOLITAN AREA OF GUADALAJARA

The collective initiative known as Wixaritari, Artistas y Artesanos Unidos en la Zona Metropolitana de Guadalajara (WAAU) is a response to some of the struggles Wixaritari face in the ZMG: discrimination at the hands of municipal authorities and the general public, and a lack of organizational unity among Wixaritari residing in the city. More specifically, WAAU addresses the needs of Wixaritari who live from the sale of arts and crafts. Being indigenous to the state of Jalisco and the neighboring states of Nayarit and Durango, the Wixaritari have a historical relationship with Guadalajara. The proximity between this city and their traditional communities has permitted a fluid relationship among those who have migrated to the city and those who have remained in their rural homeland. Nonetheless, until recently Wixaritari had been marginalized from the state and city governments' sense of identity and policy creation.

Another challenge that these artists and artisans face is the lack of public spaces where they can sell their goods. Certainly, the city has a long history of attempting to curb street-vending activities, including through the aforementioned Porfirian and postrevolutionary policies. Across political parties and governments, the municipality of Guadalajara has limited and at times prohibited the sale of arts and crafts in central public squares under the argument that the stands are synonymous with street peddling and give a poor image to the historic city center. Imposed regulations include the mandate for granting individual licenses only when indigenous artisans have previously received collective vending permits within their respective artisan collectives (de la Peña and Martínez Casas 2004, 121).[13] Most importantly, the discriminatory practices toward street vendors have had grave consequences for those artisan families that economically depend on access to public marketplaces. WAAU largely originated from these conditions to unite and mobilize Wixaritari in the ZMG with the objective of negotiating new spaces for the sale of arts and crafts under more just terms.

WAAU affirms its right to push forward this initiative by citing the International Labour Organization's convention 169, article 2, which states the government's responsibility in "assisting the members of the peoples concerned to eliminate socio-economic gaps that may exist between indigenous and other members of the national community, in a manner compatible with their aspirations and ways of life" (ILO 1989, art. 2). Additionally, WAAU's project document stresses that Wixarika migration to cities stems from decades of flawed development policies as well as the changes brought about by capitalist market penetration of their communities. As a result, increasing numbers of Wixaritari have sought economic sustenance through wage labor outside their nuclear communities. This does not mean that all Wixaritari residing in the ZMG face the same conditions; WAAU's members explicitly state that there is great heterogeneity among Wixaritari, a matter that has often created disunity.

The final objective of WAAU is to negotiate formal public spaces for the sale of their arts and crafts to "ensure the economic stability and identity of migrant Wixaritari and temporary inhabitants of the ZMG," inform truthful and respectful information about the Wixarika people to eliminate negative stereotypes, and foment greater dialogue between Wixaritari and mestizos in the city.[14] In this way, the organization's activities extended beyond securing spaces for the sale of Wixarika arts and crafts. When Guadalajara won the contract to host the 2011 Pan-American Games, it chose as one of its three mascots a pink deer with a god's eye on its forehead named Huichi. Members of WAAU swiftly criticized this unwarranted characterization of Wixarika culture. In response, organizers of the games offered their apologies for creating a "Huichol" mascot and extended an olive branch by inviting Wixarika artisans to set up vending tables at the Pan-American Games' venues. By this time, the organizers argued that they could not remove the mascot, as they had already ordered merchandise plastered with Huichi's image and designed the Mexican team's uniforms using Wixarika iconography. Paradoxically, the Pan-American Games offered a rare instance of Jalisco's recognition of Wixarika culture as one of its own. Although members of WAAU were split over whether to accept this apologetic invitation, they ultimately agreed under the condition that they could use the games as a platform for negotiating their larger demands with municipal authorities.

In the two months leading up to the games, members of WAAU mobilized to call attention to the Huichi mascot and, by extension, introduce a wider public debate around the unauthorized appropriation of Wixarika culture and aesthetics at a moment when Wixarika sacred territories were being conceded to mining and tourist corporations in Wirikuta and Haramara. At the same time, organizers of the Pan-American Games retracted their promise to Wixarika vendors amid a series of other missteps, which concluded with the flooding of the Primavera Forest with sewage from the game's facilities. To make matters worse, shortly before the games began, Wixarika vendors in downtown Guadalajara' were forcibly removed, beaten, and fined for their unsanctioned use of public space. Not surprisingly, these incidents further radicalized some members of WAAU, who have since begun work with other indigenous communities of the ZMG. Undoubtedly, during its most active years (2010–14), WAAU sought a renewed vision for urban coexistence that sustains indigenous peoples' right to the city.

UNIVERSIDAD SOLIDARIA (SOLIDARITY UNIVERSITY)

Universidad Solidaria (US) began as an initiative set in 1998 by a former ITESO chancellor with the purpose of lending support and retention for indigenous and working-class students at the university, albeit with a special interest in the ethnic background of participating students (Ceja Chávez 2014, 28). Students selected to be a part of US must participate in the organization's meetings and relate to fellow US students and to the university employee in charge of running the program and directing the students' needs to the appropriate administrative staff. These needs range from receiving financial aid and work-study opportunities to getting assistance in navigating the university's programs. Antonio Hayuaneme García, a US member, told me that he felt strange when he entered the ITESO and was directed to this specialized program. He had studied his

FIGURES 10A AND 10B Antonio Hayuaneme García demonstrating during Guadalajara's celebration of International Indigenous Peoples' Day, August 9, 2011. Antonio embroidered the following on his shirt: "Indigenous Peoples' Day—Learn the Reality" (*front*); "Sacred Sites for Sale: Wirikuta for $3 Million a Day to Remember Our Blood" (*back*). Photos by Lisbeth Bonilla.

entire life among mestizos without ever receiving "preferences" for being indigenous, whereas he now faced a situation in which he was separated from the rest of the student body based on his ethnicity (Hayuaneme García interview). Nonetheless, by the beginning of the 2009–10 academic year, the group began a process of reflection and criticism over the objective of US and the way in which the monthly meetings were run. Influenced by liberation theology, Paolo Freire, and grassroots labor struggles, the university-appointed coordinator had a long trajectory of pedagogical work with peasant communities in the Americas. While the students recognized this coordinator's good efforts in moving the group through its formative stages, they also felt the need for the coordinator and group representative to be one of the US students.

As a result of these discussions, the meetings became more participatory and horizontal, with the election of a student coordinator who brought US students to focus on channeling the needs of low-income and indigenous students to the administration and projecting a greater presence within the campus's culture (Hayuaneme García interview). US's two principal objectives include creating safe and respectful spaces for the members to share their struggles and express themselves and organizing projects and events that diversify the university's identity. To understand the weight of a student organization like US, we need only return to the aforementioned event, "The Interpellation of Differences: In Search of Intercultural Dialogue." It is important to stress that ITESO is a private university largely comprising children of the Tapatío elite. Unlike other private universities in Guadalajara, however, ITESO has set itself apart because of its Jesuit ideals and history of social engagement, whereby it has financed and coordinated numerous social welfare projects in the state of Jalisco. In fact, ITESO has been active in various projects in Wixarika communities and has acted as an important financial and human resource for the so-called intercultural schools, which have been established in these communities since the mid-1990s. Consequently, ITESO has a community of young people who have a sincere interest in service learning but nevertheless run the risk of replicating paternalist and naïve attitudes toward their less-privileged fellow citizens. This has direct repercussions in the daily experiences of indigenous students, who for better or worse are treated by their peers with a degree of difference based on their ethnoracial and socioeconomic standing.

Considering this context, the space created by the US monthly assembly allows its members to share academic, economic, and family-related concerns without fear of being judged. Under the new model headed by the students themselves, various initiatives have sprouted that seek to deepen the diversity of the university through events and activities reflecting the heterogeneity of the indigenous students at the campus. Hayuaneme García, the first student coordinator of US, is convinced that a key objective for the organization is to foment university policies that are truly inclusive so that more youth "from other places" can enter and not be identified as "special." Hayuaneme García affirms that the only way to rupture with the reproduction of prejudice is through increased student diversity on campus. Although the event organized by the philosophy students appeared to have confirmed stereotypes, US members were able to leave their mark during the closing of the program by engaging in a critical dialogue that led their peers in philosophy to recognize that greater efforts were needed to make the university an inclusive space for all its students. In 2016, the ITESO and the Wixárika Regional Council established a formal agreement to foment the yearly recruitment, admission, and retention of Wixárika students, with the added benefit of a tuition-free education.

One of the most remarkable aspects of US is that it is a space where indigenous and working-class students can critically discuss larger societal problems without losing touch with the intimate issues each member deals with daily. It is a place where they can share the alienation that they face in the halls of the university and receive ideas for overcoming personal problems that they usually cannot raise elsewhere. At the beginning of each meeting, all members are given the opportunity to share how they are doing. During one session, a mestiza student shared that she rarely had money for lunch and agonized over the difficulty she had in hiding the matter from an upper-class friend with whom she tended to spend the lunch hour. Upon sharing this anecdote, several other students spoke about how class difference permeated their campus experiences, such as not enjoying the privilege of buying lunch, driving to school, or boasting of beach vacation trips after spring break.

After observing and participating in various interracial organizations, I am struck by US as a group where members have equal representation and where questions of racism and classism in Mexican society are discussed in a clear and focused manner. Above all, it is an organization where indigenous and nonindigenous students can see eye to eye. As such, US is a poignant example of what M. Jacqui Alexander terms "pedagogies of crossing," where people of diverse backgrounds can "walk together." Alexander notes, "Ultimately, one's ability to be heard as saying what one is saying and what one intends to say is structured by one's social and legal status, one's standing" (2005, 122). For its membership, US offers a space not only where people can speak their minds, but most importantly, where people can be heard and understood.

UNFIXING THE TAPATÍO NARRATIVE

WAAU and US are two organizations that seek to promote the indigenous presence within a diversity of city spaces, including universities, public squares, and private offices. These organizations are part of a growing indigenous population in the ZMG that asserts their right to the city, a question that geographer David Harvey describes as a relegated human right: "The right to the city is far more than the individual liberty to access urban resources: it is a right to change ourselves by changing the city. It is, moreover, a common rather than an individual right since this transformation inevitably depends upon the exercise of a collective power to reshape the processes of urbanization. The freedom to make and remake our cities and ourselves is, I want to argue, one of the most precious yet most neglected of our human rights" (Harvey 2008). It is precisely the principle of making and remaking the city, ourselves, and our social relations that motivates popular organizations like WAAU and US, as they challenge a historically fragmented urban space that sustains distance between different social groups and that reproduces race and class privileges. In 2013, a new organization was formed uniting indigenous students across different ethnicities and universities under the name Young Indigenous University Students in the ZMG (Jóvenes Indígenas Universitarios, or JIU). JIU's objective is to build the dignified visibility of the indigenous presence in the metropolitan region, beginning with collaborative research programs to determine the presence and conditions that indigenous university students face (Mendoza, García, and García 2013).

Anthropologist Johannes Fabian notes that to place peoples and cultures on a different "temporal slope" produces spatial distance reflecting power hierarchies rooted in the colonial system and in capitalist development (1983, 17).[15] Both systems create a "denial of coevalness" of different subjects who have participated in the creation of colonial and capitalist enterprises, even if their participation has been unequal, forced, or oppositional (31). In the previous pages, I demonstrate how a particular Tapatío racial imaginary has been promoted since the city's colonial foundation, contributing to a series of displacements that distort the lived reality of a large segment of its society—a segment that has not always played a silent part in local and regional history. As signaled by Escobar Ohmstede in the case of the nineteenth century and Martínez Casas in the current Otomí case, the construction of a uniform ethnic identity in Guadalajara has created an environment in which many indigenous peoples identify as mestizos to access greater social mobility—an act that is the product of gross symbolic violence. Nonetheless, a history of social contention and the current demographic shifts taking place open new opportunities for indigenous residents of Guadalajara to proclaim their right to be and belong in the city.

5

MAKUYEIKA

She Who Walks in Many Places

Once law enshrines cultural identity as the basis for political identity, it necessarily converts ethnicity into a political force.
— MICHAEL WATTS, "DEVELOPMENT AND GOVERNMENTALITY"

THROUGH THE LOOKING GLASS

THE SHAMAN Chocolates website proudly proclaims to be a "Shaman-run Chocolate Company" that "helps support Huichol Indians." The image of the Indian on the chocolate bar's packaging might suggest that he and his otherworldly community will soon see those dollars converted to pesos, or perhaps back into cacao, as *these* Indians are still steeped in their pre-Hispanic economies. The company's website confidently states, "The Huichol, declared a national treasure of Mexico, are one of the few American tribes to maintain their pre-Columbian traditions. Chocolate has been a rich part of their tradition for hundreds of years, and the sweet-tasting candy is now being used to conserve their culture and lifestyle."[1] Through the logic of capitalist-enabled cultural preservation, consumption of this candy can help the Huichol continue to be Indian. Yet Shaman Chocolates claims to be unique in its philanthropy because it was founded by Brant Secunda, a "Huichol shaman" from New Jersey, who was "born into the Huichol tribe" thanks to a vision quest several decades ago. After collapsing on a rural backroad in Nayarit, Secunda was awakened by the face of an Indian, who then shared with him the most well-kept secrets of his peoples' pre-Columbian faith. Ignited by this alleged apprenticeship, over the past several decades Secunda has sold his brand of Huichol shamanic retreats in Alaska, California, and Nayarit.

To date Shaman Chocolates claims that 100 percent of their sales go toward supporting a culturally and geographically imprecise group of "Huichol Indians." Several years of probing which Wixarika communities are benefiting and how they are benefiting from these chocolate bars led me back to the same answers: an unspecified community one day will have a bead factory, and a Wixarika law student will one day get a scholarship. The company representative with whom I corresponded in June 2010 specified that they wanted to support the first Wixarika college student but had yet to turn a profit. The email thread between the representative and me ended when I responded that there are in fact hundreds of Wixarika college students, graduates, and professionals, some of whom have studied abroad. Yet the company's website, updated in 2018, continues to state that the profits are destined to projects in "three Huichol villages" that "include sending the first Huichol to college!"[2] In the meantime, the packaged faces of happy indigenous children and the stoic stare of an elderly shaman meet the normative imaginaries of a global public that easily believes that indigenous peoples are not present in spaces of higher education, and much less as arbiters in courtrooms.

I open this final chapter with a sketch of this chocolate company as a way to expose how people and goods are mobilized to sustain the entrenched fictions that continue to surround indigenous peoples. The faces that appear on the packaging of these chocolates are viewed through the looking glass held up by Western peoples enamored by the possibility of encountering an ethnic Other; while the materiality of a purchase is grounded on the existence of abstracted peoples held back in time and space. Ultimately, these abstracted peoples are real and have voices to talk back and invert the looking glass. In the following pages, I examine how Wixarika students and young professionals are negotiating their place in a world that often holds impossible expectations of who they should be as indigenous subjects. This chapter draws on ethnographic data and existing literature to demonstrate how the post-multicultural landscape has introduced new problems that indigenous peoples must strategically negotiate. Most Wixarika students and professionals living in Guadalajara and Tepic straddle several spaces and take on many roles to bridge their commitments to self, to their families, and to their ethnic community. The Wixarika concept of *makuyeika*—he or she who walks in many places—speaks to the multiple responsibilities that Wixarika students, professionals, and their organizations carry in the city and beyond. I propose that through the prism of makuyeika, one can acknowledge the geographic and cultural fluidity of the experiences of Wixarika youth. As a result, the concept of makuyeika works against the grain of racial and spatial representations of Wixaritari that continue to be grounded on the institutional legitimacy of the archive and perpetuated through the workings of the popular imagination.

This chapter is punctuated by anecdotes that Wixarika students and professionals shared with me to express their personal engagement with migration, academics, activism, and everyday life in today's Mexican cities. Listening to the voices of these Wixarika students and professionals is especially important at a time when their nation's sacred places are under unprecedented threat by mining concessions, hydroelectric dams, and tourist development. At the same time as these sacred territories are being targeted by big capital, Wixarika material and spiritual culture is being increasingly consumed by a global audience. With the public eye set on them, Wixaritari have encountered a new set of challenges and opportunities. Over the course of more than ten years, many of my research participants graduated from college and are working in the career area of their choice, directly advocating for their communities, whether in governmental or university positions, or through nonprofit or Wixarika communal positions. This is no small feat because while poor statistics are kept by university administrations on the admissions of indigenous students, on a national level this demographic makes up only 3 percent of the total university population, despite being 10 to 14 percent of the population as a whole (Foro Consultivo 2018; Martínez Casas et al. 2014). Where indigenous students are studying geographically, the type of academic institution they are at, and the existence of any direct or indirect support networks significantly shapes the outcomes of these first-generation university students. Throughout this chapter, student testimonies reflect the multiple ways in which "the psyche is interdicted by race" (Saldaña-Portillo 2016, 30) and the clear limits that liberal multicultural inclusion presents for a "deeper cultural recognition" that can shift quotidian and structural systems of racialized and spatialized power (Gómez Gallegos 2018, 200).

> During middle school I was discriminated [against]. I can say it like that. . . . All of us have suffered discrimination. I have heard it from many young [indigenous]. I did not like to go to the sierra. I was a teenager. I dressed differently. . . . I remember that I dressed like a cholo with long hair and the hanging belt, big flashy sneakers that said the brand name. I did not like to go to the sierra; my mother forced me when I was in middle school. Because that occurs when one comes [to the city], you get worried because you do not speak Spanish. During high school I continued to suffer with my peers. I do not like to mistreat others

precisely because of this. And from that time I said: "I am going to learn to speak Spanish well but never like them, never." That is because of the mistreatment, because of the experiences . . . because of the color of my skin, because of how I spoke, because of the way I dressed.

And in high school it was the same, but I slowly won over my classmates. I did not like to wear my traje [tribal dress]. I did not like going to the countryside. And I regret this because now I know what that meant. But then there was a teacher who I remember had us think about who we were, psycholog[icall]y, to learn to value ourselves, who we are, what we can do, what we can develop. And they changed. . . . I remember that in our final year, my classmates who told me things were now my friends because it was a lack of education on their part . . . because they would come and start speaking in what was supposedly my mother tongue and to imitate me, and I would tell them, "I have no idea what you are saying." And at the graduation was the first time I put on a Huichol traje in the city.

[It] was important for me, because that is where I began to completely change. I put on my traje. What's more, I did not even know how to put it on. My mom teased me when she saw the photos because I did not know how to put it on. And my classmates and the school directors told me that they wanted for me to give the graduation speech . . . with my traje. That is why I decided to put on my traje. . . . That is where everyone recognized me, everyone listened to me, even the constitutional governor of the state of Nayarit, Antonio Echevarría. . . . That is where I began to get recognized; I came out in the newspaper—for the first time a Wixarika student appeared. . . . And my peers congratulated me for who I am; that was something very important for me. Because I can be myself. In the graduation photos, everyone is wearing their black toga, and I appear with my Wixárika traje. (Journalist Ukeme Muñoz, interview by author, July 4, 2010)

RECOGNITION BEYOND AUTHENTICITY

The impossible demand placed on these and other indigenous people: namely, that they desire and identify with their cultural traditions in a way that just so happens, in an uncanny convergence of interests, to fit the national and legal imaginary of multiculturalism; that they at once orient their sensual, emotional, and corporeal identities toward the nation's and law's image of tradi-

tional cultural forms and national reconciliation and at the same time ghost this being for the nation so as not to have their desires for some economic certainty in their lives appear opportunistic.
—ELIZABETH POVINELLI, THE CUNNING OF RECOGNITION

In early 2010, I was asked to begin participating in a seminar on the presence of indigenous peoples in Guadalajara at the Centro de Investigaciones y Estudios Superiores en Antropología Social (Center for the Investigation and Study in Social Anthropology, or CIESAS). The goal of the seminar was to assess the heterogeneity of indigenous residents in the city and place it in conversation with ongoing issues of discrimination, the tension that exists between different indigenous ethnic groups in the city, and the ways in which city spaces have been appropriated by the approximately sixty indigenous groups present in Guadalajara. Note that none of us in the group identified as indigenous and that the bulk of the researchers focused on street vendors and artisans. I was asked to share my research on Wixarika university students and professionals. I attempted to underline the diversity of personal trajectories that each student has and the work that needs to be done to show both the commonalities and divergences in the experiences of young Wixaritari in Guadalajara and Tepic. I stressed that while some students' families have lived in the city for more than one generation, other students have only recently arrived to the city with the sole purpose of receiving a higher education. Despite differences in each family's history and the established network that each student has in the city, all share the common experience of discrimination and the struggle of negotiating the mestizo and Wixarika worlds they straddle.

During the question-and-answer segment of my presentation, an anthropologist dedicated to the study of rituals in one Wixarika rural community objected to the lack of cultural authenticity some Wixarika students demonstrate, claiming that some use their ethnic identity as a strategy to obtain privileges from mestizo society when, in reality, they have become *mestizoized*. To illustrate his point, he pointed to the success of one prominent Wixarika professional who at that moment led the Union of Indigenous Students for Mexico, stating that he knew this young man to be using his ethnicity to advance his personal career.

The shock of this anthropologist's comments brought up a series of important questions dealing with the judgments and types of expectations that were being held for indigenous students: Is there a different moral standard being held for indigenous students? Are indigenous students supposed to be inherently communitarian and thus not seek personal benefits? Is it intrinsically wrong to use one's cultural heritage as a stepping stone for future endeavors, be they for personal or larger communal gain?

As Elizabeth Povinelli points out in her study on the limits to recognition of Aborigines in contemporary Australia, a particular burden of purity is placed on indigenous peoples that is not applied to other members of society, as the "law and public do not require all citizens to undergo the same type of public, corporeal cleansing, the same type of psychic and historical reformation" (2002, 29). Gradients of authenticity are excessively placed on indigenous bodies irrespective of the reality that identities are in a "constant process of construction and reconstruction[;] strategic versus authentic is simply not a relevant distinction" for engaging indigenous citizenship and identity (Speed 2008, 115). Months later, the very student leader the anthropologist was accusing of ethnic opportunism shared with me that he had only refound pride in his cultural background at the end of high school, when, after years of being ashamed of being Wixarika and hiding behind a mestizo identity, he decided to wear his community's traditional attire for his graduation. This young man recounted that his initial shame emerged when he left his community and family to study at a secundaria in Tepic, Nayarit. Peers shunned him for his accent and demeanor, and by the time he entered high school, he had discovered his ability to camouflage himself as a mestizo. Evidently, this type of painful personal battle with identity and belonging were not considered under the rigidity of some anthropologists' cultural paradigms.

The fact remains that the bulk of Mexico's understanding of indigenous cultures continues to emanate from the lens of the nonindigenous. Anthropologist Juan Castillo Cocom makes this poignantly clear by critiquing what he terms the creation of "the Maya" by archaeologists, anthropologists, linguists, and historians. He argues that the contemporary indigenous peoples who have been grouped together under the Maya ethnic category may often feel the need to "travel on a map that was already previously created for them" to obtain some form of political, economic, or cultural recognition (Castillo Cocom 2005, 138). To understand the standards that have been set for recognition, one inevitably must return to the archive as the long body of scholarly and governmental work that defines tradition and authenticity (Povinelli 2002, 230). Accordingly, the archive makes recognition contingent on internalizing and carefully performing on "the nation's and law's image of traditional cultural forms and national reconciliation and at the same time ghost this being for the nation so as not to have their desires for some economic certainty in their lives appear opportunistic" (8). Saidiya Hartman problematizes our reliance on the archive as a source of knowledge by pointing to it as a "death sentence, a tomb, a display of the violated body, an inventory of property" prepared by and for those who exercise power (2008, 2). Consequently, the archive becomes a poor receptacle for understanding the experiences of the oppressed outside the margins of power. Following this logic, a successful student leader and professional is judged as being opportunistic by overperforming his Indianness and attempting to be too authentic too late.

This careful line of recognition that indigenous peoples confront exceeds the problems posed by the judgment of cultural experts, for recognition carries material stakes that can have concrete effects on livelihoods, including claims to land, access to economic programs, political representation, and entry into schools. To meet these criteria, indigenous peoples must be clearly differentiable from their mestizo counterparts, usually through dress, language, and documents validating their tribal belonging. The indigenous must appear in "contrapuntal relation" to the mestizo subject; racial alterity must be obvious (Coronil 1996, 73). So what does a judge do when he or she receives a land claim from "indigenous people who dress, act, and sound like the suburban neighbors they are" (Povinelli 2002, 13)? What happens to aspiring students who have spent their life in the city and have no immediate connection to tribal leaders who can certify their membership? And what happens to those young people who grew up ashamed to look or sound different but have rediscovered that they are in fact proud of their culture? Is it fair to then critique them for ethnic opportunism? These questions illustrate how the narrow lens that binds recognition to authenticity too easily dismisses historical legacies of political economic inequality and sociocultural domination, including the under-representation of indigenous peoples in institutions of higher education.

These problems are distinctly linked to contemporary political shifts made toward defining nation-states as comprising multicultural or pluricultural societies. In Mexico, this shift came in 1992, when the constitution officially declared that Mexico is a pluricultural nation and that, as a result, its institutions must act accordingly by facilitating the full and equal participation of all citizens, no matter their language, dress, or skin color. In part, such shifts have emerged from a need to acknowledge past harms and legacies of discrimination that informally made citizenry conditional on acculturation to the dominant culture. Throughout the twentieth century, indigenista thought and policy was based precisely on the notion of assimilating indigenous peoples into mestizo society through the disciplining technologies of education, agrarian reform, and the market. From the 1980s through the present, the classical indigenista logic began to crumble, giving way to participatory models of development accompanied by multicultural neoliberalism, a term that some Mexican scholars have also coined neoindigenismo (Hernández Castillo, Paz, and Sierra 2004). According to Héctor Díaz Polanco, the multicultural model functions as an "immense machine of universal inclusion" that creates a "smooth space without wrinkles, where identities can slip in, articulate and circulate under conditions favorable to global capital" (2006, 137). The Wixarika people's hypervisibility on public and private stages over the past two to three decades demonstrates the malleability of race and ethnicity for the purposes of institutional and financial gain, as well as the ways in which the "politics of cultural recognition" are divorced from tangible structural or redistributive policies (Díaz Polanco 2006, 174; Negrín da Silva 2015).

Despite such shifts and the acknowledgment of pluriculturalism, racial attitudes and stereotypes remain engrained across the social and political spectrum. Online and social media cultures have created new platforms for the articulation of racial and ethnic celebration and disdain, often emulated through viewer and reader comments. For instance, YouTube videos for regional Wixarika musical bands are accompanied by transnational viewer debates over the music, always with relation to perspectives that hinge on the merit of indigeneity. One 2010 news article on a robbery along a country road, which made no indication of the ethnicity of the perpetrators, was followed by the following reader comment: "I don't know how it really ended, if they are Koras [sic] or Huicholes, but I know many of those guys from the Sierra are some lazy bastards, they really only want to spend their time in the shade waiting to be taken care of" (*Nayarit en Línea*, March 10, 2010). For the segment of the population that does not access the web, television programming also aids in the circulation of particular images of indigeneity. The 1997 soap opera *María Isabel* starred fair-skinned actress Adela Noriega as a "Huichol" maid in a wealthy Guadalajara household who has a love affair with her employer. The signifiers used for this character's authentic Indianness include her thick "Indian" accent, pigtails, and a combination of innocence and incompatibility with affluent urban Mexico. Her Huicholness is suggested through her supposedly authentic attire and occasional scenes of her father's home—an equally generic and incongruous setting that is somehow meant to look indigenous. Ironically, while the soap opera intends to send a moralizing message about discrimination in modern-day Mexico, the actress chosen to play María Isabel is neither Wixarika nor indigenous, and the signifiers used to make her "Indian" reproduce age-old racial stereotypes. Nonetheless, she is loved and accepted by viewers because of her (Caucasian) beauty, her simplicity, and her handsome white employer's ability to feel compassion and fall in love with her.[3]

The looming challenge presented here is the not-so-delicate balance between positive stereotypes of the indigenous—read as colorful folklore and dignified victimhood—and negative ones, ranging from ignorance and passivity to the threatening secessionist attitudes some identify with indigenous activism. Put crudely, the authenticity that the popular imagination awaits is relegated to images of a shaman or craftsman, or a mendicant leeching society. María Elena García's analysis on indigenous citizenship in Peru stresses how "cultural difference is not only made safe for the new democratic, multicultural state, it seems to be effortlessly absorbed by it," to the point of making determinations on how to "attract visible and 'authentic' indigenous peoples into the distant and isolated halls of governance" (2005, 166). On the other hand, scholars may still be making their judgments of authenticity contingent on the work of the archive, sizing up indigenous peoples by their degrees of engagement with what is perceived as traditional or as modern. As such, much work is still needed for society to effectively transcend the enduring racial stereotypes that mold our popular and academic imaginations through everyday forms of consumption, whether these are television programs, billboards, social media, or scientific studies. Considering these circumstances, it seems highly unfair to accuse a young indigenous leader of opportunistically seizing on his ethnicity to climb educational and professional ladders, particularly because he is responding to the existing limits set within Mexican society and to the doors that have been most recently opened under the multicultural shift.

> The very first time we [indigenous students] entered [the university], you could feel that boom because it is different for our peers, who are not accustomed to interacting with urbanized people—you have to adapt little by little. I did not have that problem. I was more involved [with nonindigenous students], but my [indigenous] peers often limited their friendships. For example, when work groups are made in a classroom, usually people get together with those who they know, and if you do not know anyone, you are left on the side and are not integrated, and you feel rejected or that you are seen as strange. If you respect them generally they respect you, but one time I was able to overhear in the classroom (because

they still didn't know I was indigenous), and two mestizos with who[m] I always hung out . . . left the room saying, "It is best that they [indigenous students] not get admitted. . . . They get everything: free Internet, services, classes." And when they came back into the classroom and saw me, they were quiet, and I thought that it must be because they knew that I was indigenous. (Octavio, interview by author, May 14, 2010)

STRATEGIES FOR RECOGNITION IN A MULTICULTURAL WORLD

> *Every time that I put on my traje or my bracelets, the first thing that strangers ask me is "how much does it cost?" They see my culture and they want to purchase it: "How much does it cost? How much does it cost?"*
> —JUAN AURELIO CARRILLO RÍOS, PANEL PRESENTATION, CONFERENCE FOR THE INTERNATIONAL ASSOCIATION OF INTER-AMERICAN STUDIES, UNIVERSITY OF GUADALAJARA, SEPTEMBER 23, 2012

The discursive shifts that have emanated from the Mexican state, academic circles, and popular society have done little to alter the often stagnant cultural and spatial expectations that continue to be held of indigenous peoples. This remains true despite the push for new types of legal and cultural recognitions brought on by the multicultural turn. After the CIESAS seminar, I decided to debrief with two Wixarika students, both of whom study at a private Jesuit university in Guadalajara and whom I will name Antonio and Rosa. I asked them what they thought of the idea that wearing Wixarika attire in a mestizo setting might bring about suspicions of ethnic opportunism. Antonio and Rosa are siblings who from an early age grew up in Guadalajara and, later, in the coastal resort town of Puerto Vallarta. Their father had moved the family to the city from their home in the community of San Andrés Cohamiata because of a job he was offered as an assistant to a linguist at the University of Guadalajara. Despite their parents speaking to them in Wixarika and their mother's deep connection to Wixarika traditions, Antonio and Rosa were drawn to mestizo customs and felt quite comfortable living between the two cultures, dismissing neither. Yet Antonio points out that his first couple of years as an undergraduate student awakened a new sense of pride and curiosity in his Wixarika heritage, eventually leading him to be more outspoken about his ethnicity and driving him to interact more readily with other Wixarika residents of Guadalajara. This type of self-affirmation transcends racial and geographic barriers and is likely a trait of early adulthood, when one becomes more conscious of personal identity and the political economic and cultural contexts that surround one's articulation of identity. In this way, we can understand the move toward ethnic visibility to be far more textured and not merely a strategy for receiving goods and services from a newly declared multicultural society purportedly seeking to undo past harms.

Antonio was careful to point out that this ethnic "coming out" is differentially interpreted and received by classmates and professors, becoming an illuminating moment of interracial relations where both positive and negative stereotypes are enunciated. Many Wixarika students speak of the immediate relation that their peers make between "Huichol culture" and the hallucinogenic peyote cactus or the beadwork that many Wixaritari make and sell. While these cultural references are not necessarily offensive and can be broached in a sincere manner, they can easily become objectifying and demeaning; this is especially true when a Wixarika student is then expected to perform on these referenced cultural markers. Because peyote and beaded crafts have become the hypervisible markers of Huicholness, the assumption then becomes that the students in question are also artisans or that they can speak on the experience of using peyote and even invite their peers to a "peyote ceremony." Returning to the words of Castillo Cocom, in these contexts, Wixarika students find themselves traveling "on a map that was already previously created for them," or, at the very least, negotiating with these preordained identities that they are supposed to embody (Castillo Cocom 2005, 138).

The epigraph to this section further illustrates how the objectification of the ethnic Other is intimately connected to the commoditization of indigenous culture, summoning what Diane Nelson calls the "fetish effect" of indigeneity (1999, 163). It is not uncommon for Wixaritari to be approached and asked whether they are willing to sell their clothes and jewelry, sometimes off their backs. In Juan Aurelio's case, strangers fail to consider the symbolic value that a bracelet made by a relative possesses. As struggles to defend Wixarika land, particularly the endemic territory of the peyote in Wirikuta, gain national and international traction, Wixaritari are increasingly targeted to pose for photographs and sell ethnic crafts.

Surely these moments are differentially interpellated and may or may not lead to formal contestation by the stereotyped. In fact, with so many people eager to pay their way to some state of nirvana, some Wixaritari have seized on the popular imaginary that is held of Huichol spiritual culture for personal economic gain, leading to intensifying internal debates surrounding the willingness by some to commodify spiritual practices for profit. In the past decade or so, the Wixarika word *mara'akame*, or shaman, has been appropriated for a couple of marketing schemes. The first is a state-run alcohol and substance abuse treatment program in Nayarit called Marakame, which uses the symbol of the *muwieri*, or healing wand, as its emblem. The second example, the Gran Maracame tequila brand, stands in ironic juxtaposition to the rehabilitation program in Nayarit. Gran Maracame claims to be rooted in Jalisco's indigenous traditions; each bottle comes with a beaded sash aimed to help solve "the troubled reality of many indigenous families in Mexico."[4] The product's website espouses the beauty of the isolationist and resistant Wixarika culture to the tune of tantric tabla drumming. Beyond Shaman Chocolates and Gran Maracame tequila are ample examples of public and private marketing endeavors that use some aspect or image of Wixarika culture, often through the guise of philanthropy (Negrín da Silva 2015). It should come as no surprise that many Wixaritari see economic opportunities in this overt public consumption of the multicultural that targets their visual and spiritual traditions.

In the political sphere, Castillo Cocom's essay "'It Was Simply Their Word': Yucatec Maya PRInces in YucaPAN and the Politics of Respect" argues that the legacy of indigenismo and its multicultural reformulation as neoindigenismo has allowed some individuals to use their Mayanness to climb the political ladders of the PRI and PAN (Castillo Cocom 2005). This becomes a two-way political game, in which the political party gains cultural points by having indigenous membership and backing, and the given indigenous candidate or partisan worker can gain cultural, economic, and political privileges. Likewise, some Wixarika professionals in the state of Nayarit have debated the ways in which political parties "fish" for Wixarika students at the state's autonomous university to offer them positions where they can act as intermediaries between their communities and the given political party. Occasionally this may include having the designated student recruit other indigenous students to rally for and endorse a particular political candidate. These newly hired party representatives undoubtedly have the right to take pride in their duties and may see no problem in employing their ethnic heritage as an instrument for economic and political mobility. Playing on the convergence of established stereotypes and the nation's pluricultural status can work in myriad ways, as leftist activist organizations that champion indigenous causes often hold imaginaries of indigeneity similar to those of their conservative counterparts. Gayatri Chakravorty Spivak describes this position in the context of progressive academic tendencies in the Global North: "The current mood, in the radical fringe of humanistic Northern pedagogy, of uncritical enthusiasm for the Third World, makes a demand upon the inhabitant of that Third World to speak up as an authentic ethnic fully representative of his or her tradition" (Spivak 1999, 60).

On the other hand, some Wixarika students express outright rejection of the notion of performing "authenticity" for a mestizo public. Tutupika is a UAN graduate and currently teaches statistics and language courses for master's students at the university. As someone who for several years has been involved in Wixarika student and professional organizations, Tutupika is weary of the fine line that he must walk as a Wixarika professional living in Tepic. To this end, he is adamant about determining when and where he is willing to distinguish himself as Wixarika. For instance, he was offended when coworkers asked him to use Wixarika attire for the faculty group photograph despite his daily use of "mestizo" clothing. For Tutupika, this request was a clear indication of his colleagues tokenizing him as a "diversity hire." Conversely, one specific university professor has repeatedly questioned his presence in faculty and staff-only rooms, indicating disdainful surprise when he reiterates his legitimate belonging to these spaces. Yet while Tutupika may be seen as completely mestizoized by some, lacking sufficient pride to dress up for the cameras, he is deeply engaged with the Wixarika communities in Tepic and in the sierra. What is important for Tutupika is that these moments of cultural affirmation be set on his own terms.

Intentionally or not, the present multicultural climate has led to numerous, often contradictory, responses across the social and political spectrum. The multicultural turn regarding indigenous peoples has largely exposed what Philip Deloria terms the "paradox of racial thinking," made evident in the ways in which the desires of some individuals to shield the Indian from modernity are trumped by others who see the Indian's only path to be that of total assimilation. As Deloria points out,

> Such cultural expectations and social relations exist in dialogue with economic, political, and legal structures. The same unarticulated expectations that surround

the war chant (not honor and courage, let's admit, but Indian violence, transmuted to sports) help explain the seeming naturalness of Indian poverty and the active hostility to the very idea of Indian wealth and modernity. They help explain the indignant opposition to indigenous people's efforts to move from the political margins by contributing to political campaigns or the efforts to roll back the legal rights embedded in treaties, including those to hunt and fish. Expectations, in short, exist in relation to concrete actions. (2004, 225)

While this paradoxical contrast of nonindigenous expectations of the indigenous is nothing new, the growth of rural to urban migrations and networks, coupled with the increasing centrality of Internet-based technologies, has made such expectations ever more inconsistent. García argues that the current IT landscape, coupled with redefinitions of indigenous identities has provided some indigenous professionals and intellectuals with more visible social and political roles (M. E. García 2005, 143). Despite changes on the national discursive level, policy continues to deprioritize indigenous rights, as evidenced by Jalisco's congressional failure in 2015 and 2016 to get enough votes to modify the state's indigenous law, thereby converting indigenous citizens from "subjects of public interest" to "subjects of law" (like all other citizens). As such, racialized imaginaries continue to be more than mere rhetorical enunciations and have direct implications for indigenous rights. These expectations illuminate the profoundly static social and political economic borders that continue to be erected irrespective of individual and collective transformations, such as a growing and active heterogeneous indigenous population in Mexico's urban centers.

Perhaps this heterogeneity is what is so difficult for Mexican society to grasp. From a young age we are taught to admire the Aztec Empire as the foundation of our national pride, yet we are simultaneously bombarded by the tropes of indigenous rusticity and poverty. Most significantly, we are taught that indigenous peoples' cultural, economic, and political barriers are so dire that they can only surmount them through our helpful mestizo hands. When the Zapatistas erupted on the political scene in the 1990s, mestizos (with the clear exception of Subcomandante Marcos) were not the protagonists and were not the movers and shakers of the movement. While a large segment of the Mexican population sympathized and even appropriated Zapatista imagery, a perhaps equal portion of society read the uprising and ensuing mobilizations as proof of indigenous peoples' inability to adapt to normative citizenship. Specifically, many were troubled at the Zapatista demand that indigenous peoples be recognized as equal citizens of the nation while also being granted rights to sustain political, economic, and cultural autonomy. The notion that a people desire to be respected as equal while being given the space to affirm their difference is too perplexing within the context of deeply engrained liberal binaries that structure society.

Anthropologist Charles R. Hale tackles these questions surrounding ethnic and cultural alterity within the context of multicultural neoliberalism, understood as the tense interplay between postassimilationist celebrations of diversity and the social, political, and economic impacts of the free market on these celebrated cultures. Hale explores the racial ambivalence of ladinos (mestizos) in the face of Maya ascendancy in post–civil war Guatemala and finds that while ladinos claim to embrace antiracism and multiculturalism, they maintain long-held racist views of indigenous peoples and a desire to preserve their racial privileges by arguing that academic, governmental, and nongovernmental institutions favor all that which concerns indigenous peoples and funnel countless resources to indigenous peoples that ladinos do not have the opportunity of obtaining. Hale's exploration of racial ambivalence thus refers to the "political sensibilities that encompass both the support for the principle of cultural equality and deep commitments to the social conditions that preserve ladinos' material and ideological advantage. By extension, the term applies to those who express solidarity with Indians, but as innocent victims rather than protagonists, as acts of benevolence deployed from a higher rung in the social hierarchy" (2006, 108). In a similar vein, Diane Nelson notes that the articulation of Mayan identity in Guatemala partly emerges from the "hostile markings" of colonial and postcolonial experiences that ambivalently mark the indigenous body as both attractive and repulsive (1999, 129).

The concepts of racial ambivalence can help us understand why so many claim compassion and respect for indigenous peoples while finding it difficult to come to terms with the idea that they can hold similar occupational positions as mestizos. In this light, the previously cited anthropologist's critique of ethnic opportunism fails to consider the competing expectations that an indigenous student must negotiate within a multicultural society: failure to be "authentically Huichol" likely will close doors of opportunity, while too much pride in ethnic heritage invokes suspicion.

> I have been in Guadalajara since August 28, 2000. On September 2 of that same year, I entered a high school affiliated with the University of Guadalajara, but I could not finish the [final] year for lack of economic resources. I lost a semester

because I had to work, and then I returned for the last semester.... In high school nobody knew that I was indigenous ... nobody even imagined it, only an English teacher knew.... At my university nobody knows [that I am indigenous], much less at my work because at my previous job, they knew that I was indigenous, and for that reason they took advantage of me: I was not insured; I worked from 7:00 am until 5:00 in the afternoon; and I was fired without severance pay. For this reason I try to avoid these types of situations. I don't do it out of shame but rather because I am reserved about certain issues.

I tell this because it is what has maintained me firm without forgetting my customs, traditions, dress, language. This is why I have directed my current interest toward advocating for higher education among indigenous migrants in the city, not just for Wixaritari ... but without forgetting our cultures and traditions. After learning of the challenges that I have confronted and the experiences I have gained, ... I am conscious of the inequity that affects indigenous populations because racism in Mexico is a problem that exists due to the lack of dissemination that informs the public about diversity and about relations between mestizos and the indigenous. (Tacho, Wixarika student and worker residing in Guadalajara, interview by author, January 25, 2010)

AWAKENINGS TO THE URBAN HUSTLE

We need to buy books, we need to buy poster board, school materials and the organization's materials. We need to go and be connected with the [Wixarika] communities, go to the assemblies.... If we wanted computers, we needed to petition the ITESO and move things as we could. You had to find solutions by any means possible, but in reality, you needed to dedicate time to the organization. I studied all the time, I worked all the time and I dedicated myself to the organization. These were three loads for me to carry.
—SANTOS DE LA CRUZ CARRILLO, INTERVIEW BY THE AUTHOR, JUNE 4, 2010, SPEAKING ABOUT HIS EXPERIENCE AS A LAW STUDENT AT THE ITESO AND THE ORGANIZATIONAL WEIGHT NEEDED TO MAINTAIN THE UNION OF YOUNG WIXARIKA STUDENTS

Guadalajara's Jesuit university, ITESO, has set itself apart from other private institutions of higher education in Guadalajara by holding a track record of welcoming a small number of indigenous university students—twelve total for academic year 2013–14 (Mendoza, García, and García 2013, 25). While the numbers are small, the initiatives to become a more accessible and inclusive educational space have been propelled by the hard work of the indigenous university students themselves. The Union of Young Wixárika Students (Unión de Jóvenes Estudiantes Wixaritari, UJEW) was a short-lived organization supported by the chancellor's office as a way to assist Wixárika students' entrance to the university and receive financial support while giving something back to their home communities. UJEW's slogan was "For the development of the Wixárika people," whereby each student carved a distinct utilitarian professional path in their communities: law, accounting, architecture, engineering. From its foundation in 2000 until its eventual dissolution in 2005, members of UJEW split their time between school, work, and the duties required to maintain their organization. This included selling Wixárika beadwork to help pay for school materials. By no means were these duties easy to juggle, as Santos notes in this section's epigraph. Wixárika students did not have the privilege of focusing on any one aspect of their new student lives. While some had spent significant time living in Guadalajara prior to their entry into ITESO, others were recent city residents and had little to no financial or social support network, making them particularly vulnerable when any one of their occupations faltered. More importantly, balancing these various responsibilities was a high-stakes situation, as failure at school, work, or in the organization would likely mean an end to their path toward a degree. In other words, these responsibilities were mutually contingent: not meeting academic requirements meant losing scholarships and university privileges, while failure at their respective off-campus jobs would lead to their inability to pay for housing, food, and transportation needs.

Former member of the UJEW Pascual notes that the organization dissolved from a combination of factors, not least of which was its membership's struggle to balance their duties as students, workers, and organizers (Pascual, interview by author, February 5, 2010). As much as the students attempted to act as a unified group, some succeeded more than others, and eventually, Santos notes, ITESO shifted its commitment from supporting the group as a whole to supporting the individual students who held continued academic promise (Santos de la Cruz Carrillo, interview by author, June 24, 2010). Additionally, UJEW's membership lacked experience administering an organization and could not consistently count on the university's staff to orient and monitor their activities. UJEW's brief trajectory illustrates the hustle that many Wixarika students face, particularly those who are newcomers to the city and who feel an obligation to their families and home communities. Although only three of the five initial members finished their bachelor's degrees, UJEW brought together a small but crucial community for this group of Wixarika students, all of whom have since become involved in coordinating educational, legal, and economic initiatives in their home communities.

ITESO professor Rocío de Aguinaga recalls how UJEW emerged from the clear need for the university to support the admission and retention of indigenous students (Rocío de Aguinaga, interview by author, May 31, 2010). Beyond basic economic needs, prospective Wixarika students, particularly those coming from rural schools, faced the uphill battle of passing the entrance exam. As a result of this reality, a few devoted professors with previous experience working in Wixarika communities helped prepare a handful of Wixaritari for the entry exam. De Aguinaga recalls how these prospective students worked day and night to bring themselves up to par with their mestizo competitors, most of whom spent their lives attending private schools in Guadalajara. Nonetheless, those who passed the admissions exams continued to face the educational inequities of the Mexico they grew up in: "It was difficult because they still held a low academic preparation. One thing is that dear Juan is a brilliant young man, but like Carlos, he still failed classes. Very brilliant young people, but they had to work very hard, and it was difficult for them, psychologically, socially; these were important efforts on their part" (de Aguinaga interview). As de Aguinaga points out, the steep academic climb that UJEW's students faced was only one of several factors that brought anxiety to Wixarika students, as social, cultural, and economic differences shrouded much of their experiences on campus.

Whether they attend public or private universities, one of the repeated stories that I hear from Wixarika students relates to their difficulty making ends meet away from their families and in the city. Particularly in the urban sprawl of Guadalajara, students often have to choose between being able to buy lunch or take public transport between their home, work, and school.[5] At a private institution like ITESO, differences of economic and social capital are especially sharp. Located off the peripheral highway of Guadalajara, many ITESO students commute to school by car, are financially supported by their parents, and, as a result, do not need to hold a job. Santos recalls how his mestizo peers often had long gaps between classes that they used to socialize, return to their homes for lunch, or nap. He, on the other hand, had to take classes back to back, between work, or use a gap in his schedule to go to the library, where he could study from the books he could not afford to purchase. For Santos, his experience at ITESO underlined the differences between Wixarika and Western ways of being:

> There I learned what the Western and Wixarika cultures are. They are totally different cultures; it is an impact to go from one culture to the other. [In Wixarika territory] we fight for collective interests, and here it is about individual rights, from the first day of classes. [Mestizo students] never invited me [to hang out] on the weekends, only from Monday to Friday, because on the weekends they went to [Puerto] Vallarta, to Mazatlán, to Acapulco, and they would come back really tan, and they would ask you, "And what did you do?" And in the summertime, they would go to the United States, Europe, Germany, Venice, all of those places. "And you?" "Me? I was in the sierra working." Many times conversations were about "What did you do?" I tell you it is another world, but even so I struck up a good dialogue. I was never hard on them. (de la Cruz interview)

Undoubtedly, Santos's experience at ITESO offered him valuable insight into the race and class dynamics that permeate social relations in Guadalajara.

With the advent of intercultural middle and high schools established in Wixarika communities in the mid-1990s, a new generation of Wixarika students has arrived in the city without having attended schools with non-Wixaritari, as had previously often been the case.[6] Anita, a business administration student, recalls her initial month at ITESO: "Upon the start of the school year, the days were very difficult. I had never had classes with mestizos. I was very nervous. I thought I would fail the courses; I did not understand the classes; I missed my community; and I was alone. . . . At the beginning I did not know how the mestizo professors taught and evaluated or graded [student work]. With time I made the effort to analyze what expectations they held of me" (Anita, interview by author, June 22, 2010). One of the starkest contrasts that Anita faced was that her motivation for studying business administration deviated from that of her peers, who already had access to family businesses and were mainly interested in "making money." Conversely, she wanted to obtain the tools to return to her home community and work in administering community development funds that were historically poorly managed by mestizo outsiders or ill-equipped Wixaritari. Anita knew that her transition to Guadalajara would be more difficult than to a smaller city like Tepic, which has a strong network of Wixarika students. But this challenge was precisely what motivated her to move away from her community, into a stranger's house, and study among the elite of Guadalajara. After graduation, Anita spent two years working in accounting for the CIESAS research institute and is now working for the state's Secretary of Culture developing a peyote conservation project for Wixarika communities, bridging traditional and scientific methods too slow the sacred plant's rapid decline.

But not all Wixarika students are new urban migrants, and the distinction between newly arrived Wixarika university students and their urbanized counterparts can be significant in their ability to perform in the classroom or in the urban workplace. This distinction also holds in each person's relationship with Wixarika culture and his or her ability to meet expectations for proper "Huicholness." This is especially the case in Tepic, where several Wixarika students have spent the bulk of their lives living outside the sierra communities.

Sandra comes from an educated upwardly mobile family. Both of her parents were career teachers, and in 2010 her father became the first Wixarika congressional state representative serving Nayarit. Sandra's older brother Arturo studied law at UAN, spent two years working as the first Wixarika-Spanish bilingual public defender in the state of Jalisco, and has since held similar positions in other neighboring states. This family not only has broken several educational barriers in Mexico, but has also challenged stereotypes through their middle-class lifestyle, which has allowed them to travel domestically and make consumer purchases that most Wixaritari could only dream of. Sandra simultaneously studied two degrees—one at the UAN in communications and the other at the Pedagogical University of Nayarit (Universidad Pedagógica de Nayarit), in education sciences, where more than 95 percent of the student body is indigenous (Juan Aurelio Carrillo Ríos, personal communication, November 30, 2018). After her undergraduate studies, she completed a master's degree in pedagogical technologies at the University of Guadalajara to pursue her interest in designing literacy software for use in the rural indigenous classrooms where she has since worked (Sandra, interview by author, July 4, 2010). Despite Sandra's unique familial and educational background, she has faced repeated discrimination for being indigenous; more so, she states, than for being a woman. She was particularly taken aback when she petitioned to wear her Wixarika traje for her graduation from UAN and was met by the explicit opposition of her classmates, even when her professors supported her request.[7] Despite moments of discrimination, Sandra is optimistic about the paths that so many young Wixaritari are taking in higher education and notes that young Wixarika women who migrate to the city face more "opportunities and security" today than they did a generation ago, when they often were pulled into "centers of vice" (Sandra interview).

Contrary to state and popular imaginaries, the stories that Wixarika students and graduates shared with me undoubtedly point to the dynamic heterogeneity of this demographic. While some were born in the city, others arrived at an early age alongside their families, and yet another segment of the population moved to Tepic or Guadalajara as young university students embarking on their new lives. Although slight differences in class, culture, and regional geography differentiate these young Wixaritari, there is a tendency for them to unite under the umbrella of shared ethnic identity and the positive and negative experiences that this brings them as individuals and as a collective. Efforts toward forging a better future and the shared experience of ongoing discrimination are the impetus behind the numerous Wixarika organizations that have been established in recent years in both Tepic and Guadalajara. The following section discusses how some students became involved in claiming their rights to be active participants on their campus and in the city, and how the practice of activism can reconstitute notions of racial and spatial belonging in post-multicultural Mexico.

> The city is really big, and I am always looking for Wixas, but I don't always find them because there are not many spaces where Wixas get together.[8] I have heard that on Sundays they get together at a certain place to play soccer, but I don't know where. Downtown you can find Wixas but only older ones, but I still always go to talk with them or at least see them because it motivates me to continue doing what I am doing. I know that many live here in the city, but I have not been able to find out where. Some say that there are many in Tesistán [at the northern edge of the metro region], but I don't know how to get there. Also many from the sierra stay in the Casa Huichol [a boarding house for Wixaritari], but I have not gone there yet.
>
> A little while back I began attending the meetings of artisans (craftsmen and women) and I met more Wixas, even though many of them are very different from me, to the point that I feel as if I am not with Wixas, because they have spent a long time living here, and they think differently from those in the [sierra]. I would like to meet more young people who are just arriving to the city, especially if they

are students; that way I can accompany them and help them not feel as lonely. (Anita interview)

CLAIMING SPACE AND IDENTITY THROUGH ACTIVISM

The entrenched racial imaginary refashioned under new political economic models be they indigenista, neoindigenista, assimilationist, or pluricultural have been readily engaged by indigenous peoples. This holds true with the most recent national political shift toward the Left, led by Andrés Manuel López Obrador and MORENA (Movimiento Regeneración Nacional, or National Regeneration Party, whose acronym denotes brown complexion). As discussed in the previous sections, these engagements are manifold, ranging from those who find opportunity in these models to those who remain neutral and those who are ignited to speak and mobilize against what they believe to be the continuation of dispossessing policies. Through the creation of distinct organizations, many Wixarika university students and professionals are gradually finding ways to make interventions within their rural and urban communities, often times drawing links between spaces that are understood as antagonistic. Remember that Wixarika engagement with mestizo spaces and customs is not a new occurrence. The conception that Wixarika communities have been resistant to outside impositions, from the precolonial period to the present market system, has often led government officials and citizens to see Wixaritari as a static people, while in fact they have long engaged and negotiated with peoples and systems outside their communal territories. One need only consider the sacred territories that span multiple states in northwestern Mexico to understand that mobility and engagement with the so-called outside world is integral to Wixarika social history; once again, the term *makuyeika*, "he or she who walks in many places," is reflective of the nonmonolithic pathways toward relations with other geographies and peoples.

Historical patterns of mobility have increasingly become conjoined with more recent temporary and permanent migrations that stem from structural changes in Mexico's economic system, particularly since the 1970s. As discussed in chapter 2, the 1970s ushered in a combination of state development projects (e.g., Plan Huicot and the Aguamilpa Dam) and private market interventions that sent many community members to seek work in neighboring towns, cities, and coastal tobacco plantations (Díaz Romo 1994; Talavera Durón 2003;

Negrín da Silva 2004). Some of the current generation of Wixarika students and professionals are a product of these migrations, including children whose families worked in Nayarit's plantations and those whose parents became part of the government's rural teaching programs, which often shuffled indigenous teachers to different regional communities. As a result, the current generation of Wixarika youth attending Tepic's and Guadalajara's universities has been raised to coexist between multiple spaces and identities.

While Mexico's racial geography continues to place indigenous peoples in fixed locations and read their existence outside these spaces as a form of deterritorialization, scholars have also pushed for a more critical conception of the relation between identity and place, stressing that these movements are creating a reterritorialization of culture and belonging (Ferguson and Gupta 1997; Greene 2007; Castellanos 2010). According to James Ferguson and Akhil Gupta's influential text on the matter, "reterritorialized space . . . forces us to reconceptualize fundamentally the politics of community, solidarity, identity, and cultural difference" (1997, 37). In this sense, while deterritorialization connotes displacement and implies a final point of loss and eternal liminality, reterritorialization considers the ways in which peoples construct new places and networks that, among other things, have the potential to invoke their heritage while affirming their belonging to a larger national body. Additionally, the concept of reterritorialization allows for a more dynamic understanding of migration, urban struggles for recognition, and indigenous peoples engagements with "the modern." As M. Bianet Castellanos indicates in her study on Maya migration from the town of Kuchmil to Cancún, contrary to the popular and governmental imagination, "indigenous peoples have always been central to Mexico's efforts to become modern" (2010, 178). So while President Felipe Calderón Hinojosa (2006–12) dressed in Wixarika attire and declared that the indigenous group's state of unmoving poverty and lack of access to the modern world would be resolved through *his* new social initiatives, hundreds of Wixarika youth are carving out paths, often independently from state-orchestrated initiatives.

Reterritorializations of culture and belonging undoubtedly summon reformulations around identity as equally fluid and changing. In "Maya Scenarios: Indian Stories in and out of Contexts," Castillo Cocom weaves together a series of meditations on the multiple identities that one must carry in present-day Mexico, from the vantage point of an indigenous scholar who is conscious of the judgment he receives from whites and mestizos as well as from the friends and family he grew up with in his hometown of Xocenpich, Yucatán (Castillo

Cocom 2007). Castillo Cocom exposes the "inconstancy of Maya cultures and identities in their construction," stressing that identity is contingent on given social situations, social landscapes, and social contexts that frame the ways in which a person self-identifies and the ways in which others identify that person (13). As Stuart Hall has eloquently pointed out, identity is "lodged in contingency"; it is the work of suturing together, "binding and marking symbolic boundaries," which produce "frontier effects" of difference (Hall and du Gay 1996, 3). In this light, identity is not essential but strategic and positional, fragmented and multiplying across the difference of discourses, practices, and positions. Hall thus prompts us to understand the process of identity formation as one that is very much steeped in the politics of power and representation, which summon actions of performativity, negotiation, resistance, and accommodation (4).

We must not forget that on a personal level, identity can be quite painful. The desire to be recognized as belonging to particular spaces and the sense of liminality that this longing for recognition can create is wrought by the need to perform, negotiate, resist, or accommodate. Castillo Cocom makes this especially clear when speaking about the position he holds in his home community: "When I am reminded of what my real 'status' in Xocenpich is, I get upset and I do not know what to think. But one thing is for sure: it hurts—identity, sometimes, hurts. Many Xocenpicheños reject me, not as a person, but as a Xocenpicheño. I think that is ridiculous because I grew up there, I grew up with them: I speak the same languages, they were my friends, and still they are my friends" (Castillo Cocom 2007, 27). Upon returning to their home communities, many Wixarika students and professionals share this same sense of distance and alienation. Martín is a recent graduate from a career college affiliated with the University of Guadalajara. Despite having spent nine years studying in Guadalajara, he returned to his ranch in the sierra every summer and is looking at possibilities for applying his accounting degree in his community. Nonetheless, he has a difficult time reconnecting and feeling accepted by his old friends who remained in the sierra. Martín believes that his alienation is a result of people feeling like he has a sense of superiority over them because of his advanced degree. At the same time, Martín feels a level of embarrassment because he no longer is literate in communal affairs and happenings. In this way, he feels equally displaced in Guadalajara as he does in his home of Tuapurie. Martín hopes that he can regain a sense of belonging in the sierra through the formation of a nonprofit that will manage the material needs of the local autonomous high school, created by another Guadalajara-educated peer, yet in 2018 he remained underemployed in Guadalajara (Martín, interview by author, November 6, 2009). Examples such as these can help inform conceptualizations of identity as related to the habitation of multiple spaces, illustrating the difficult and often painful coexistence between fluidity and fixity.

Antonio Hayuaneme García is a formidable example of how some youth have reterritorialized their identities through the practice of using resources based in the city to conduct service work in sierra communities. When Hayuaneme was in the process of finishing his high school education in Puerto Vallarta, his mother took the family back to Guadalajara, where the children had spent most of their lives. Once in Guadalajara, Hayuaneme had a chance meeting with the director of the "intercultural" secundaria school, Tatutsí Maxakuaxí, located in the Wixarika locality of San Miguel Huaixtita, near his family's home in San Andrés Cohamiata. The director offered Hayuaneme an opportunity to work on an administrative project for the school that was being managed by ITESO. After spending a year and a half working at Tatutsí Maxakuaxí through ITESO, Hayuaneme applied and was accepted to this university, where he began studying industrial engineering before switching to political science. For several years economic and personal challenges extended his years of study while he continued to work intermittently on educational programming at the secundaria in San Miguel Huaixtita, allowing him to actively engage with local matters in this area of the sierra while helping him consolidate the connection he long wished to have with Wixarika youth and elders in traditional communal territory.

For some time, Hayuaneme and other fellow Wixarika students from ITESO participated as active members and coordinators of ITESO's Universidad Solidaria (US), discussed in chapter 4. Their first campus event in February 2010 celebrated the International Day of Mother Tongues and showcased the wealth of indigenous languages through brief lessons in Wixarika, Mixtec, Ch'ol, and Tzeltal, as well as a forum on the importance of preserving these languages, especially for those indigenous peoples who live in cities and do not have access to bilingual and bicultural education. The event also invited mestizos to learn an indigenous language as a way to better understand the richness and complexities of Mexico's indigenous culture.

Outside the university, Hayuaneme, his sister Rosa, and Anita connected with Wixarika artisans and members of Wixaritari, Artistas y Artesanos Unidos en la Zona Metropolitana de Guadalajara (WAAU). While Hayuaneme

FIGURE 11 Mixtec, Wixarika, and Tzeltal students at the International Day of Mother Tongues, ITESO, Guadalajara, February 2010. Photo by author.

and others had been actively involved in US, the chance to work with a diverse multigenerational group of Wixarika residents in Guadalajara offered them a new perspective on the challenges that indigenous peoples face in the city—a large group of artisans who have been increasingly prohibited from selling their work in public spaces. Through WAAU, Hayuaneme was pushed to think more critically about how he and fellow Wixarika university students and future professionals could help push for indigenous peoples' rights to the city while drawing closer ties with the struggles their fellow Wixaritari face in the traditional territories of the sierra.

Hayuaneme recalls his initial interventions at the WAAU meetings as transformative experiences for him and the larger group:

> One time I had a stronger participation when [members of WAAU] were criticizing mestizo agencies that have treated them poorly. That is where I was able to contribute a little, no? Basically it happened that I drew the globe on the blackboard, and I began to explain about the Spaniards, very generally, but it gave them a panorama of why; not just that the mestizos are bad and that things are bad for us, but that this is the fruit of many things that we have not known about, and it

helped give a view of the circumstances that they currently experience. It is as if we visualized many things that had not yet been considered, so [the meeting] lasted many hours, from nine in the morning until five in the afternoon. And that is where I discovered how the experience of coordinating Universidad Solidaria had given me tools through which I could coordinate this other assembly as well. . . .

A lot of reflections were made about one's identity. At first they only wanted to search for a space to sell as Wixaritari and as artisans, a place to sell, to make ends meet, no? And then we began to discover all the cultural questions, and the following meetings were very rich because we began to ask ourselves what it means to be Wixarika, what is Wixarika culture, what is the actual landscape for artisans, and why are they artists of culture? (Hayuaneme García interview)

For Hayuaneme, the WAAU assemblies provided him with the opportunity to showcase his knowledge as a Wixarika trained in the modern education system. His knowledge of world history and specialization in political science gave him the tools through which he could critically discuss the web of power and subjectivity in contemporary Mexico—the same web that perpetuates the hierarchies Wixarika artisans experience in Guadalajara. After his activities in WAAU, Hayuaneme took an active role in the JIU (Jóvenes Indígenas Universitarios, or Young Indigenous University Students) project, conducting quantitative and qualitative research on indigenous university students in the ZMG. He also held a multiyear cargo for the Tateikié community, serving as an *agente* for the community's urban population through fundraising for sierra projects and cultural events in the city. In 2017, Hayuaneme and a Nahua professional from JIU were hired to work for Jalisco's public defense entity, leading workshops on indigenous rights and culture for staff, police forces, and the interested public. In this capacity, Hayuaneme has also acted as a bilingual interpreter for Wixarika defendants.

When asked about his career objectives, Juan Aurelio Carrillo Ríos answers using the standard warm professionalism that has propelled him into leadership positions at UAN:

[I] have always proposed to myself . . . to go to a community and speak with [the people] and present my achievements and bring something of what I have earned. And that is what I have proposed to myself because indigenous education is very deteriorated; it has many holes in the sense that projects appear and money arrives but is lost because there is no follow through. It is full of holes that need to be first and foremost sutured well in order for those things that are built to remain with the people. And now that I am finishing my degree, I want to support indigenous communities. (Juan Aurelio Carrillo Ríos, interview by author, December 19, 2009)

Juan Aurelio's ideal of applying his education to work for indigenous communities is rooted in his mother's career as a rural teacher and fed by several years of work with UAN's indigenous student body. When he was appointed the new coordinator for Indigenous Issues (Asuntos Indígenas, later renamed Gestión Estudiantil Indígena, and currently Interculturalidad) through UAN's student union, Juan Aurelio was driven not only to deal with the academic and financial struggles of indigenous students at the university but also to travel to rural communities to promote higher education. As coordinator of Asuntos Indígenas, Juan Aurelio has worked with the university's administration to facilitate the continued entry and retention of indigenous students. Within the last ten years, the number of indigenous students at UAN has increased from a few dozen in the 1990s to close to 300 in 2009, out of a total population of 12,760 (Universidad Autónoma de Nayarit 2011).[9]

But what does it mean to support indigenous communities, and how different are the interventions proposed by these young professionals from those made by mestizos? Over the years UAN has housed several Wixarika student activists who individually and collectively dream of ways to use their skills for the economic, political, and social advancement of Wixarika and other indigenous communities. Among these efforts, student-led organizations have attempted to gain and reuse public spaces through the use of multiple mediums, including the Internet, radio, academic conferences, and cultural festivals. At the Fifth Annual Meeting of Indigenous Youth, held on October 25, 2009, Arturo, who served as president of the Union of Indigenous Professionals of Nayarit (Unión de Profesionistas Indígenas de Nayarit, UPIN), summarized this issue as follows:

> Where does the idea that we are youth, we are students and we want to do something originate from? Or for example, the fact that we emigrate from our communities and need to be in the city . . . get a degree in order to be able to say that we want to do something. But above this, the dilemma of what to do when I belong to an indigenous community? When I say, "Okay, I am from an indigenous community and what is it that I need to return?" Or "What will my role be as someone who is educated, who is a student, who is a professional? What is it

that *I* am going to do?" And that is how our idea was born, from this question of what needs to be done.

In the past several years, students and graduates of UAN have carried out these goals by initiating projects ranging from attempts to restore the traditional Wixarika justice system in Nayarit to workshops that address violence against women and alcoholism, and the development of school curricula that is culturally, linguistically, and geographically relevant for rural Wixarika communities. These activities have taken many of Tepic's Wixarika students to different states and countries to participate in cultural exchanges, conferences, and sporting tournaments. Through these efforts, spaces previously experienced as ones of loneliness and suffering are increasingly becoming spaces of opportunity and self-expression (Bonilla et al. 2017).

Temari Waniuki (The voice of the youth), a radio program initiated by several Wixarika students at UAN, is an example of the space these students and professionals have gained by consolidating their projects. Tukarima, a law graduate from UAN, explained how in 2001 Nayarit's 1530 AM radio station, Radio Aztlán, gave *Temari Waniuki* five minutes a week to broadcast to Nayarit's indigenous communities on the coast and in the sierra from their position as indigenous university students.[10] Soon enough, the students successfully petitioned for thirty minutes of air time a week and currently have received one hour of air time every Saturday. A daily hour-long morning broadcast by *Temari Waniuki* could also be heard on a popular Wixarika-run website Indigenous Peoples, www.puebloindigena.com, later reconfigured as www.wixarika.mx. On Sunday mornings, members of UPIN host a separate radio show on Radio Aztlán called *Voces Indígenas* (Indigenous voices). The goal, according to Tukarima, is to eventually have an independent indigenous radio station for Nayarit.

The activities of these organizations also speak out against the ongoing racial hierarchies reproduced through acceptable everyday speech, aesthetics, and political economic decision making that equate indigeneity with poverty, ignorance, and underdevelopment. Wixarika students and professionals repeatedly are met with surprise from mestizos and whites who hold on to notions of indigenous peoples as inherently pastoral and illiterate. In this light, Juan Aurelio believes that indigenous peoples cannot wait for Mexican society to transform its racial imaginary: only through indigenous self-representation and cultural exchange can these stereotypes be broken (Carrillo Ríos interview). Displays of cuisine, dance, storytelling, and artisanal goods are some of the activities that set out to educate the general public about the diversity of the country's indigenous peoples. While these organizations host friendly programs based on cultural exchange, they remain vocal about the injustices they live by organizing demonstrations, letter-writing campaigns, and forums. These political manifestations help advance public knowledge of territorial encroachments, unwanted development, and racist media portrayals that affect indigenous peoples. Within the educational system, Fragoso and Domínguez argue against the deracialized, or colorblind, curricula, emphasizing the need for antiracist work to continually accompany indigenous space making (2018, 26), this includes direct conversations on the history of racism in Mexican society and how it is perpetuated across scales that include individual acts of discrimination and large-scale dispossession, such as the threat of mining in Wirikuta.

This sketch of Wixarika youth organizations in Tepic and Guadalajara illustrates the efforts that are being made on multiple scales to address the challenges and opportunities that new generations of Wixaritari are facing in Mexico's cities and in their traditional territories. Like UJEW, a handful of urban Wixarika organizations have dissolved within a couple of years of their formation. The inability to consolidate organizational projects is largely attributed to the discursive and practical divisions that emerge among the membership. For instance, WAAU faced a significant internal divide in 2012 between those who wanted to strictly focus on the vending rights of artisans and those who sought a larger sociopolitical platform regarding indigenous rights. Sharper divisions among Wixarika activists have surfaced amid the ongoing defense of Wixarika sacred lands in Nayarit and Wirikuta. Despite these organizational bumps along the road, Wixarika students and professionals continue to be idealistic about what the future holds as their population grows and diversifies its interests. If anything, movements such as these may well be the answer for carving out new forms of ethnic recognition that affirm the equality of all citizens while permitting cultural, economic, and political autonomies that are vital for indigenous peoples in Mexico and elsewhere.

STUDENT 1: I am a critic of my own religion, of my own ethnic group. Why do I say this? I am Huichol, since I have been studying, since elementary school I said I would study a degree, and I had this objective. My objective was not to help out the people, no. My objective is to fill my pockets; that is my objective. And here where are we going? To the person who defends their community? No! It is to fill our pockets. That is how things are. That is how life is. Religion and culture are like that. As indigenous people they offer us an [outside] religion—and this I say because I am a critic of my community, of my people—outsiders arrive and they tell you they are offering you this, this, and that, and they leave food. What we want is to fill our stomachs, fill our hands and our pockets.

STUDENT 2: Well, it is not so much for that, I don't know, in my case [I am studying] not as much because I want to fill my pockets on the day that I finish my degree. I chose this major because I think it is something useful, but I want to comment that I did it for my people because many of us know that we do not receive good treatment; that is where I am going. I did not do it because I want to have a lot of money. It is true that many do it to fill their pockets, but I want to give a service because I want to support my people.

STUDENT 1: I said this because I am poor and this is my interest. The first. The other thing is that I am a nursing student, and I am doing things in my community. We are creating an organization of indigenous advisers; . . . these are things that we are dealing *on the side*. Personal matters are very different. To help is another issue. (Taller de diálogo, National Autonomous University of Nayarit, April 17, 2010)

WITH AND AGAINST THE ARCHIVE

At the end of the summer of 2010, Wixarika authorities were alerted to twenty-two mining concessions in their sacred pilgrimage site of Wirikuta, in the northeastern state of San Luis Potosí. These concessions were awarded by the Mexican government to a Canadian transnational corporation operating through its Mexican subsidiaries. Within weeks, a coalition of nongovernmental organizations united to "Save Wirikuta," promising to follow the leadership of Wixarika communal authorities. Wixarika students and professionals quickly added their voices to the struggle by organizing forums on their campuses and sending letters of opposition on behalf of their respective organizations. A handful of these students have been particularly vocal, using the scholarly expertise gained in the classroom and the cultural knowledge gained in their homes and communities to bring attention to the cause. Speeches, letters, conference calls, and countless interviews have led them to international conferences, the Mexican senate, and to the offices of numerous organizations. Time and again, these activists have called on Mexico's constitutional recognition of pluriculturalism and its related guarantees for the rights of indigenous peoples, which rest on the coexistence of equal citizenship and the recognition of their cultural autonomy and difference. At the same time, many national and international organizations and media outlets have responded to the alert, reflecting some of the benefits that have resulted from the hypervisibility of "Huichol" culture at home and abroad. In this case, the ironic benefit of what some may call ethnic opportunism has allowed for a broad coalition based on the territorial and cultural defense of indigenous patrimony against a transnational corporation.

I mention this struggle because it reflects some of the dilemmas discussed in this chapter, namely, the challenges and opportunities that Wixaritari face in contemporary Mexico, as well as the tense negotiations they must undergo to respond to and transcend ingrained expectations held by the nonindigenous segment of society. The conflict over the mining concessions brings to the fore Philip Deloria's "paradox of racial thinking" and Charles R. Hale's discussion of racial ambivalence in a multicultural world, which signal contrasting challenges to the ways in which state and society comprehend indigenous peoples to be equal but different citizens enjoying the privileges that this status affords them, including protections for their ancestral lands and sacred places. As Wixaritari enter and exit these spaces of activism, they are faced with the multiple expectations that continue to structure racial relations, by placing the indigenous as either noble savages who are intrinsically allied to land and nature or as barriers to modernity who stand in the way of economic progress, in this case, resource extraction. Furthermore, the recognition of their legitimate claims to Wirikuta as a sacred place rests on ghosting an authentic being for the nation (Povinelli 2002) and therefore using particular signifiers that will convince senators and the corporation's shareholders alike that the mining project is an illegal affront to native culture and territory.

Finally, what this current struggle signals is the increasing strategic importance of spatial linkages that the Wixaritari have forged and that Wixarika university students and professionals have seized on in particular. Returning to Gupta and Ferguson, these efforts show how the reterritorialization of space and ethnic belonging "forces us to reconceptualize fundamentally the politics of community, solidarity, identity, and cultural difference" (Ferguson and Gupta 1997, 9). The many hats that urban Wixarika citizens wear contest enduring notions of static indigenous belonging by demonstrating that identities are indeed, as Stuart Hall tells us, strategic and positional, fragmented and multiplying across the difference of discourses, practices, and positions (Hall 1996).

As Shannon Speed notes with relation to indigenous social justice struggles in contemporary Mexico, "Indigenous people actively take part in the dual process of reconstituting globalized discourses and reasserting local identities in the context of struggle and negotiation with the Mexican State. In these reassertions, they also alter the discourse of rights in ways that can be reactionary, progressive, or radically challenging to the discourses and structures of power within which they are articulated" (2008, 32). The stories outlined in this chapter shed some light on the coexistence of multiple spatial and cultural belongings that, while painful, have the ability to become productive forces in shifting Mexico's ingrained racial and spatial imaginary by recognizing indigenous peoples as complex and heterogeneous citizens of the nation. The case of Wixarika culture is illustrative for exposing how the hypervisibility of targeted cultural traits and traditions intensify state and popular expectations of who Wixarika people are supposed to be, while turning a blind eye to their territorial and political struggles. As such, a more ample discussion of how different Wixarika actors respond to these expectations can bring new insight into how authenticity, identity, space, and cosmopolitics (Liffman 2011) intersect to become accommodated or challenged at different conjunctures.

CONCLUSION

Walking Together

Crossings are never undertaken all at once, and never once and for all.
—M. JACQUI ALEXANDER, *PEDAGOGIES OF CROSSING*

PUSHING THE LIMITS OF MULTICULTURALISM: NUNCA MÁS UN MÉXICO SIN NOSOTROS

ON DECEMBER 9, 2016, I attended the ITESO graduation ceremony to congratulate Imelda and Rosa, two indigenous women who successfully earned their bachelor's degrees in education and communications, respectively. Despite the economic challenges that were always present, their individual commitment to earn a degree while being activists in their urban and rural communities was on display as their families and friends accompanied them. Imelda was one of the student keynote speakers. She stood in her black toga and recounted her path as a Mixtec woman at one of Guadalajara's most elite educational institutions. She spoke of her family as both migrant and local and of Universidad Solidaria's role in creating community for ITESO students who come from underrepresented backgrounds. Finally, she urged the crowd to work toward decolonizing educational models that reproduce capitalist, patriarchal, and racist epistemologies and practices. A finely dressed white couple sitting inches in front of me turned toward each other astonished and whispered in disapproval after Imelda's remarks. I sat next to Santos, now a Wixarika alumni of ITESO and an active lawyer; he smiled and nodded in affirmation of Imelda's frank diagnosis of an educational model that forecloses other forms of knowing and doing. As if Imelda's words had come and gone in a flash, the next student speaker was a fair-skinned girl who talked of the nostalgia she already felt for her campus after spending so many days under its trees with friends, chuckling about the long nights studying. College had been a dream come true for both young women, yet their everyday struggles and victories were starkly different.

That night Rosa donned a skirt embroidered by her grandmother, who had not been able to make the trip from Tateikié to Guadalajara. In the crowd of black togas, her traje was a bright interruption. After the ceremony pictures were taken, balloons and flowers were handed to the graduates in the courtyard outside the auditorium. The elegant Tapatío families walked by and watched as Rosa's family celebrated in their fine trajes. Some stepped away from their circles to personally congratulate Rosa's mother for such a grand accomplishment; she smiled back awkwardly yet proud.

In *Pedagogies of Crossing* (2005), M. Jacqui Alexander critically addresses the limits of liberal discourse and practice that have cemented ideas of individual rights, including our right to travel across geographic spaces and our freedom to enunciate our personal views. Yet this liberalism reaches its limit once nonnormative subjects, discourses, and practices make these same physical and articulatory movements. Alexander illustrates this argument through an analysis of the processes and outcomes of activism at the New School for Social Research in New York, where students, faculty, and staff struggled to articulate and understand one another's demands for respecting and transcending differences of race, class, gender, and sexuality. Perhaps one of the most formidable obstacles of this struggle was to overcome the dismissals by those who supposed that social equality had been consolidated through the university's radical origins and the ascendancy of American multiculturalism. In this vein, additional demands made on the state and private sector (an institution of higher education) were viewed not only as superfluous but as examples of the reactionary and separatist stances held by women, people of color, low-income people, and the LBGTQ community.

Most importantly, Alexander describes how institutional diversity discourses were employed to delegitimize the New School activists' call for equity, whereby diversity was whittled down to the "counting of bodies of color" (2005, 133). While the New School's activists were given the chance to enunciate their demands, the discursive work of institutionalized diversity and multiculturalism effectively limited their opportunity to be listened to and have their claims fully understood. Through the tropes of diversity and multiculturalism, the university effectively sought to dismiss the "lived experience of everyday oppressions within the institution" (125).

I refer to Alexander's analysis of the New School's struggle over diversity because it poignantly highlights the inconsistencies of liberal multiculturalism on a global level. Mexico's constitutional embrace of pluriculturalism in 1992 was in many ways a rhetorical move—an attempt to quell rising popular anger at the country's political, economic, and cultural inequality on the eve of the five hundredth anniversary of the Spanish conquest. Mexico's "pluricultural constitution" legally mandated that indigenous peoples have a right to protect and promote their languages, customs, natural resources, and forms of political and social organization (León-Portilla 2012). In effect, this constitutional amendment has become a crucial, albeit contested, legal tool for indigenous communities as they continue to defend their aboriginal territories and cultures from encroachment and obliteration. But twenty-five years later, the Mexican people and the institutional bodies that govern them still struggle over the philosophical meaning and material substance of living in a pluricultural nation. Questions surrounding the rights and privileges of indigenous communities become visible in different moments of major public debates over development projects, or in more intimate and quotidian interactions at work or school. Should the government continue to tolerate the semiautonomy of indigenous communities? Do indigenous communities have the right to thwart development projects that place their sacred sites in peril but are said to bring economic benefits to the nation? Is it fair to waive testing and fees for aspiring indigenous university students? And should mestizo students be encouraged to embrace a fellow indigenous student who chose to wear native clothing during graduation?

As I have argued throughout the present work, racial alterity has always existed at the core of Mexico's pursuit of nation building. Indigenous peoples' demands to be recognized as culturally autonomous but equal citizens have certainly tested the limits of the liberal nation-state. The unfolding of the Zapatista movement since 1994 can tell us a lot about how the Mexican government and public have come to understand indigenous demands for treatment as separate but equal citizens. The Zapatista call of *"nunca más un México sin nosotros"* (never again a Mexico without us) expresses this pursuit by indigenous peoples to be recognized as full Mexican citizens at the same time that it speaks to another, more complex demand based on respect for indigenous peoples' differences. This delicate interplay between autonomy and inclusion best illustrates the political and social landscape that Wixaritari navigate as they push against development projects in their sacred lands or call for respect and recognition within Mexico's cities. What is perhaps most difficult to assimilate for both the government and the general population is the fact that within this call for indigenous peoples as full but autonomous citizens lies each indigenous community's distinctive historical geographic engagement with Mexico and Mexicanness. In this light, I call for the importance of anchoring the stories of Wixarika university students and professionals to the specific geographic and interpersonal trajectories that reveal the heterogeneity of Wixarika experiences in contemporary Mexico and, by extension, the heterogeneity of all Mexicans.

Through grounded engagement with these experiences, the pluricultural nation can begin to have discursive and practical significance. Indeed, Mexico has come a long way from the time that the centralist state forced mestizaje as *the* desired national identity. In 2010, Mexico celebrated two hundred years of independence and one hundred years since the Revolution. While still moving within the margins of sanctioned historical narratives, the traveling multimedia spectacle that commemorated these anniversaries portrayed a diverse country where differences in race, class, gender, and age are respected. Even more notable was the presidential inauguration of López Obrador on December 1, 2018, which was marked by the elected official's accompaniment of dozens of indigenous representatives, burning incense and praying in what some called an unprecedented public neoindigenista ceremony. Compared to the assimilationist tendencies of yesteryear, this respect for and celebration of difference should perhaps be appreciated for its progress. But as Alexander's analysis suggests, the institutionalization of diversity discourse and multicultural politics poses new challenges for those who continue to suffer discrimination. Undoubtedly, the state continues to enact policies that undermine the political, cultural, and territorial integrity of the country's indigenous peoples. Similarly, the popular imagination still fixes indigenous peoples and indigeneity to age-old stereotypes that perpetuate both everyday racist encounters as well as institutional forms of racism. As Allan Pred notes, "stereotypes that Universalize" render invisible the lived experiences of the stereotyped (2004, xii). But today, the voices of the stereotyped, of the discriminated against, and of the colonized have access to more outlets through which they can contest their invisibility and break the silences that surround their hardships.

Mexico's multicultural turn and spectrum of ethnic identification have occurred unevenly depending on regional political and cultural dynamics (Martínez Casas et al. 2014, 53; Fragoso and Domínguez 2018, 26). The cases of Tepic and Guadalajara allow us to discern, at both a local and a regional level, the types of opportunities and foreclosures that have arisen as a consequence of these new cultural politics. A promotional video created in December 2012 by the government of Nayarit reflects the state's celebration of racial and geographic diversity. In this video, Nayarit's progress and modernity is reached through embracing its multiracial and multilingual population. One scene depicts a Wixarika man dressed in a traje on a stretcher, being airlifted from his remote homeland to receive medical services. Reminiscent of Aguirre Beltrán's call for reaching the country's "regions of refuge," the video's message promotes the idea that modernity and progress imply providing essential infrastructure and health services to the most isolated of its population. Strikingly, the video is accompanied by the state's anthem sung in Spanish, Wixarika, and Náayeri. In August 2016, Guadalajara launched its new city brand with a musical video that invited Mexican musicians of various genres to interpret "Guadalajara, Guadalajara," the famous mariachi anthem composed by Pepe Guízar. Venado Azul, the best known of the "regional Wixárika" indigenous musical groups, open the video, decked in white-and-blue embroidered trajes on the stage of Guadalajara's most elegant venue, the locally celebrated neoclassical Teatro Degollado. Yuawi, the child lead singer, opens with the Wixarika greeting "*ke'aku*" before launching into Guízar's song. After showcasing various musicians singing throughout Guadalajara's plazas and nearby tourist attractions, the video returns to Venado Azul in the theater, as they conclude the anthem and Yuawi shouts, "*Pamparius!*" (Thank you!). The camera then follows the band as they walk off the stage. The Guadalajara city brand thus appears to place the Wixarika center stage; they are the opening and the closing act that invites future investments and tourism to the metropolitan region.

These shifts have not originated behind the closed doors of the hegemonic state; they are the product of public debates and the longtime work of indigenous peoples who have sought wider visibility. At the same time, government policies demonstrate that the multicultural turn is a poorly disguised strategy to continue to dispossess indigenous peoples of their territorial, political, economic, and cultural sovereignty. In this way, Nayarit and Jalisco's celebration of diversity on the public stages of YouTube or sporting events is of little significance in the face of the lukewarm reception if not complete rejection by state authorities to the ongoing political, economic, and cultural demands of indigenous peoples. The struggle for equality is far from ending when Wixarika citizens continue to be denied service at local restaurants and are victims of the denigrating stares and insults of their lighter-complexioned countrymen and women.

WIXARIKA CLAIMS TO THE CITY

The present book seeks to demonstrate why understanding the experiences and negotiations of urban Wixaritari within the context of particular places and situations is essential. Examining the historical construction of racialized identities in Guadalajara and Tepic allows us to understand how each city has imbued the landscape with particular signifiers. For instance, the hypervisibility of the "Huicholito" and "Corita" in Tepic may render the diversity of the city's indigenous population invisible by promoting an ethnic Other suitable for the tourism industry, through the depiction of the city's "Huicholitos" and "Coritas" as attached to ethnic neighborhoods and as holding ethnic-appropriate occupations. Conversely, Guadalajara appears to be slowly shedding its historical identity as a whiter and more Catholic enclave with a new generation of interethnic and young progressive political leaders who discursively welcome the presence of indigenous peoples, Central American migrants, and global tech workers. As noted by Marisol de la Cadena and Orin Starn, "Indigenous self-representation implies wide collaborative networks that include persons from many walks of life, indigenous and non-indigenous" (2009, 215).

By emphasizing the conjuncture between the historical conditions and identities of these two cities and the current experiences of their Wixarika residents, we can move away from perceiving the presence of indigenous peoples in cities as a form of displacement and deterritorialization. As discussed in chapter 5, Wixarika struggles to carve out spaces of inclusion and cultural recognition within the urban setting demonstrate the active work of emplacement and reterritorialization that is occurring through both the intimate individual and the collective organizational efforts of Guadalajara's and Tepic's Wixarika youth. Arturo Escobar contends that present-day agendas and demands surrounding identity reflect a "multilayered entanglement" of actors whose claims evolve and are situated around the production of spatial and historical assemblages (2008, 273, 287). From this perspective, Escobar argues that the "metaphor of the rhizome" reveals the "networks of heterogeneous elements that grow in unplanned directions, following the real life situations they encounter" (274). Escobar's analytic can help us make sense of the particular conditions that distinguish the experiences and modes of action of Wixaritari residing in Tepic from those in Guadalajara.

As my research with Wixarika university students and professionals deepened, I came to realize the formative role that the political, economic, and cultural landscapes of each city had on the outlook of my story's protagonists. Early on, I was advised by a Wixarika professor in Tepic that too many of the city's Wixarika university students and professionals were being sucked into political partisanship. At the time, I understood this matter to be primarily a problem of certain students not finishing their degrees because they had been "fished out" by a political party, or of too many Wixarika professionals serving the state as opposed to their communities—becoming development intermediaries to the detriment of their tribal lands. As time passed, I realized that this matter marked a key difference between Wixarika students, professionals, and organizations based in Tepic from those in Guadalajara. The inclusion and celebration of Wixarika heritage in Tepic has given Wixaritari a certain cultural leverage, reflected in the local university's affirmative action–type policies and in the increasing presence of indigenous peoples holding government positions. As a result of this and the city's smaller bureaucracy, Wixarika organizations in Tepic have less difficulty accessing public spaces and may often be less critical of the government.

Guadalajara presents a strikingly different panorama for its Wixarika inhabitants. Undoubtedly the city's physical and demographic magnitude affects the conditions and types of political and cultural organizing that occurs among its Wixarika population. But Guadalajara's dismissal and mistreatment of its indigenous residents fosters a more cynical stance from Wixarika youth. In contrast to Wixarika students in Tepic, those in Guadalajara often belong to organizations that hold more critical views of the city, state, and nation's political agenda. Consequently, many Wixarika students who enter the political arena in Guadalajara do so via the nongovernmental sector and hold more radical visions for the future. This was palpably visible in the way urban Wixarika organizations mobilized marches to call on the defense of Wirikuta in 2010–12, as opposed to the relative silence on the matter in Tepic. Furthermore, the scale of Guadalajara's private and public institutions as well as the dispersion and ethnic diversity of indigenous communities within the metropolitan area present significant challenges for its local indigenous organizations. Yet recent panindigenous organizing among students and artisans in the metropolitan area reflect the urgency of Guillermo de la Peña's "ethnic citizenship," expressed through more dignified public visibility; political, economic, and social equity; as well as the opportunity and space to continue to reproduce their cultural traditions (de la Peña 2013).

I mark these differences with a broad brushstroke to emphasize the articulatory work of space and place in the trajectories of urban Wixaritari. I do so knowing that these trajectories are also rhizomatic, fluid, and in constant construction. The highly contentious movement to defend Wirikuta from the encroachment of capital exposes these differences, as some Wixarika activists based in Tepic have shown more willingness to listen to and work with the government, while Guadalajara has produced some of the most radical Wixarika leaders of the movement. Finally, a finer brushstroke allows us to see that even the most "pro-government" and radical Wixarika students and professionals demonstrate shifting discourses and practices.

As the Mexican state and population continues to struggle over the meanings and implications of its pluriculturalism, its colors oscillate—they bleed together to form complex hybrids, but they also stay vividly vibrant in their difference. As we recognize the threads that lead us to our shared futures, we must take on the difficult and always unfinished work of walking together, even in our differences. To borrow the words of M. Jacqui Alexander, "Crossings are never undertaken all at once, and never once and for all," for the geographies that construct our individual and collective identities reflect the dynamic colors of the ever-changing Mexican landscape.

NOTES

INTRODUCTION

1 The Wixárika Research Center is a nonprofit foundation established in Oakland, California, in 2001 to consolidate the vast multimedia archive that Juan and Yvonne Negrín have gathered over the decades and to support Wixarika communal initiatives like forestry conservation, territorial defense, and student scholarships.
2 *Criollo* refers specifically to the descendants of Spaniards born in the Americas.
3 I was inspired by the concept of hypervisibility from the work of M. Jacqui Alexander, who discusses it within the context of the United States' 2001 invasion of Afghanistan, where the hypervisibility of the image of the oppressed Muslim woman was deployed as one of several justifications for military intervention (Alexander 2005, 185).
4 Mexico offers several types of institutions for higher education, including the robust autonomous university public system, various private institutions, and thirteen intercultural indigenous universities (*universidades interculturales indígenas*) located throughout the country. There are multiple types of national, state, and institution-specific scholarships, yet most of these do not fully cover the tuition and cost of living, making higher education a costly endeavor for indigenous students, the poorest demographic within Mexican society.
5 This musical genre *música regional wixárika* has a regional folkloric sound that uses some traditional violin and brings in a strong *grupero* influence, sung in Wixarika and Spanish. The genre exploded in the early 2000s with Venado Azul and Huichol Musical as the most popular acts, both of whom claim authorship of the international hit "La cusinela."

CHAPTER 1

1 *Güero* is a widely used colloquial Mexican term that refers to a range of people of light complexion and light-colored eyes. In areas of the country that have higher indigenous populations, *güero* may be used to refer to any nonindigenous person no matter their complexion. *Ojos* are eyes, thus the column's name roughly but poorly translates to "The Eyes of the Light Skinned." A *mayate* is a type of beetle and a highly denigrating term often used to describe any spectrum of nonbinary sexuality in Mexico. Within the United States, it is occasionally used by some Mexican Americans as a derogatory slur for African Americans. As an insult, *mayate* connotes bestial (or literally insectlike) tendencies, including direct references to the sexual appetite of a group of people.
2 Although the United States and Mexico have distinct racial legacies, critical hemispheric scholarship on race and ethnicity are gaining traction and decentering mestizaje's historical weight, shaping Mexico's debates on race and racism.
3 Gramsci explains hegemony not as complete and coherent power exercised by a monolithic dominant class, but rather as a process through which ruling classes and ideas are constructed and upheld through society's "common sense," which is constructed and deconstructed in historically and geographically specific ways.
4 Stuart Hall describes Antonio Gramsci's concept of ideology as one in which the world is mobilized into cultural, faith-based, and political movements that produce social practice (1986, 20). Using this framework, *indigenismo* can be considered an ideological current.
5 In Mexico, all private and public schools use the textbooks issued by the SEP, and within this system, each student is guaranteed a copy of each textbook per year. The SEP's history, geography, and literature textbooks reflect Mexico's postrevolutionary nationalism and replicate the nation's foundational mythologies and officially sanctioned historical narratives.
6 During the seventeenth century, Mexico heavily engaged in the slave trade from Africa.
7 Within the casta system, it was determined that it took three generations for the Spanish-Indian mixture to return to being denominated Spanish.
8 The social causes of the Mexican Revolution are overwhelmingly attributed to the thirty-year Porfirian regime; however, the political economic engine behind social dispossession was set during the early years of independence and catalyzed with Juárez's Reforma. Historian Aldana Rendón affirms that Juárez and Díaz "travelled on the same economic project ... understanding progress in the same way." For this reason, the Revolution of 1910 should be understood not solely as movement that rose up against Díaz but as one that questioned the political economic program of liberalism (Aldana Rendón 2007, 20).
9 On September 14, 1866, Maximilian decreed the Agrarian Law, which, according to Meyer (1993, 351–53), became a strong precedent for the postrevolutionary Agrarian Reform.

CHAPTER 2

1 Peter Wade (1997) offers a concise overview of twentieth-century scholarly debates that brought the question of class to the forefront of discussions on race and ethnicity under the argument that economic inequity is the primary enabler of racial injustice.
2 Michael Watts notes that one form of power is not fully displaced by another, but rather a "complex triangulation" is produced that sustains "many forms of power put to the purpose of security and regulation" (2003, 14). In the context of state-indigenous relations in Mexico, this analysis provides a more nuanced view of how new indigenous authorities surreptitiously mediated debates between traditional tribal authorities and the different scales of government.
3 Not all indigenous dress was equal in the eyes of the indigenista observer. In Chiapas, considerable effort was made to have male coffee workers use "proper" pants, while in coastal Oaxaca, the INI designed shirts for bare-breasted women. Many case studies note that these changes in dress were not wholly embraced by all indigenous peoples, particularly by the older generations. Hernández Castillo points out how Chiapas' governor Victórico Grajales (1932–36) ordered the burning of Mam clothing after officials had distributed mestizo clothes to the population (2004, 25).
4 The entrenched local power dynamics and inequities that restricted indigenista interventions in the 1960s came at the same time as the broader postrevolutionary nationalist project began to rupture as a result of the coercive state apparatus.
5 A native of Guadalajara, Echeverría's wife, Esther Zuno de Echeverría, was fond of Wixarika culture and had a Wixarika ceremonial center, or *calihuey*, built at the presidential residence of Los Pinos (Durin 2008, 353).
6 For more on the conjuncture of neoliberalism, decentralization, and the rise of non-governmental and "community-based" development initiatives, see James Petras's "Imperialism and NGOs in Latin America" (1997).
7 Fikes decries how the drug culture of whites and mestizos lead to the penalization of peyote as a controlled substance and the subsequent harassment of Wixarika pilgrims by Mexican law enforcement (1993, 131).
8 Arturo Escobar (1995) maintains that the insertion of indigenous and rural peoples into an (inter)national consumer society is a fundamental precept of global developmentalist politics.
9 Tania Murray Li's *The Will to Improve* (2007) provides an excellent analysis of the ways in which development projects can often dispossess the same populations they purport to be "improving."
10 This includes the seasonal labor migrations, when the entire family travels outside their community to work.
11 Some government emissaries in charge of development projects were known for extreme corruption. A veterinarian in charge of introducing high-grade cattle (and one of anthropologist Karen Reed's informants) was imprisoned for nine months

for selling the improved cattle stock designated for the Wixarika and replacing it with tuberculosis-infected cattle, which caused a devastating epidemic in Wixarika communities during the 1970s (Juan and Yvonne Negrín, interview by author, March 2, 2004).

12 The UCIHJ was established as an interlocutor of Wixarika communities of Jalisco, while the Unión de Comunidades y Ejidos Indígenas (UCEI), its counterpart in Nayarit, included Náayeri and Mexicanero Nahuas (Liffman 2011, 216).

13 Paul Liffman (2011) analyzes how Wixarika territoriality is articulated through complex practices anchored in the ceremoniality that reflects ancestral relations to the land, as well as historically sedimented relations with the state and more recent appropriations of global identity politics.

14 Norwegian ethnographer Carl Lumholtz, followed by anthropologists Léon Diguet, Theodor Konrad Preuss, and Howard Mowry Zingg, collected, described, and made illustrations of Wixarika offerings and textiles. These collections largely remain in U.S. and European museums.

15 De la Torre was commissioned to create one of his signature beaded murals at the Louvre Museum metro station in Paris, a matter documented in the 2014 film *Eco de la Montaña*. Ramón Medina is said to have served as Carlos Castaneda's template for his Yaqui medicine man, Don Juan, while Castaneda was an understudy of Peter Furst.

16 Negrín's collection of paintings from artists José Benítez Sánchez, Guadalupe González Ríos, Juan Ríos Martínez, Tutukila, and Pablo Taizán (a.k.a. Yauxali) resulted from close friendships formed through Negrín's participation in numerous pilgrimages as well as service to Wixarika communities.

17 Talavera Durón notes that the use of indigenous laborers in the tobacco plantations coincides with the commercialization of the crop between 1933 and 1966 (Talavera Durón 2003, 16).

18 Durin (2008) notes that Wixaritari who seasonally travel to and permanently live in the northern city of Monterrey have pushed for the Cañón de Guitarritas, located in the city's outskirts, to be recognized as a sacred Wixarika site.

CHAPTER 3

1 Lozada was recognized as a general by Maximilian I and decorated by the Legion of Honor of Napoleon III (González Navarro 1994, 27).

2 Nineteenth-century Mexican writer Manuel Payno denominated Lozada a *"forajido comunista,"* or "communist outlaw" (Meyer 1969, 536).

3 It is difficult to ascertain whether Juárez (who was Zapotec) tolerated Lozada's movement out of a suppressed affinity for his indigenous compatriots. As the principal face of nineteenth-century Mexican liberalism, however, Juárez is ultimately judged by his policies, which directly undermined indigenous territorial organization and consequently attacked the central political, economic, and cultural tenets of this population.

4 Much of what we know about Lozada's rise and fall is owed to the work of historian Jean Meyer, whose careful archival and ethnographic work have brought to light new hypotheses for understanding the nature of this agrarian struggle and why it came to a seemingly abrupt end.
5 Among other things, the Plan Libertador called for a representative government based on direct elections as well as the end to domestic customs.
6 Historian Beatriz Rojas notes that the majority of Wixaritari that made up Lozada's bases came from Guadalupe Ocotán and Tenzompa; the latter town has since become a mestizo settlement. Wixaritari from Wautɨa, Tateikié, and Tuapurie occasionally participated in the battles (Rojas 1993, 259–60).
7 During a conference held in March 1950, Ricardo Lancaster Jones, the grandson of Corona's friend who owned the property of La Mojonera, pointed to Vega's pact with Jalisco's liberal political leaders to sabotage Lozada's troops by calling for their retreat (cited in Meyer 1969, 546–47). This may suggest that Corona's victory was far less glorious than popular legend holds.
8 The creation of the state of Nayarit in 1883 fueled years of disputes between the political and economic elites of Tepic and Guadalajara. Those in Tepic argued that the leadership of Guadalajara had permitted Tepic and its surrounding region to fall into years of lawlessness during Lozada's reign. Meanwhile, those from Guadalajara asserted that Tepic had neither the necessary population nor administrative know-how to effectively lead a region that was intrinsic to the West's economic sustenance (S. García 1878, 30–31).
9 Governor of Nayarit Gilberto Flores Muñoz (1946–51) used Lozada as a controversial "political banner" during his inaugural campaign (Agraz García de Alba 1997, 21).
10 The earliest Spanish chroniclers underlined the region's large native population, which over the next century would be decimated through murder, disease, and enslavement. Although the Spanish Crown prohibited slavery in 1530, it rescinded the law four years later as a consequence of the wanton murder of an indigenous population viewed as holding no value for the Spaniards as long as their labor could not be forcibly conscripted (López González 1984, 14). In 1536, slavery was once again prohibited after Friar Bartolomé de las Casas's famous intervention. Notwithstanding, Guzmán turned a blind eye to these decrees and continued to enslave thousands of people until his arrest by the Crown in 1537 (15).
11 This letter was compiled by Friar Antonio Tello for his *Crónica miscelánea*, second book, chapter I72. Dana Velasco Murillo's discussion of the use of *vecino* within colonial Zacatecas signals that the term could "encompass people from all social statuses and ethnicities" (2016, 7) and that it gained popular usage for those who settled in the new urban barrios.
12 Salvador Gutiérrez Contreras (1974) states that Xícora, or Xícori, in Náayeri means peyote, showing strong similarities to the wixarika *hikuri*.
13 Documents from the period state that King Nayar died sometime between 1624 and 1626, during a war between the Huaynamotecos and the Náayeri, suggesting that King Nayar was at least 134 years old at the time of his death (Gutiérrez Contreras 1974, 110–11)!

14 As a lesson in the penalties of idolatry and rebellion, Spanish authorities made sure that indigenous prisoners were present at the burning.
15 Not all Wixaritari communities fully cooperated with the Spaniards as indios fronterizos. Those from Tuapurie and Wautia were far more rebellious and were not pacified until 1733, by Captain Antonio Escobedo (Torres Contreras 2009, 175).
16 Authorship of "Son de la negra" is most commonly attributed to Blas Galindo, who brought it to the world stage in a 1940 New York City performance. Anthropologist Jesús Jáuregui's extensive research on the matter, however, demonstrates that the song's origins are more correctly attributed to popular regional mariachi variations found throughout Mexico's western states, particularly in Nayarit and Jalisco (2010). Jáuregui notes that the lyrical emphasis on the silk shawl from Tepic clearly dates the song's origins to the years of independence at the height of San Blas's trade with Asia and Tepic's short-lived but vibrant bazaar (Jáuregui 2010, 309).
17 After several chapters in which Forbes tells of California's promising land and unquarrelsome Indians, he concludes his book by stating, "The cession of such a disjointed part of the republic as California, would be an advantage. In no case can it ever be profitable to the Mexican republic. . . . Therefore, by giving up this territory for the debt, would be getting rid of this last for nothing" (Forbes [1839] 1937, 92).
18 The Arellano and Gayou firms were two of the primary beneficiaries of these practices (Meyer 1990, 33).
19 He would later form the Partido del Pueblo Mexicano (Party of the Mexican People) and in 1979 helped form the Coalición de Izquierda (Coalition of the Left) along with the Communist Party of Mexico. In a 1992 interview, Gascón Mercado underlined how Nayarit's electoral system obeyed the orders of the federal government and therefore denied the needs of the state's population. The PPS emerged in the 1960s with strong support from the teachers' union and an "organizational strategy between the working class neighborhoods of Tepic to defend the electoral vote" (Pacheco Ladrón de Guevara 1992, 7). This party's failure to effectively contest the PRI's hegemony led its dissidents to search for new party affiliations based on a working-class constituency. With some exceptions, the parties of the Left eventually were consolidated into the Partido de la Revolución Democrática (Party of the Democratic Revolution, or PRD).
20 Mackinlay cites a study conducted by the Autonomous University of Tepic that found 69 percent of the indigenous laborers to be Wixarika (Mackinlay 2008, 129).
21 Initial steps toward the city's expansion outside the city center's limits began in 1838, when the government of Tepic gave a large segment of land located on the northern stretch of the Tepic River (now the Mololoa River) to Barron, Forbes and Company. In this location the firm established the Jauja textile factory, which in turn helped urbanize this area (López González 1996, 12).
22 Tutupika de la Cruz Carrillo, the son of one of Colonia Zitakua's founders and a professor at the Autonomous University of Nayarit, suggests that Sitakwa or Xitakwa are the more correct spellings for the word. Xitakwa is derived from *xita*, meaning corn silk, and *takwá*, which means outside, or "in the patio." The eventual spelling

of Zitakua (or Zitacua) is a simplified version of the former. I use the spelling Zitakua when referring to this neighborhood as it is the officially used spelling.
23 Although Zitakua houses a calihuey, or *tuki*, it does not have the accompanying ancestral houses that make up the traditional tukite of the highland communities. Zitakua's calihuey bears little resemblance to those found in the highland ceremonial centers, yet it symbolizes the efforts of Zitakua's founders to re-create ethnic spaces outside nuclear communities. Paul Liffman notes that since the 1980s, "new *tukipa* style organizations" not linked to a set community and civil-religious cargos have been established in different places, including Zoquipan, in Guadalajara, and Zitakua (Liffman 2011).
24 Benítez Sánchez's work won him exhibitions at prestigious museums in Mexico, the United States, and Europe. He brought a unique aesthetic to Wixarika yarn paintings, and his name was read into the U.S. Congressional Record by Republican senator Jesse Helms on May 19, 1983, where the senator described him as the "Picasso of Huichol art."
25 The city of Puerto Vallarta is located in the state of Jalisco, yet the resort area has expanded northward to various towns in Nayarit, including Nuevo Vallarta, Bucerías, and Cruz de Huanacaxtle.
26 Brant Secunda, a self-proclaimed "Huichol Shaman" from New Jersey, has capitalized on the popularity of Wixarika shamanism by leading "shamanic retreats" through his Dance of the Deer Foundation.
27 Many have nicknamed the statue El Chamán Güero (The White Shaman) because of the statue's European features and light complexion.
28 In 2019, Yukaima González became the first indigenous woman to win a beauty contest in the state of Nayarit. Many credited the recent success of Mixtec actress Yalitza Aparicio for shifting public views on indigenous beauty.
29 *Ladino* is a term used in southern Mexico and Central America to refer to the nonindigenous.
30 Traditional Wixarika dress is not uniform and has significantly changed over the past couple of centuries. The more elaborate and quite expensive embroidered attire is worn only on special occasions.

CHAPTER 4

1 *Tapatío* is a word that has been used since the colonial era to designate all that comes from the Mexican city of Guadalajara. According to the *Diccionario de mejicanismos*, by Francisco Santamaría (1959), the word has its origin in the measurement of three tortillas as well as in three units of cacao used by the natives of the region of Jalisco.
2 Ramón Corona's description of the battle places his force numbers at 2,241 and Lozada's at more than 6,000 (Corona 1873, n.p.).

3 "Conmemora Zapopan 137 aniversario de la Batalla de la Mojonera," Gobierno de Zapopan, January 28, 2011, www.zapopan.gob.mx.
4 Corona's political ambitions and perceived popularity made President Porfirio Díaz weary of the competition of another soldier who had fought the French Empire and the conservative cause (Peregrina 2004, 111).
5 Other reforms included abolishing sales taxes in 1888 and establishing Monte de Piedad and Caja de Ahorros branches, both of which offered loans and credit to the working class at an annual interest rate of 12 percent (Peregrina 2004, 112).
6 Guadalajara of the Indies was the name used to differentiate this city from its Spanish counterpart.
7 The First Audience was the maximum tribunal of the Spanish Crown.
8 The etymological roots of the name Guadalajara come from the Arabic, *Wadal-Hachara*, meaning river of rocks (González y González 1994, 100).
9 Brian Connaughton's (2003) study on clerical ideology in Guadalajara argues that despite appearances, the Catholic Church was not monolithic, and demonstrates that a significant portion of the clergy embraced liberalism as long as they did not lose their privileged social status (9), a matter Raymond Buvé describes as "liberalism à la carte" (2007, 97).
10 *Pelado* was a derogatory term used to describe the poor.
11 Salinas de Gortari's modification of the constitution's twenty-seventh amendment facilitated the dramatic transfer of ejido land to private hands.
12 Sinarquismo is a far right, antistatist political and cultural movement that emerged in 1937 and holds ideological parallels with fascism.
13 Indigenous artisan collectives generally manage these collective vending permits by alternating the schedules of the vendors of the same collective in a given stand. In theory, this ensures each artisan equal access to customers and an equitable distribution of money.
14 WAAU project document, presented to the Ministry of Culture in Jalisco in 2010, 16.
15 As suggested by Henri Lefebvre and David Harvey, and affirmed by the WAAU project, urban processes cannot be disconnected from capitalist development, which has restructured the countryside. In this way, development in the country and the city are closely linked—a matter that is intensely reflected in the experiences of indigenous populations.

CHAPTER 5

1 Shaman Chocolates home page, accessed June 7, 2010, http://www.shamangoods.net.
2 Shaman Organic Chocolates home page, accessed December 6, 2018, http://www.shamanchocolates.com.
3 Adela Noriega won Best Young Lead Actress at the 1998 TV y Novelas Awards for her performance as María Isabel. The celebrated 2018 Mexican film *Roma*, directed by

Alfonso Cuarón and starring Mixtec actress Yalitza Aparicio, made a significant contribution to discussions around race, beauty, and the film industry, while also demonstrating the existence of racial, gender, and class hostility.

4 Gran Maracame homepage, accessed July 20, 2010, http://www.maracame.com.

5 The fares for public transportation have quickly risen in Guadalajara, where current bus fares average fifty cents per bus, compared to Mexico City's fare of twenty-two cents. Most students I interviewed need to take a minimum of four buses per day, bringing their daily transportation costs to two dollars, a heavy price in a region where the minimum wage is about five dollars per day ("Tabla de Salarios Mínimos Generales y Profesionales por Áreas Geográficas," Comisión Nacional de los Salarios Mínimos, last updated January 8, 2019, https://www.gob.mx/conasami/documentos/tabla-de-salarios-minimos-generales-y-profesionales-por-areas-geograficas).

6 Until the establishment of middle and high schools in sierra communities, Wixarika youth had to continue their studies in mestizo towns and cities. The bulk of my informants studied outside their communities before going to college in the first decade of this century.

7 Diane Nelson discusses how the indigenous traje is similarly fixed to particular nonurban and nonmodern geographies. Within the context of contemporary indigenous activism, however, reclaiming the traje is a political statement for the urban indigenous professional (1999, 197, 199).

8 Wixas is colloquial for Wixaritari.

9 Figure given at the Fifth Annual Meeting of Indigenous Students, October 25, 2009, Tepic, Nayarit.

10 Speech given by Tukarima at the Fifth Annual Meeting of Indigenous Youth, October 25, 2009, Tepic, Nayarit.

REFERENCES

Adelantos y mejoras materiales realizados durante la administración del Senor General Mariano Ruiz, jefe político y de las armas del territorio de Tepic, 1905–1908. 1909. Tepic: Imprenta del Gobierno.

Agraz García de Alba, Gabriel. 1997. *Quienes resistieron al sanguinario Tigre de Álica en Tequila y lo vencieron en la batalla de la Mojonera.* Mexico City: G. Agraz García de Alba.

Aguirre Beltrán, Gonzalo. 1967. *Regiones de refugio.* Mexico City: Instituto Nacional Indigenista.

Aguirre Beltrán, Gonzalo. 1988. "Formación de una teoría y una práctica indigenistas." *Instituto Nacional Indigenista: 40 años,* edited by Lourdes Herrasti Maciá, 11–40. Mexico City: Instituto Nacional Indigenista.

Aldana Rendón, Mario A. 1983. *Manuel Lozada y las comunidades indígenas.* Guadalajara: Centro de Estudios Históricos del Agrarismo en México.

Aldana Rendón, Mario A. 2004. "Las correrías de Manuel Lozada." *Viñetas de Guadalajara,* edited by José María Murià, 105–10. Guadalajara: Ayuntamiento de Guadalajara; El Colegio de Jalisco.

Aldana Rendón, Mario A. 2007. *Manuel Lozada hasta hoy.* Zapopan: El Colegio de Jalisco.

Alexander, M. Jacqui. 2005. *Pedagogies of Crossing: Meditations on Feminism, Sexual Politics, Memory, and the Sacred.* Durham, N.C.: Duke University Press.

Anderson, Benedict. 1991. *Imagined Communities: Reflections on the Origins and Spread of Nationalism.* London: Verso.

"Apuntes biográficos relativos a Ramón Corona." 1885. Hubert Howe Bancroft Collection. University of California, Berkeley.

Arana Cervantes, Marcos. 1990. *Cien años de vida en Guadalajara.* Guadalajara: Cámara Nacional de Comercio en Guadalajara.

Arriaga, Ingrid, and Diana Negrín. 2018. "Arte y procesos creativos en la circulación de la espiritualidad wixárika." In *Entre trópicos: Diálogos de estudios Nueva Era entre México y Brasil,* edited by Carlos Alberto Steil, Renée de la Torre, and Rodrigo Toniol, 411–40. Mexico City: CIESAS.

Baldwin, James. (1955) 1984. "Preface to the 1984 Edition." *Notes of a Native Son.* Boston, Mass.: Beacon Press, ix–xvi.

Baronnet, Bruno, Gisela Carlos Fregoso, Fortino Domínguez Rueda, eds. 2018. *Racismo, interculturalidad y educación en México.* Xalapa: Universidad Veracruzana.

Barthes, Roland. 1957. *Mythologies.* Paris: Editions du Seuil.

Belgodere, Francisco. 2005. *Guadalajara: Historia y geografía*. Guadalajara: Ayuntamiento Constitucional de Guadalajara.

Benítez, Fernando. 1975. *Viaje al centro de México*. Mexico City: Fondo de Cultura Económica.

Blackwell, Maylei, Floridalma Boj López, and Luis Urrieta Jr. 2017. Introduction to "Critical Latinx Indigeneities," special issue, *Latino Studies* 15 (2): 126–37.

Bonfil Batalla, Guillermo. 1988. "Notas sobre civilización y proyecto nacional." In *Instituto Nacional Indigenista: 40 años*, edited by Lourdes Herrasti Maciá, 121–40. Mexico City: Instituto Nacional Indigenista.

Bonfil Batalla, Guillermo. 1990. *México profundo: Una civilización negada*. Mexico City: Grijalbo.

Bonilla, Lisbeth, Marina Carrillo, Tutupika Carrillo, Ana García, Antonio García, Isaura García, Maximino Muñoz, and Diana Negrín. 2017. "Voces universitarias: Trayectorias, logros y retos en el Occidente Mexicano." In *Juventude indígena: Estudos interdisciplinares, saberes interculturais, conexões entre Brasil e Mexico*, edited by Assis Oliveira and Lúcia Rangel, 224–49. Rio de Janeiro: E-Papers Serviços Editorais.

Boyer, Christopher. 2003. *Becoming Campesinos: Politics, Identity, and Agrarian Struggle in Postrevolutionary Michoacán, 1920–1935*. Stanford, Calif.: Stanford University Press.

Brodie, John Pringle. 1824–1919. John Pringle Brodie Journals and Related Materials: Typescripts, 1824–1919. Bancroft Library, University of California, Berkeley.

Buvé, Raymond. 2007. "Pueblos indígenas de Tlaxcala, las leyes liberales juaristas y la Guerra de Reforma: Una perspectiva desde abajo, 1855–1861." *Los pueblos indios en los tiempos de Benito Juárez*, edited by Antonio Escobar Ohmstede, 91–121. Oaxaca: Universidad Autónoma Benito Juárez de Oaxaca.

Calvo, Thomas. 1990. *Los albores de un nuevo mundo: Siglos XVI y XVII*. Guadalajara: Universidad de Guadalajara.

Calvo, Thomas. 1992. *Guadalajara y su región en el siglo XVII: Población y economía*. Guadalajara: Ayuntamiento de Guadalajara.

Camus, Manuela. 2015. *Vivir en el coto: Fraccionamientos cerrados, mujeres y colonialidad*. Guadalajara: Universidad de Guadalajara.

Castellanos, M. Bianet. 2010. *A Return to Servitude: Maya Migration and the Tourist Trade in Cancún*. Minneapolis: University of Minnesota Press.

Castelló Yturbide, Teresa. 1998. "La indumentaria en las castas del mestizaje." *Artes de México*, no. 8, 73–78.

Castillo Cocom, Juan. 2005. "'It Was Simply Their Word': Yucatec Maya PRInces in YucaPAN and the Politics of Respect." *Critique of Anthropology* 25 (2): 131–55.

Castillo Cocom, Juan. 2007. "Maya Scenarios: Indian Stories in and out of Contexts." In *Mayab Bejlae: Yucatan Today*, edited by Beatriz Reyes-Cortés and Timoteo Rodriguez, 13–35. Kroeber Anthropological Society Papers 96. Berkeley, Calif.: Kroeber Anthropological Society.

Ceja Chávez, Brenda. 2014. "Educación e identidad de jóvenes de origen indígena miembros de la Asamblea Universidad Solidaria del Instituto Tecnológico y de Estudios

Superiores de Occidente en el period 2006–2013." Master's thesis, El Colegio de Jalisco.

Chakrabarty, Dipesh. 2000. *Provincializing Europe: Postcolonial Thought and Historical Difference*. Princeton, N.J.: Princeton University Press.

Clavijero, Francisco. 1944. *Capítulos de historia y disertaciones*. Mexico City: Ediciones de la Universidad Autónoma de México.

Clavijero, Francisco. (1780) 1945. *Historia antigua de México*. Mexico City: Editorrial Porrúa.

Comisión Nacional para el Desarrollo de los Pueblos Indígenas (CDI). 2005. *Dinámica de la población indígena en centros urbanos: Zona Metropolitana de Guadalajara, Jal*. Mexico City: Dirección General de Investigación del Desarrollo y las Culturas Indígenas.

Comisión Nacional para el Desarrollo de los Pueblos Indígenas (CDI). 2006. *Percepción de la imagen del indígena en México: Diagnóstico cualitativo y cuantitativo*. Mexico City: Comisión Nacional para el Desarrollo de los Pueblos Indígenas.

Comisión Nacional para el Desarrollo de los Pueblos Indígenas (CDI). 2010. *Plan Nacional para el desarrollo de los pueblos indígenas, 2009–2012*. Mexico City: Comisión Nacional para el Desarrollo de los Pueblos Indígenas.

Connaughton, Brian F. 2003. *Clerical Ideology in a Revolutionary Age: The Guadalajara Church and the Idea of the Mexican Nation, 1788–1853*. Translated by Mark Healey. Boulder: University Press of Colorado.

Cornejo Franco, José. 1959. "El conquistador, de Guadalaxara colonial." In *Testimonios tapatíos*, by José Cornejo Franco and Luis Pérez Verdía, 11–53. Guadalajara: Ediciones del Gobierno del Estado de Jalisco.

Cornejo Franco, José, and Luis Pérez Verdía. 1959. *Testimonios tapatíos*. Guadalajara: Ediciones del Gobierno del Estado de Jalisco.

Corona, Ramón. 1873. *Parte detallado de la batalla de la Mohonera dada el día 28 de enero de 1873 por las tropas del gobierno al mando del c. General Ramón Corona, contra las de Lozada*. Mexico City: Imprenta del Gobierno.

Coronil, Fernando. 1996. "Beyond Occidentalism: Toward Nonimperial Geohistorical Categories." *Cultural Anthropology* 11 (1): 51–87.

Craib, Raymond B. 2004. *Cartographic Mexico: A History of State Fixations and Fugitive Landscapes*. Durham, N.C.: Duke University Press.

Degollado, Santos. 1857. *Reseña documentada que el c. Santos Degollado, gobernador y comandante general que fue el Estado de Jalisco: Hace a la representación nacional, para que en calidad de gran jurado decida sobre su responsabilidad oficial, por haber prohibido a los estrangeros Barron y Forbes que volviesen a Tepic entre tanto el supremo gobierno resolvía lo conveniente*. Mexico City: Imprenta de I. Cumplido.

de la Cadena, Marisol, and Orin Starn. 2009. "Indigeneidad: Problemáticas, experiencias y agendas en el nuevo milenio." *Tabula Rasa* 10:191–223.

de la Cruz, Sor Juana. 1998. "Castas en los villancicos de Sor Juana." *Artes de México* 8:36–39.

de Orellana, Margarita, Thomas Gage, and Eraclio Zepeda. 1998. "La fiebre en la imagen en la pintura de castas." Artes de México, no. 8, p. 50-59.

de la Peña, Guillermo. 1988. "Gonzalo Aguirre Beltrán." In *Instituto Nacional Indigenista: 40 años*, edited by Lourdes Herrasti Maciá, 355–82. Mexico City: Instituto Nacional Indigenista.

de la Peña, Guillermo. 1990. "La cultura política entre los sectores populares de Guadalajara." *Nueva antropología* 11 (38): 83–107.

de la Peña, Guillermo. 1999. "Territorio y ciudadanía étnica en la nación globalizada." *Desacatos* 1:1–16.

de la Peña, Guillermo. 2002. "Apuntes sobre los indigenismos en Jalisco." *Estudios del hombre 13 y 14, Jalisco al cierre del siglo XX*, 95–118. Lecturas antropológicas. Guadalajara: Universidad de Guadalajara.

de la Peña, Guillermo. 2013. "Ciudadanía étnica: Un modelo pertinente para América Latina." Red de Investigaciones sobre América Latina, la Universidad de Guadalajara, and CIESAS, Guadalajara, September 4–6.

de la Peña, Guillermo, and Regina Martínez Casas. 2004. "Migrantes y comunidades morales: Resignificación, etnicidad y redes sociales en Guadalajara." In *Ciudad, pueblos indígenas y etnicidad*, edited by Pablo Yanes, Virginia Molina, and Oscar González, 89–149. Mexico City: Universidad de la Ciudad de México.

de la Torre, Renée, and Juan Manuel Ramírez Sáiz. 2001. *La ciudadanización de la política en Jalisco*. Guadalajara: Instituto Tecnológico de Estudios Superiores de Occidente.

Deloria, Philip J. 2004. *Indians in Unexpected Places*. Lawrence: University Press of Kansas.

Díaz Polanco, Héctor. 2006. *Elogio de la diversidad: Globalización, multiculturalismo y etnofagia*. Mexico City: Siglo XXI Editores.

Díaz Romo, Patricia, dir. 1994. *Huicholes y plaguicidas*. Texcoco: RAPAM. VHS.

Díaz Romo, Patricia, and Samuel Salinas Álvarez. 2002. *Plaguicidas, Tabaco y salud: El caso de los jornaleros huicholes, jornaleros mestizos y ejidatarios en Nayarit*. Oaxaca: Asociación Mexicana de Arte y Cultura Popular.

Diguet, Léon. 1992. *Por tierras occidentales entre sierras y barrancas*. Translated by Aurelia Álvarez Urbajtel. Compiled by Jesús Jáuregui and Jean Meyer. Mexico City: Centro de Estudios Mexicanos y Centroamericanos de la Embajada de Francia en México.

Du Bois, W. E. B. (1903) 1994. *The Souls of Black Folk*. New York: Dover.

Durin, Séverine, ed. 2008. *Entre luces y sombras: Miradas sobre los indígenas en el área metropolitana de Monterrey*. Mexico City: Publicaciones de la Casa Chata, CIESAS.

Earle, Rebecca. 2007. *The Return of the Native: Indians and Myth-Making in Spanish America, 1810–1930*. Durham, N.C.: Duke University Press.

Escobar, Arturo. 1995. *Encountering Development: The Making and Unmaking of the Third World*. Princeton, N.J.: Princeton University Press.

Escobar, Arturo. 2008. *Territories of Difference: Place, Movements, Life, Redes*. Durham, N.C.: Duke University Press.

Escobar Ohmstede, Antonio, ed. 1993. *Indio, nación y comunidad en el México del siglo XIX*. Mexico City: Centro de Estudios Mexicanos y Centroamericanos.

Escobar Ohmstede, Antonio, ed. 2007. *Los pueblos indios en los tiempos de Benito Juárez*. Oaxaca: Universidad Autónoma Benito Juárez de Oaxaca.

Estados Unidos Mexicanos, Poder Ejecutivo Federal. 1966. *Plan Lerma Asistencia Técnica: Operación Huicot*. Guadalajara: Plan Lerma Asistencia Técnica.

Fabian, Johannes. 1983. *Time and the Other: How Anthropology Makes Its Object*. New York: Columbia University Press.

Falck Reyes, Melba, and Héctor Palacios. 2009. *El japonés que conquistó Guadalajara: La historia de Juan de Páez en la Guadalajara del siglo XVII*. Guadalajara: Universidad de Guadalajara.

Fikes, Jay C. 1993. *Carlos Castaneda, Academic Opportunism and the Psychedelic Sixties*. Victoria, BC: Millenia Press.

Fikes, Jay C. 2011. "Scrutinizing Self-Proclaimed Shamans and Appropriations of Huichol Peyote Pilgrimages, Making Apprentice-Shamans Chic." *The American Mosaic: The American Indian Experience*. Database. https://www.abc-clio.com/ABC-CLIOCorporate/product.aspx?pc=AMINW.

Florescano, Enrique. 2002. *Historia de las historias de la nación mexicana*. Mexico City: Taurus.

Flores de San Pedro, Juan. (1722) 1964. *Autos hechos por el capitán Don Juan Flores de San Pedro sobre la reducción, conversión y conquista de los gentiles de la provincia del Nayarit en 1722*. Guadalajara: Librería Font.

Forbes, Alexander. (1839) 1937. *California: A History of Upper and Lower California*. San Francisco, Calif.: J. H. Nash.

Foro Consultivo Científico Tecnológico. 2018. *Boletín No. 278*, August 9.

Foucault, Michel. 2007. *Security, Territory, Population: Lectures at the Collège de France, 1977–78*. Edited by Michel Senellart. Translated by Graham Burchell. Basingstoke, England: Palgrave Macmillan.

Fragoso, Gisela Carlos, and Fortino Domínguez. 2018. "Cruce de vías: Genealogías teórica sobre el racism para entender el problema de la educación en México." In *Racismo, interculturalidad y educación en México*, edited by Bruno Baronnet, Gisela Carlos Fregoso, and Fortino Domínguez, 17–37. Xalapa: Universidad Veracruzana.

Furst, Peter T. 1972. *Flesh of the Gods: The Ritual Use of Hallucinogens*. New York: Praeger.

Furst, Peter T. 2003. *Visions of a Huichol Shaman*. Philadelphia: University of Pennsylvania Museum of Archaeology and Anthropology.

Furst, Peter T. 2006. *Rock Crystals and Peyote Dreams: Explorations in the Huichol Universe*. Salt Lake City: University of Utah Press.

Furst, Peter T., and Stacy B. Schaefer. 1996. *People of the Peyote: Huichol Indian History, Religion, and Survival*. Albuquerque: University of New Mexico Press.

Fusco, Coco, and Brian Wallis. 2003. *Only Skin Deep: Changing Visions of the American Self*. New York: Abrams.

Galindo Gaitán, Manuel. 2002. *Estampas de Guadalajara*. Guadalajara: Ediciones Pacífico.

Gallagher, Kevin P., and Lyuba Zarsky. 2007. *The Enclave Economy: Foreign Investment and Sustainable Development in Mexico's Silicon Valley*. Cambridge, Mass.: MIT Press.

Gámez, Miguel N. 1863. *Ligera reseña de los últimos acontecimientos que han tenido lugar en el estado de Sinaloa y el cantón de Tepic; y refutación a los cargos que formula el jefe, Ramón Corona, al gobernador de aquel estado, general ciudadano Plácido Vega, hoy en jefe de la Tercera División del Ejército del Centro*. Mazatlán: Tip. del Gobierno a Cargo de M. F. Castro.

Gamio, Manuel. (1916) 1960. *Forjando patria*. Mexico City: Editorial Porrúa.

Gamio, Manuel. 1948. *Consideraciones sobre el problema indígena*. Mexico City: Ediciones del Instituto Indigenista Interamericano.

García, María Elena. 2005. *Making Indigenous Citizens: Identities, Education, and Multicultural Development in Peru*. Stanford, Calif.: Stanford University Press.

García, Silverio. 1878. *Cuestión de Tepic: Artículos publicados en "El Estado de Jalisco."* Guadalajara: Tip. de Banda.

Gascón Mercado, Julián. 1959. *Acuarelas sociales*. Mexico City: Gascón Mercado.

Gascón Mercado, Julián. 1975. *El payaso mexicano*. Mexico City: Editorial Diana.

Gibbon, Eduardo. 1893. *Guadalajara (La Florencia mexicana) Vagancias y recuerdos: El Salto de Juanacatlán y el mar Chapalico*. Guadalajara: Imprenta del "Diario de Jalisco," P. Sánchez.

Gilly, Adolfo. 1971. *La revolución interrumpida—México, 1910–1920: Una guerra campesina por la tierra y el poder*. Mexico City: Ediciones El Caballito.

Gilly, Adolfo. 2001. *El cardenismo: Una utopía mexicana*. Mexico City: Ediciones Era.

Gilly, Adolfo, Arnaldo Córdova, Armando Bartra, Manuel Aguilar Mora, and Enrique Semo. 1979. *Interpretaciones de la revolución mexicana*. Mexico City: Nueva Imagen.

Glissant, Édouard. 1997. *Poetics of Relation*. Ann Arbor: University of Michigan Press.

Godoy, Bernabé. (1954) 1992. *La batalla de la Mojonera*. Zapopan: Colegio de Jalisco.

Gómez Gallegos, María de los Ángeles. 2018. "El racismo de la inteligencia en las interacciones en el aula entre docentes y estudiantes universitarios." In *Racismo, interculturalidad y educación en México*, edited by Bruno Baronnet, Gisela Carlos Fregoso, and Fortino Domínguez, 199–226. Xalapa: Universidad Veracruzana.

Gómez Vírgen, Fernando. 1878a. *Ensayo histórico político sobre la situación de Tepic, en distintas épocas, en sus relaciones con la situación general del país: Juicio crítico*. Guadalajara: Antigua Imprenta de Dionisio Rodríguez.

Gómez Vírgen, Fernando. 1878b. *Tepic, estado independiente*. Guadalajara: Antigua Imprenta de Dionisio Rodríguez.

González Gamio, Ángeles. 1988. "Manuel Gamio." In *Instituto Nacional Indigenista: 40 años*, edited by Lourdes Herrasti Maciá, 442–58. Mexico City: Instituto Nacional Indigenista.

González, Mariana. 2003. "El rechazo a los indígenas en Providencia, reflejo del país." *Gaceta Universidad de Guadalajara*, November 3. http://www.gaceta.udg.mx/Hemeroteca/paginas/320/320-7.pdf.

González Navarro, Moisés. 1994. "Vallarta y Lozada." *La academia mexicana de historia en Guadalajara*, edited by José María Murià, 22–31. Guadalajara: H. Ayuntamiento de Guadalajara.

González y González, Luis. 1994. "Guadalajara en el siglo de las luces." *La academia mexicana de historia en Guadalajara*, edited by José María Murià, 98–105. Guadalajara: H. Ayuntamiento de Guadalajara.

Greene, Shane. 2007. "Introduction: On Race, Roots/Routes and Sovereignty in Latin America's Afro-Indigenous Multiculturalisms." *Journal of Latin American and Caribbean Anthropology* 12 (2): 329–55.

Gupta, Akhil, and James Ferguson. 1997. *Culture, Power, Place: Explorations in Critical Anthropology*. Durham, N.C.: Duke University Press.

Gutiérrez Contreras, Salvador. 1974. *Los coras y el Rey Nayarit*. Tepic: Impre-Jal.

Guzmán, Nuño Beltrán de. (1530) 1952. *Proceso contra Tzintzicha Tangaxoan, El Caltontzin, formado por Nuño de Guzmán, año de 1530*. Edited by France Acholes and Eleanor Adams. Mexico City: Porrúa y Obregón.

Guzmán, Nuño Beltrán de. (1531) 1937. *Nuno de Guzmán contra Hernán Cortés, sobre los descubrimientos y conquistas en Jalisco y Tepic*. In *Boletín del Archivo General de la Nación, México* 8 (3): 365–576.

Guzmán Pérez Peláez, Fernando. 2001. "Desarrollo humano integral y acción ciudadana: el DHIAC." Renée de la Torre and Juan Manuel Ramírez Saíz La ciudadanización de la política en Jalisco, Guadalajara, Jal: Instituto Tecnológico de Estudios Superiores de Occidente, pp. 149-192.

Hale, Charles A. 1989. *The Transformation of Liberalism in Late Nineteenth-Century Mexico*. Princeton, N.J.: Princeton University Press.

Hale, Charles R. 2006. *Más que un indio: Racial Ambivalence and Neoliberal Multiculturalism in Guatemala*. Santa Fe, N.Mex.: School of American Research Press.

Hall, Stuart. 1986. "Gramsci's Relevance for the Study of Race and Ethnicity." *Stuart Hall: Critical Dialogues*, edited by David Morley and Kuan-Hsing Chen, 411–40. London: Routledge.

Hall, Stuart, and Paul du Gay. 1996. *Questions of Cultural Identity*. London: Sage.

Hartman, Saidiya. 2008. "Venus in Two Acts." *Small Axe* 2 6:1–14.

Harvey, David. 2008. "The Right to the City." *New Left Review* 53 (September–October). https://newleftreview.org/issues/II53/articles/david-harvey-the-right-to-the-city.

Hernández Castillo, Rosalva Aída. 1997. "El zapatismo en la era de la autonomía." *Este país* 80 (November). http://archivo.estepais.com/inicio/historicos/80/18_galaxia_zapatismo_aida.pdf.

Hernández Castillo, Rosalva Aída. 2007. "La Guerra sucia en contra de las mujeres." *Ojarasca/La Jornada* 121:n.p .

Hernández Castillo, Rosalva Aída, Sarela Paz, and María Teresa Sierra, ed. 2004. *El Estado y los indígenas en tiempos del PAN: Neoindigenismo, legalidad e identidad*. Mexico City: Cámara de Diputados.

Hernández Silva, Héctor. 2007. *Los mil rostros de Juárez y del liberalismo mexicano*. Mexico City: Universidad Autónoma de México.

Hernández Larrañaga, Javier. 2001. *Guadalajara: Identidad perdida, transformación urbana en el siglo XX*. Guadalajara: Agata El Informador, Secretaría de Cultura de Jalisco.

Herrasti Maciá, Lourdes, ed. 1988. *Instituto Nacional Indigenista: 40 años*. Mexico City: Instituto Nacional Indigenista.

Ignorosa Mijangos, Oscar, ed. 1994. *Aguamilpa: Ojo de luz en territorio mágico*. Mexico City: Comisión Federal de Eléctricidad and Grupo ICA.
Instituto Nacional de Geografía y Estadística (INEGI). 1995. *Conteo Nacional de Población y Vivienda*. Aguascalientes: Instituto Nacional de Geografía y Estadística.
International Labour Organization (ILO). 1989. *Indigenous and Tribal Peoples Convention, 1989 (No. 169)*. Adopted June 27, 1989. Geneva: ILO. https://www.ilo.org/dyn/normlex/en/f?p=NORMLEXPUB:12100:0::NO::P12100_ILO_CODE:C169.
Jáuregui, Jesús. 1999. "El recuerdo del señor Manuel Lozada está todavía patente." *Manuel Lozada: Luz y Sombra*, edited by Manuel Salinas Solís, 259–93. Tepic: Universidad Autónoma de Nayarit, Cámara de Diputados.
Jáuregui, Jesús. 2010. "El son mariachero de la negra: De gusto regional independentista a aire nacional contemporáneo." *Revista literaturas populares* 10 (1–2): 270–318.
Jáuregui, Jesús, and Jean Meyer. 1997. *El Tigre de Álica: Mitos e historias de Manuel Lozada*. Tepic: SEP; CONAFE.
Jiménez Pelayo, Agueda, Jaime Olveda, Beatriz Núñez Miranda. 1995. *El crecimiento urbano de Guadalajara*. Zapopan: Colegio de Jalisco.
Joseph, Gilbert M., and Daniel Nugent, eds. 1994. *Everyday Forms of State Formation: Revolution and the Negotiation of Rule in Modern Mexico*. Durham, N.C.: Duke University Press.
Katz, Friedrich. 1998. *The Life and Times of Pancho Villa*. Stanford, Calif.: Stanford University Press.
Katzew, Ilona. 2004. *Casta Painting: Images of Race in Eighteenth-Century Mexico*. New Haven, Conn.: Yale University Press.
Keith, Michael, and Steve Pile, eds. 1993. *Place and the Politics of Identity*. London: Routledge.
Kindl, Olivia. 2003. *La jícara huichola: Un microcosmos mesoamericano*. Mexico City: Instituto Nacional de Antropología e Historia.
Knab, Tim. 1981. "Artesanía y urbanización: El caso de los huicholes." *América Indígena* 41 (2): 231–43.
Knight, Alan. 1986. *The Mexican Revolution*. 2 vols. Lincoln: University of Nebraska Press.
Laclau, Ernesto, and Chantal Mouffe. 1985. *Hegemony and Socialist Strategy: Toward a Radical Democratic Politics*. London: Verso.
Lagos de Moreno, Citizens. 1886. "Esta redacción, haciéndose eco de las aspiraciones del pueblo de Jalisco, postula para Gobernador del Estado en el próximo periodo constitucional al intachable Ciudadano General Ramón Corona." Lagos de Moreno, Jalisco, January 6. Bancroft Double Folio. Bancroft Library, University of California, Berkeley.
Lefebvre, Henri. (1974) 2000. *La production de l'espace*. Paris: Anthropos.
Li, Tania Murray. 2007. *The Will to Improve: Governmentality, Development, and the Practice of Politics*. Durham, N.C.: Duke University Press.
Liffman, Paul. 2011. *Huichol Territory and the Mexican Nation: Indigenous Ritual, Land Conflict, and Sovereignty Claims*. Tucson: University of Arizona Press.

Limón Rojas, Miguel. 1988. "El indigenismo: Un imperative nacional." In *Instituto Nacional Indigenista: 40 años*, edited by Lourdes Herrasti Maciá, 81–104. Mexico City: Instituto Nacional Indigenista.

Lomnitz, Claudio. 2001. *Deep Mexico, Silent Mexico: An Anthropology of Nationalism*. Minneapolis: University of Minnesota Press.

López Almaraz, Raúl. 1984. *Ramón Corona: Autopsia psicológica de su asesino*. Guadalajara: Gobierno de Jalisco Secretaría General Unidad Editorial.

López González, Pedro. 1984. *La población de Tepic bajo la organización regional (1530–1821)*. Tepic: Universidad Autónoma de Nayarit.

López González, Pedro. 1996. *El centro histórico de la ciudad de Tepic*. Tepic: Ayuntamiento de Tepic.

López González, Pedro. 1999. Xalisco, el original. Xalisco, Nay.: XXXIV H. Ayuntamiento de Xalisco.

López González, Pedro. 2000. El centro histórico de la ciudad de Tepic. México: XXXV H. Ayuntamiento de Tepic.

López González, Pedro, and José María Murià. 1994. *Tepic, el Vigía del Nayar*. Guadalajara: El Colegio de Jalisco.

Lumholtz, Carl. 1903. *Unknown Mexico: A Record of Five Years of Exploration among Tribes of the Western Sierra Madre; in the Sierra Caliente of Tepec and Jalisco; and among the Tarascos of Michoacán*. 2 vols. London: Macmillan.

Luna Jiménez, Pedro. 1999. *Tepic: Aproximación a su historia urbana*. Colección Rescate 2. Tepic: Fundación Nayarit.

Mackinlay, Horacio. 2008. "Jornaleros agrícolas y agroquímicos en la producción de tabaco en Nayarit." *Alteridades* 18 (36): 123–43.

Manzanares Monter, Sara Alejandra. 2009. "Staging Indigeneity, Expressing Mestizaje: Dress and Identity in Nayarit, Mexico." Master's thesis, University of Oslo.

Mariátegui, José Carlos. (1928) 1979. *Siete ensayos de interpretación de la realidad peruana*. Caracas: Biblioteca Ayacucho.

Martínez Casas, Regina. 2007. *Vivir invisibles: La resignificación cultural entre los otomíes urbanos de Guadalajara*. Mexico City: Publicaciones de la Casa Chata, CIESAS.

Martínez Casas, Regina, Emíko Saldívar, René Flores, and Christina Sue. 2014. "The Different Faces of Mestizaje: Ethnicity and Race in Mexico." *Pigmentocracies: Ethnicity, Race, and Color in Latin America*, edited by Edward Telles, 36–80. Chapel Hill: University of North Carolina Press.

Martínez Novo, Carmen. 2006. *Who Defines Indigenous? Identity, Development, Intellectuals, and the State in Northern Mexico*. New Brunswick, N.J.: Rutgers University Press.

Mayo, John. 2006. *Commerce and Contraband on Mexico's West Coast in the Era of Barron, Forbes and Co., 1821–1851*. New York: Peter Lang.

Mayo, Milca, Isaura García, and Antonio García. 2014. *Porticus: Educación no formal estudiantes indígenas urbanos en la zona metropolitan de Guadalajara (ZMG)*. Guadalajara: Instituto Tecnológico y de Estudios Superiores de Occidente, Centro de Investigación y Formación Social.

MacLean, Hope. 2012. *The Shaman's Mirror: Visionary Art of the Huichol.* Austin: University of Texas Press.

Melgoza, Ángel. 2005. "El parquet de las gatas: racism en Guadalajara." *Revista territorios* 4:n.p.

Mendoza Mayo, Milca, Isaura García Hernández, and Antonio García Mijarez. 2013. *Jóvenes Indígenas Urbanos en la Zona Metropolitana de Guadalajara.* Guadalajara: ITESO and CIFS.

Meyer, Jean. 1969. "El ocaso de Manuel Lozada." *Historia mexicana* 8 (4): 535–68.

Meyer, Jean. 1974. *La Cristiada.* Vols. 1–3. Mexico City: Singlo Veintiuno Editores.

Meyer, Jean. 1989. *Esperando a Lozada.* Guadalajara: Universidad de Guadalajara.

Meyer, Jean. 1990. *De cantón de Tepic a estado de Nayarit, 1810–1940.* Guadalajara: Universidad de Guadalajara.

Meyer, Jean. 1993. "La junta protectora de las clases menesterosas: Indigenismo y agrarismo en el Segundo Imperio." *Indio, nación y comunidad en el siglo XIX*, edited by Antonio Escobar Ohmstede, 329–64. Mexico City: Centro de Estudios Mexicanos y Centroamericano.

Meyer, Jean. 1997. *Breve historia de Nayarit.* Mexico City: El Colegio de México.

Mora, Mariana. 2018. *Kuxlejal Politics: Indigenous Autonomy, Race, and Decolonizing Research in Zapatista Communities.* Austin: University of Texas Press.

Morley, David, and Kuan-Hsing Chen, eds. 1996. *Stuart Hall: Critical Dialogues in Cultural Studies.* London: Routledge.

Mundy, Barbara E. 1996. *The Mapping of New Spain: Indigenous Cartography and the Maps of the Relaciones Geográficas.* Chicago: University of Chicago Press.

Murià, José María. 1989. "Homenaje a Ramón Corona." In *Homenaje a Ramón Corona en el primer centenario de su muerte*, edited by Angélica Peregrina and Cándido Galván, 11–20. Guadalajara: Gobierno del Estado de Jalisco, Secretaría de Educación y Cultura.

Murià, José María. 1993. *San Blas de Nayarit.* Zapopan: El Colegio de Jalisco.

Murià, José María. 1994a. "Guadalajara y la Rebelión de los Cazcanes." *La academia mexicana de historia en Guadalajara*, edited by José María Murià, 11–21. Guadalajara: Ayuntamiento de Guadalajara.

Murià, José María, ed. 1994b. *La academia mexicana de historia en Guadalajara.* Guadalajara: Ayuntamiento de Guadalajara.

Murià, José María. 2004a. *Sucesos históricos de Guadalajara.* Guadalajara: Ayuntamiento de Guadalajara.

Murià, José María. 2004b. *Viñetas de Guadalajara.* Guadalajara: Ayuntamiento de Guadalajara.

Napolitano, Valentina. 2002. *Migration, Mujercitas, and Medicine Men: Living in Urban Mexico.* Berkeley: University of California Press.

Negrín, Juan. 1985. *Acercamiento histórico y subjetivo a los huicholes.* Guadalajara: Universidad de Guadalajara.

Negrín, Juan. 2003a. "Early History." Wixárika Research Center. Accessed April 12, 2019. http://www.wixarika.org/early-history-juan-negrín.

Negrín, Juan. 2003b. "Recent History." Wixárika Research Center. Accessed April 12, 2019. http://www.wixarika.org/recent-history-juan-negrín.

Negrín, Juan. 2006. "¿Qué atrae a los indígenas huicholes hacia el Océano Pacífico?" In *Huicholes y plaguicidas*, directed by Patricia Díaz Romo. Oaxaca: Ojo de Agua Comunicación Indígena.

Negrín da Silva, Diana. 2004. "Toward a New Relation? The Struggle to Preserve Huichol Self-Sufficiency in the Face of the Developmentalist Politics of the Mexican State." Bachelor's honors thesis, University of California, Berkeley.

Negrín da Silva, Diana. 2015. "El indio que todos quieren: El consumo de lo huichol tras la defensa de Wirikuta." *Sociedad y ambiente* 1 (8): 54–74.

Nelson, Diane. 1999. *A Finger in the Wound: Body Politics in Quincentennial Guatemala.* Berkeley: University of California Press.

Neurath, Johannes. 2002. *Las fiestas de la casa grande: Procesos rituales, cosmovisión y estructura social en una comunidad huichola.* Mexico City: Instituto Nacional de Antropología e Historia.

Olveda, Jaime. 1991. *La oligarquía de Guadalajara: De las reformas borbónicas a la reforma liberal.* Mexico City: CONACULTA.

Olveda, Jaime. 1996. *Economía y sociedad en las regiones de México: Siglo XIX.* Zapopan: Colegio de Jalisco.

Olveda, Jaime. 2000. *Guadalajara: Abasto, religión y empresarios.* Guadalajara: Ayuntamiento de Guadalajara.

Orozco y Berra, Manuel. 1880. *Historia antigua y de la conquista de México.* Mexico City: Tip. De G.A. Esteva.

Pacheco Ladrón de Guevara, Lourdes, ed. 1992. *Como votamos en Nayarit en 1991.* Tepic: Fundación Cultural "Antonia Pérez Cisneros."

Parra, Francisco. 1805-10. "Conquista de la Provincia de Xalisco, nuevo reyno de Galicia y fundación de su capital, Guadalaxara: Narración poético sencilla distribuida en XXXI cantos." Hubert Howe Bancroft Collection. Bancroft Library, University of California, Berkeley.

Peregrina, Angélica. 2004. "Mataron a Ramón Corona." In *Viñetas de Guadalajara*, edited by José María Murià, 111–14. Guadalajara: Ayuntamiento de Guadalajara.

Peregrina, Angélica, and Cándido Galván, eds. 1989. *Homenaje a Ramón Corona: En el primer centenario de su muerte.* Guadalajara: Secretaría de Educación y Cultura.

Pérez Ruiz, Maya Lorena. 2001. Review for *Reforma del Estado. Política social e indigenismo en México.* 1988-1996. Alteridades, no. 21, p. 117-120.

Petras, James. 1997. "Imperialism and NGOs in Latin America." *Monthly Review* 49 (7): 10–27.

Plascencia Flores, Julio A. 1984. *Industria textil y movimiento obrero en Tepic.* Tepic: Universidad Autónoma de Nayarit.

Polanyi, Karl. (1944) 2001. *The Great Transformation: The Political and Economic Origins of Our Time.* Boston, Mass.: Beacon Press.

Poole, Deborah. 1997. *Vision, Race, and Modernity: A Visual Economy of the Andean Image World.* Princeton, N.J.: Princeton University Press.

Postero, Nancy Grey. 2007. *Now We Are Citizens: Indigenous Politics in Postmulticultural Bolivia.* Stanford, Calif.: Stanford University Press.

Povinelli, Elizabeth. 2002. *The Cunning of Recognition: Indigenous Alterities and the Making of Australian Multiculturalism.* Durham, N.C.: Duke University Press.

Pozas, Ricardo. 1988. *Juan Pérez Jolote: Biografía de un tzotzil.* Mexico City: Fondo de Cultura Económica.

Pred, Allan. 2004. *The Past Is Not Dead: Facts, Fictions, and Enduring Racial Stereotypes.* Minneapolis: University of Minnesota Press.

Razo Zaragoza, José Luis. 1970. *Crónicas de la conquista del nuevo reyno de Galicia.* Mexico City: Instituto Jalisciense de Antropología e Historia.

Reed, Karen. 1972. *El INI y los huicholes.* Mexico City: Secretaría de Educación Pública, Instituto Nacional Indigenista.

Reina Aoyama, Leticia. 1993. "Introducción." *Indio, nación y comunidad en el México del siglo XIX,* edited by Antonio Escobar Ohmstede, 11–17. Mexico City: Centro de Estudios Mexicanos y Centroamericanos.

Reynoso, Salvador. 1964. *Autos hechos por el capitán don Juan Flores de San Pedro: Sobre la reducción, conversión y conquista de los gentiles de la provincia del Nayarit en 1722.* Guadalajara: Font.

Rhoux, Rhina. 2005. *El príncipe mexicano: Subalternidad, historia y estado.* Mexico City: Ediciones Era.

Rivière d'Arc, Hélène. 1973. *Guadalajara y su región: Influencias y dificultades de una metrópoli mexicana.* Translated by Carlos Montemayor and Josefina Anaya. Mexico City: Secretaría de Educación Pública.

Robles Vásquez, Héctor, and Mónica Pérez Miranda, eds. 2017. *Breve panorama educativo de la población indígena.* Mexico City: Instituto Nacional para la Evaluación de la Educación.

Rodríguez, Luis Eloy. 1994. *Los huicholes y su relocalización involuntaria por el proyecto hidroeléctrico Aguamilpa, Nay. Y con algunas particularidades en los ejidos de Colorado de la Mora y Playa Golondrinas.* Undergraduate Thesis, Universidad Autónoma Nacional de México.

Rojas, Beatriz. 1993. "Los huicholes: Episodios nacionales." *Indio, nación y comunidad en el siglo XIX,* edited by Antonio Escobar Ohmstede, 253–65. Mexico City: Centro de Estudios Mexicanos y Centroamericanos.

Roseberry, William. 1994. "Hegemony and the Language of Contention." *Everyday Forms of State Formation: Revolution and the Negotiation of Rule in Modern Mexico,* edited by Gilbert M. Joseph and Daniel Nugent, 355–66. Durham, N.C.: Duke University Press.

Rus, Jan. 1994. "La 'Comunidad Revolucionaria Institucional': The Subversion of Native Government in Highland Chiapas, 1936–1968." In *Everyday Forms of State Formation: Revolution and the Negotiation of Rule in Modern Mexico,* edited by Gilbert M. Joseph and Daniel Nugent, 265–300. Durham, N.C.: Duke University Press.

Sahagún, Bernardino de. (1590) 1829. *Historia de la conquista de México.* Vols. 1–3. Mexico City: Impr. de Galvan à cargo de M. Arévalo.

Sahagún, Bernardino de. 1990. *Breve compendio de los ritos idolátricos que los indios de esta Nueva España usaban en tiempo de su infidelidad.* Mexico City: Lince Editores.

Said, Edward W. (1978) 1994. *Orientalism*. New York: Vintage Books.
Saldaña-Portillo, María Josefina. 2016. *Indian Given: Racial Geographies across Mexico and the United States*. Durham, N.C.: Duke University Press.
Sánchez Montes, Ignacio de Jesús. 2009. "Juan Kaiser: Editor e impresor de papel moneda y tarjetas postales en Guadalajara." *Boletín Eclesiástico, Arzobispado de Guadalajara* 120 (5). https://arquidiocesisgdl.org/boletin/2009-5-7.php.
Santamaría, Francisco J. 1959. *Diccionario de mejicanismos, razonado: Comprobado con citas de autoridades, comparado con el de americanismos y con los vocabularios provinciales de los más distinguidos diccionaristas hispanoamericanos*. Mexico City: Editorial Porrúa.
Santana, José Epigmenio. 1930. *Nuño Beltrán de Guzmán y su obra en la Nueva España*. Mexico City: Museo Nacional de Arqueología, Historia y Etnografía.
Speed, Shannon. 2008. *Rights in Rebellion: Indigenous Struggle and Human Rights in Chiapas*. Stanford, Calif.: Stanford University Press.
Spivak, Gayatri Chakravorty. 1999. *A Critique of Postcolonial Reason: Toward a History of the Vanishing Present*. Cambridge, Mass.: Harvard University Press.
Stepan, Nancy Leys. 1991. *"The Hour of Eugenics": Race, Gender, and Nation in Latin America*. Ithaca, N.Y.: Cornell University Press.
Stoler, Ann Laura. *Along the Archival Grain: Epistemic Anxieties and Colonial Common Sense*. Princeton, N.J.: Princeton University Press.
Talavera Durón, Luis Francisco. 2003. *Las venas del tabaco: La migración de los wixaritari en la costa de Nayarit*. Bachelor's thesis, Escuela Nacional de Antropología e Historia, Mexico City.
Taussig, Michael. 1987. *Shamanism, Colonialism, and the Wild Man: A Study in Terror and Healing*. Chicago: University of Chicago Press.
Tays, George. 1941. "Reconnaissance of the Mexican Territory of (Tepic) Nayarit. A Study Done for the Commission on National Defense, Chairman Major General David P. Barrows, at the Request of the Chief of Staff of the United States Army General George C. Marshall, in 1941, when the Defense Program Was Beginning." Bancroft Library, University of California, Berkeley.
Telles, Edward. 2014. *Pigmentocracies: Ethnicity, Race, and Color in Latin America*. Chapel Hill: University of North Carolina Press.
Topete Bordes, Luis. 1944. *Jalisco precortesiano: Estudio histórico y etnogénico*. Mexico City: El Sobre Azul.
Torres Contreras, José de Jesús. 2000. *El hostigamiento a "el costumbre" huichol: Los procesos de hibridación social*. Zamora: El Colegio de Michoacán.
Torres Contreras, José de Jesús. 2009. *Relaciones de frontera entre los huicholes y mestizos—Santa Catarina y Huejuquilla el Alto*. Zapopan: El Colegio de Jalisco.
Torres Sánchez, Rafael. 2001. *Revolución y vida cotidiana: Guadalajara, 1914–1934*. Mexico City: Galileo Ediciones.
Universidad Autónoma de Nayarit. 2011. "Universidad Autónoma de Nayarit, Plan de Desarrollo Institucional, Visión 2030." *La Gaceta*, April 15.
Valerio Ulloa, Sergio. 2002. *Empresarios extranjeros en Guadalajara durante el porfiriato*. Guadalajara: Universidad de Guadalajara, CUCSH.

Vasconcelos, José. (1948) 2007. *La raza cósmica*. Mexico City: Editorial Porrúa.
Velasco Murillo, Dana. 2016. *Urban Indians in a Silver City: Zacatecas, México, 1546–1810*. Stanford, Calif.: Stanford University Press.
Villoro, Luis. (1950) 1987. *Los grandes momentos del indigenismo en México*. Mexico City: Colegio de México.
Wade, Peter. 1997. *Race and Ethnicity in Latin America*. London: Pluto Press.
Warman, Arturo, Margarita Nolasco Armas, Guillermo Bonfil Batalla, Mercedes Olivera de Vázquez, and Enrique Valencia. 1970. *De eso que llaman antropología mexicana*. Mexico City: Editorial Nuestro Tiempo.
Watts, Michael. 2003. "Development and Governmentality." *Singapore Journal of Tropical Geography* 24 (1): 6–34.
Weckman Muñoz, Luis. 1994. "Florecimiento y decadencia del espíritu caballeresco en la Guadalajara del siglo XVI." *La academia mexicana de historia en Guadalajara*, edited by José María Murià, 117–20. Guadalajara: Ayuntamiento de Guadalajara.
Winichakul, Thongchai. 1994. *Siam Mapped: A History of the Geo-Body of the Nation*. Honolulu: University of Hawai'i Press.
Womack, John. 1969. *Zapata and the Mexican Revolution*. New York: Knopf.

INDEX

Acapulco, 96, 98, 100, 129
acción indigenista, 9, 53–54, 58, 62–63, 76
activism, 16, 18, 64–67, 152, 170–182, 184
Africans: in casta paintings, 35; cultural obliteration of, 42; in Guadalajara, Jalisco, 118–19; in Mexico, 96–97; racial stereotypes of, 29, 35; second class citizenship of, 62; in Tepic, Nayarit, 85
agrarianism, 62–63
agribusinesses, 105–6, 108, 110, 122
Aguamilpa hydroelectric dam, 74–76, 108, 171
Aguirre Beltrán, Gustavo, 52, 58, 62–64
Aguirre monopoly, 103–4
Alexander, M. Jacqui, 112, 147–48, 184–85, 190
Alta California, 96, 99
alterity, 33–34, 49, 52, 54, 164
anthropology, 14, 58, 61, 63–64
archives, 155, 158
assimilation, 17, 58, 157
authenticity, 14–15, 32, 86, 113, 154–59, 161–62, 164
Autonomous University of Nayarit (UAN), 3–4, 108, 162, 169, 176–78
Aztecs, 8, 25–26, 29, 31, 163

Barron, Eustace, 98–102
Barron, Forbes and Company, 88, 99–100, 103, 131
Barthes, Roland, 24, 26, 30–31
Battle of La Mojonera, 11, 48, 86, 89–90, 119–123
beaded crafts, 81, 108, 160
Bellavista, 100, 102–3, 110
belonging, 142–43, 172, 188–190
Benitez Sánchez, José, 108, 111
Black Legend, 25, 28, 56
Bourbon Reforms, 36, 97, 128
British American Tobacco, 82, 105–6
Brodie, John Pringle, 81, 96, 100

capitalism, 53–54, 63–64, 99–100, 132, 149
Cárdenas, Lázaro, 58, 60, 69, 104
cartography, 45, 100–102
casta paintings, 24, 32, 34, 50
castas, 29, 36–37
Castillo Cocom, Juan, 15, 155, 160–61, 172–73
Catholic Church, 7, 10, 91, 94, 120, 124, 135, 139–140
Caxcan Rebellion, 126. *See also* Mixtón War

Center for the Investigation and study in Social Anthropology (CIESAS), 154, 159, 169
Centro Coordinador Indigenista Cora-Huichol, 68, 70, 78
Centro de Investigaciones y Estudios Superiores en Antropología Social (CIESAS), 154, 159, 169
Chiapas, 12, 56, 62–63, 110
Chichimec, 42, 126–27
Cihuapili Tzapotzintli, 124–25
citizenship, 16, 32, 44, 50, 76, 142–43, 158
Clavijero, Francisco Javier, 27–30, 41–43
colonialism, 6, 39–40, 77–78, 87, 149. *See also* Spanish colonialism
Colonia Zitakua, 108–14
Comisión Federal de Electricidad (CFE), 75
Comisión Nacional para el Desarrollo de lost Pueblos Indígenas (CDI), 66, 72, 138
Comité de Estudio y Deslindes (committee for Study and Demarcation), 89
Consejo Supremo Huichol, 71–72
contraband markets, 87, 98–100, 131
Corona, Ramón, 11, 88–90, 120–23
Cortés, Hernán, 29, 31, 39–41, 123
Cuauhtémoc, 30–31

de la Cadena, Marisol, 26, 31, 188–89
de la Peña, Guillermo, 53, 66, 74, 135, 142–43
Deloria, Philip J., 16, 162–63, 181
Díaz, Porfirio, 27, 47–50, 103, 122, 130–31, 133–34, 143–44
discrimination: anxieties of the dominant class and, 142; classism and, 147–48; in education, 138–140, 152–53, 155, 169–170; exclusion as, 117, 138–140, 142, 147–48; of indigenous peoples, 169–170, 187; institutional, 7–8; popular, 7–8; "positive," 116–17, 145–46, 158–59; of Wixarika, 7–8, 155, 169–170, 187. *See also* racism

Echeverría, Antonio, 111, 153
Echeverría, Luis, 65, 104

education: activism and, 170–180; as an assimilation tool, 17, 53, 58; attendance rates, 17, 69, 169; boarding schools and, 69; community service after, 168–69, 176–77, 188–89; cultural, 17; discrimination in, 138, 152–53, 155, 169–170; exclusion from, 138; failure of, 69; funding of, 167–68; graduation rates, 17; in Guadalajara, Jalisco, 17; primary schools and, 31; racism in, 83–84; research on, 17–18; rural, 5, 53–54, 58, 68–69, 169; teacher-promotores and, 68–69; in Tepic, Nayarit, 17; of Wixarika, 16–19, 78
ejido system, 62, 105, 136
El Güerote Chulote, 22–24, 49
El Tigre de Álica, 48, 88, 120–23. *See also* Lozada, Manuel
enslaved Africans, 8, 29

Fabian, Johannes, 11, 149
Ferguson, James, 15, 143, 172
fetish effect, 160–61
fiFcAtCiTonS, 23, 90
Florescano, Enrique, 27–28
Flores Muñoz, Guillermo, 104, 106
Forbes, Alexander, 99–102
forced labor, 30, 101, 127
Foucault, Michel, 53–54
Franciscans, 73, 78, 93

Gamio, Manuel, 26, 44, 58–59, 61–63, 65, 70, 73
García Cubas, Antonio, 45–46
Gascón Mercado, Alejandro, 104–5, 108
Glissant, Édouard, 38, 41
Green Revolution, 65, 137
Guadalajara, Jalisco: Africans in, 118–19; agribusinesses in, 122, 129–130; arts and crafts sales in, 143–45; autonomy of, 128–29; barrios of, 136–37; Battle of La Mojonera and, 119–123; bribery in, 131; California and, 136; Catholic Church and, 10; city geography of, 131–140;

classism in, 139–140; colonialism in, 6; colonization and, 127; commercial ventures of, 129–130, 135; conservatives of, 120, 139–140; contraband markets in, 131; corruption in, 131; as a criollo city, 118, 127–28, 134; demographics of, 12, 118–19, 128, 131–32, 138–140; description of, 12, 132–33; development of, 128; discrimination by, 143–44; economic development of, 94, 128–29; ejido system in, 136; electronics industry of, 136; expansion of, 131–140; exploitation of laborers in, 131; expropriation of land in, 129–130, 132, 136; foreign investments in, 129–131, 134–35; founding of, 124; growth of, 12, 135; heterogeneity of, 118; Hispanicized goal for, 126, 134, 149; historical development of, 6, 10–11; housing in, 131–32; identity of, 118–19, 122, 132, 134; immigration to, 128–135; importance of, 96, 126; indigenous peoples in, 131–141, 154; information technology industry of, 136; invasion of, 47–48; land dispossession in, 128; land ownership in, 128; liberalism in, 119–120, 130, 139–140; location of, 10; Manuel Lozado and, 47–48, 88–89, 120–23; Mexican Revolution in, 133–34; mining and, 127, 129–130; modernity and, 134; monopolies in, 131; Nahuas in, 137, 139–140; nicknames for, 134, 136; normative identity of, 119; Nuño Beltrán de Guzmán and, 123–25; peninsulares and, 128; people of African descent in, 12; Plan Libertador and, 120–21; political development of, 11, 128–29; political economy of, 6; populism in, 134; race in, 11, 122, 132; racism in, 138–140; railroad and, 102, 122; Ramón Corona and, 120–23; regulation of, 134, 143–44; *repartimiento* system and, 127; research on, 6; segregation of, 134; self-identification of, 118; shops in, 130–31; social development of, 6; socioeconomic hierarchy of, 127–28, 139–140, 149; spacial production of, 13; Spanish colonialism in, 123–26; suburbanization of, 136–37; Tapatio families of, 129; Tepic, Nayarit and, 10, 122; urbanization of, 127, 129, 133–140; whitening of, 118–19; Wixarika in, 151, 189–190. *See also* Andalusia of Mexico; City of Lights; Mexican Florence; Pearl of the West

Gupta, Akhil, 15, 143, 172
Guzmán, Nuño Beltrán de, 87, 90–92, 123–26

Hale, Charles R., 115–16, 164, 181
Hall, Stuart, 15, 143, 173
Hartman, Saidiya, 8–9
Harvey, David, 148–49
Huichi, 144–45
hunger, 87, 93
hypervisibility, 13, 32, 67, 111, 182

identity: activism and, 171–180; Akhil Gupta and, 143; development of, 15–16; as dynamic, 142–43; ethnic, 142–43; Guillermo de la Peña and, 143; of indigenous peoples, 188–89; James Ferguson and, 143; Juan Castillo Cocom and, 172–73; multiple, 143, 172–73; as performative, 15; as potentially painful, 173; reconnection with, 173–75; space and, 15; Stuart Hall and, 143; of Wixarika, 188–89

Incas, 8, 26, 29
"Indian problem," 30, 44, 51, 54, 60, 66, 76
indigeneity, 21, 31, 115, 157, 160
indigenismo: agrarianism and, 62–63; as bourgeois, 64; chronology of, 25; critiques of, 64; definition of, 25–26; as an epistemic system, 8; first moment of, 39–41; functionalism of, 60; iconography and, 25; "Indian problem" and, 54; indigenous peoples and, 57–58; legacy of, 161; Luis Echeverría and, 104; Luis Villoro and, 25; Mexican Revolution (1910) and, 53; modern developmentalism and, 62;

as neocolonial, 64; paternalism and, 73; research on, 8; second moment of, 41–43; space and, 38; termination of, 66; third moment of, 44–50; time and, 38; visual representations and, 25

indigenous peoples: academic studies of, 14; acculturation of, 53, 57–58, 60–61; activism of, 64–67, 170–180; alterity and, 33–34, 49–50, 52; archives as problematic for, 156; assimilation of, 58, 157; authenticity of, 14–15, 32, 86, 113, 154–59, 164–65; Benito Juárez and, 48; as "biologically deficient," 61; bravery of, 27–28; categories of, 35–36, 54; citizenship of, 60; civil rights of, 137; classifications of, 59, 132; classified as "bad," 35–36, 45, 49, 91, 94; classified as "good," 35–36, 45, 49, 91, 94; commodification of, 140–41; communal landholdings of, 30, 44–51, 54, 100–102; communication with, 145; contemporary representations of, 7; conversions of, 39, 93, 95–96; cooperatives and, 65; cultural identity of, 63, 137, 154; cultural obliteration of, 42; culture of, 53, 57–58; defense of, 25–26; as different, 52, 117; discrimination against, 138–140, 147–48, 169–170, 187; dispossession of, 42, 44–50, 57, 100–102, 129–130, 132, 136–37; as docile, 47; education of, 64, 138; enslavement of, 59, 92, 123, 125; exclusion of, 13, 138–140, 147–48; as exclusively rural, 11, 14–15; folklore of, 53; forced acculturation of, 42; forced labor of, 30, 101, 127; in Guadalajara, Jalisco, 12, 131–32, 134–140, 154; health of, 64; in higher education, 158–59, 164–172; hypervisibility of, 13; identity and, 181–82, 188–89; identity politics and, 9; as ignorant, 73; inclusion of, 188–89; indigenismo and, 25–26, 57–58; as inferior, 23, 43, 59; intercommunal political bodies of, 72; internal cultural differences of, 154; ladinos and, 115–16, 164; land disputes and, 72; land ownership by, 87; land use by, 73–74; languages of, 140–41; lasting impact of colonialism on, 149; leadership of, 70–72; as malleable, 36, 47; Manuel Gamio and, 61; marginalization of, 142; in Mexico, 183–87; Mexico and, 66–67; migration to cities by, 11, 137–38; mobility of, 126; mobilization of, 9; models of governance of, 73–74; modernity and, 63; murder of, 42, 92–93; nationalist histories and, 24; natural resources of, 73–74; oppression of, 58; othering of, 24–25, 33, 38, 114, 141, 151; as passive, 73, 92, 125; performance and, 161–62; political mobilization of, 161; positive discrimination and, 145–46, 158–59; power structures and, 31; racial ambivalence and, 115–16, 141, 164, 181; racial stereotypes and, 11, 14, 27–28, 73, 138–142, 161–62, 169, 178, 181–82; racism and, 59, 138–140; recognition of, 155–56; reconnection with, 173–75; rejection of, 142; religion of, 39; representations of, 63, 157–58; research on, 42, 158; resistance by, 23, 25, 29, 42, 44–50, 52–53, 87, 92–93, 125–26; rights of, 87, 163; as seasonal migratory workers, 63–64; segregation of, 30; self-determination of, 66; social media and, 157–58; social mobility of, 149; space and, 32; Spanish colonialism and, 8, 10; stigmas facing, 142; subordination of, 40–41; on television, 157–58; Tepic, Nayarit and, 12–13, 18; territorial autonomy of, 9; as threatening, 29; tourism and, 24; traditional attire of, 140–41; as unproductive, 65; in urban geographies, 6–7; urban studies and, 21; as used in advertisements, 158; violence against, 8, 44, 48, 64; as wage laborers, 42; workers rights and, 65

indios amigos, 45, 49, 91, 94
indios de guerra, 45, 49, 91, 94

Instituto Nacional Indigenista (INI): assimilation by, 53–54, 58; centro coordinador indigenista of, 63–64, 66–68; coordinating model and, 66; defunding of, 65–66; education and, 83; Guillermo de la Peña and, 66; nation building through, 53–54; rural education and, 5, 53–54, 58, 68–69; sectarian model of, 66; self-determination model of, 66; termination of, 66, 72; Wixarika and, 54, 78

Instituto Tecnológico y de Estudios Superiores de Occidente (ITESO), 18, 20, 140–41, 145–48, 166–68, 183

Jóvenes Indígenas Universitarios (JIU), 18, 149, 176, 179

Jauja, 100, 102–3

Juárez, Benito, 47–50, 59, 88, 99, 122, 132

King Nayar, 12, 90, 93–94, 117

Laclau, Ernesto, 15–16
ladinos, 115–16, 164
la cuestión indígena. See "Indian problem"
Lerdo de Tejada, Sebastián, 88–89
Lerdo Law, 46–47
Límon Rojas, Miguel, 65–66
Linnaeus, Carolus, 36
Loera, Ernesto, 78
logging, 73–74
López Obrador, Andrés Manuel, 56, 67, 171
Lozada, Manuel, 10–12, 21, 44–50, 86–90, 99, 117, 120–23. See also El Tigre de Álica

makuyeika, 16, 151, 171
mariachi, 31, 187
Marxism, 52, 63–64, 104
Maximilian I, 47, 121
Mayans, 8, 45, 115, 155, 161, 164, 172
Medina Silva, Ramón, 67, 79
mestizaje, 60–61, 64
mestizo: celebration of, 26; central role of, 8; nationalism and, 66–67; the Other and, 38; as the quintessential hybrid Mexican, 26, 52, 66–67, 142; as teacher-promotores, 68; as unifying identity, 32

Metropolitan Zone of Guadalajara (ZMG), 18, 91, 136–37

Mexica, 27–29, 32, 34–35, 38, 41, 45

Mexican Revolution, 17, 26, 31–32, 53, 57, 60, 98, 103, 133–34

Mexican West, 9, 11, 30, 86, 90, 93, 96–97, 122–23

Mexico: Africans in, 96–97; agrarian conflicts in, 87–90; agrarian reform in, 104; allocation of resources, 65; alterity and, 52, 54; art of, 56; auto-da-fé in, 94; cartography and, 100–102; citizenship of, 50, 53; classism in, 147–48; class struggle within, 52; commodification of land by, 43–50; communal landholdings of, 11, 30, 44–50, 52, 71, 105–6, 120; communities of African descent, 62; conservatives of, 44–50; constitution of, 52, 54, 60, 105, 156; demographics of, 96; diplomatic relations with France of, 130–31; economic development of, 54, 96; ejido system in, 62, 105; foreign invasions of, 42–47, 121; foreign investments in, 44–47, 99–100, 103–4; formation of Nayarit, 90; founding myth of, 27, 30–31, 41, 43–44, 56; growing independence of, 97; heterogeneity of, 14, 23, 25, 31–34, 52, 61, 66–67, 76, 96; independence from Spain of, 44, 46, 87; indigenous peoples and, 61, 66–67; indigenous peoples in, 183–87; industry regulation and, 82; internal conflict of, 42–43; land ownership in, 87, 100–102, 120; land reforms of, 54–55; land tenure system in, 87, 105–6; lasting impact of colonialism on, 54, 149; leftists and, 64–65, 104–5; liberals of, 44–50, 99–101; local support by, 76; as Machiavellian, 54; management of indigenous peoples by, 44; mestizos and, 52, 142; models of

governance of, 71, 100; modernity and, 54, 57, 187; modernization of, 102–8; national identity of, 52–53, 58, 60–61, 114, 183–87; nationalism and, 29, 54, 62–63; nation building by, 185; nongovernmental organizations (NGOs) and, 76; as a pluricultural nation, 14, 156, 183–87; political economy of, 44–47; poverty in, 87; power inequities within, 20; primary schools in, 33; racial ambivalence in, 115–16, 141, 164, 181; racial formation of, 11; racial geography of, 5, 30; racial privilege in, 115; racial stereotypes and, 11, 14, 27–28, 73, 76, 138–142; racism in, 19, 60, 83–84, 147–48; raw materials of, 129–130; redistribution of land in, 87–90, 104–5; social hierarchies in, 33–34; use of cartography by, 45; violence against indigenous peoples by, 44; Wixarika and, 76, 183–87; workers rights and, 82
Meyer, Jean, 47, 49, 90
Mier, Teresa de, 41–43
mining, 9, 94–95, 98–100, 102, 127, 129, 145
Ministry of Public Education (SEP), 17, 31, 56, 83
miscegenation, 30, 34–36, 50, 52, 60–61, 117–19
Mixtecs, 137, 143
Mixtón War, 89, 93, 126. *See also* Caxcan Rebellion
Moctezuma, 30, 39
Mouffe, Chantal, 15–16
Movimiento Regeneración Nacional (MORENA), 171
multiculturalism, 31–32, 66, 115, 151, 183–87
muralist movement, 24, 56, 60
Muriá, José María, 118, 126
Museo de Artes Populares, 78–79
myth, 24, 26, 30–31

Náayeri, 13, 68, 72–73, 77–78, 85, 94
NAFTA, 136
Nahuas, 137, 139–140, 176
Nayarit, 90, 93, 100–101, 105, 107, 161, 187. *See also* Tepic, Nayarit
Nelson, Diane, 160, 164
neoindigenismo, 15
neoliberalism, 9, 14, 54, 65, 115
New School for Social Research, 184–85

Orellana, Margarita de, 33–34
Orientalism, 24–25
Orozco y Berra, Manuel, 41–43, 45
Other, 24–25, 33, 38, 114, 141, 151
Otomís, 137–38, 149
Our Elder Brother Wind Neighbor, 81
Our Mother Ocean, 81, 102

Pacheco, Gabriel, 83, 111
Pan-American Games, 144–45
Partido Acción Nacional (PAN), 54, 139, 161
Partido Popular Socialista (PPS), 104–5
Partido Revolucionario Institucional (PRI), 54, 104–5, 107, 161
paternalism, 47, 61, 73, 140–41
Pearl of the West, 119, 128–133. *See also* Guadalajara, Jalisco
pedagogies of crossing, 147–48
peyote, 22–23, 67, 160
Philip Morris International, 82, 105–6
Plan Huicot, 65, 72–74, 171
Plan Libertador, 89, 120–21
Plaza de las Artesanías, 111
pluriculturalism, 31, 156–57
Polanyi, Karl, 46–47
populism, 104, 134
poverty, 14, 66, 87, 142
Povinelli, Elizabeth, 14–15, 32, 155
Pred, Allan, 7, 23, 36, 49, 141–42, 186
psychedelic movement, 67, 79
Puerto Vallarta, 108, 110, 159
Purhépecha, 124, 137, 143

racial stereotypes: of Africans, 29, 35; casta paintings and, 24; in Guadalajara, Jalisco, 138–140; of indigenous peoples, 138–140,

161–62, 181–82; material consequences of, 23; in popular culture, 24; of Wixarika, 7, 158, 161–62, 181–82
racism, 19, 60, 79, 115, 138–142, 147–48. *See also* discrimination
Reform Laws of 1857, 11, 42, 49, 100, 133
regions of refuge, 52, 54, 62–64
representations, 32–35, 39, 63
Ríos Martínez, Juan, 3–4

Sahagún, Bernardino de, 39–41
Said, Edward, 24–25, 38
Saldaña-Portillo, María Josefina, 6–7, 23, 30, 40
Salinas de Gortari, Carlos, 66, 105, 137
San Blas (port), 11, 48, 81, 95–97, 102, 117, 129–130
Santiago Mexquititlán, 137, 142–43
Seven Cities of Cíbola and Quivira, 126–27
Shaman Chocolates, 150–51, 161
social media, 156–57
Solidarity University (US), 140–41, 145–49, 174–76
space: activism and, 171–180; for critical discussions, 147, 175–76, 179–180; division of, 112; as exclusionary, 148–49; identity and, 15; importance of, 20; as inclusive, 147; indigeneity and, 21; indigenous peoples and, 32; nativization of, 112; power structures and, 149; race and, 7–8, 30; as respectful, 146; reterritorialization of, 172; as safe, 146; social production of, 13
Spanish colonialism: of California, 95; conversions and, 39, 91, 95; decline of, 97; disease and, 93; in Guadalajara, Jalisco, 123–26; hunger and, 93; miscegenation and, 52; resistance to, 10–12, 29, 35–36, 42, 91, 93, 125–26; Tonallán and, 91; violence during, 33, 39–40, 42, 92–93, 123–26; Wixarika and, 77–78
Speed, Shannon, 9, 182
Starn, Orin, 26, 188–89
sugar production, 103, 108

Tabamex, 105–6
Talavera Durón, Francisco, 81–82
Tamatsi Eakatéiwari, 81
Tapatío coloniality, 12, 119
Tatéi Haramara, 81, 102
Tenochtitlán, 27, 30–31, 39
Tepehuan, 72–73
Tepic, Nayarit: Africans in, 85; agribusinesses in, 105–6, 108, 110; Aguamilpa hydroelectric dam and, 75; autonomy of, 129; colonialism in, 6, 87; colonization of California and, 95; communal landholdings of, 105–6; contraband market of, 87, 98–100; cultural identity of, 12, 86; culture of, 114; decline of, 100, 102, 129; demographics of, 12–13, 85–86, 100, 107–8; description of, 12–13, 91–92; drug trafficking and, 106; economic development of, 87, 95, 97, 100, 114, 128–29; ejido system in, 105–6; employment in, 107; encroachment on indigenous lands in, 94; exclusion from, 114; expansion of, 106; founding of, 92; geography of, 86; growth of, 105–6; Guadalajara, Jalisco and, 10, 122; heterogeneity of, 85–86; historical development of, 6, 10–11; historic buildings of, 106–8, 110; identity of, 106; inclusion in, 114; indigenous peoples and, 12–13, 18, 85–86; international chain stores in, 107–8; invasion of, 47–48; land tenure system in, 103–6; as lawless, 87; livestock and, 97; location of, 10; Manuel Lozado and, 12, 47–48, 86–90; mining in, 94–95, 98–100; natural resources of, 103, 107; political development of, 11, 128–29; political economy of, 6; political parties of, 104–5; politics of, 114; presidios in, 94; racial discrimination and, 13; racial formation of, 11; racial stereotypes and, 86; railroad and, 102–3; redistribution of land in, 104–5; research on, 6, 86; resistance to Spanish colonialism of, 12; resorts in, 108; rural populations of, 107;

social development of, 6; spacial production of, 13; suburbanization of, 105, 108–14; sugar production and, 103, 108; textile industry of, 100, 102–3; tobacco plantations and, 97; tomato farms of, 105–6; tourism and, 85–86, 108–14; trade and, 96–98; urban revitalization of, 106; Wixarika in, 85, 110–11, 151, 189–190
textile industry, 100, 103
"The Interpellation of Differences: In Search of Intercultural Dialogue," 140–41, 146–47
tobacco plantations, 81–83, 97
Torres Contreras, José de Jesús, 77–78
tourism, 19–20, 24, 57, 67, 73–74, 102, 108–14, 145
Tuapurie, 70, 74

Unión de Comunidades Indígenas Huicholes de Jalisco, 71–72
Unión de Jóvenes Estudiantes Wixaritari (UJEW), 166–67
Unión de Profesionistas Indígenas de Nayarit (UPIN), 177–78
Union of Indigenous Professionals of Nayarit, 22–23
Union of Indigenous Professionals of Nayarit (UPIN), 177–78
Union of Young Wixarika Students (UJEW), 166–67
Universidad Solidaria (US), 145–48, 174–76

Vallarta, Ignacio, 47–48, 120, 122, 132
Vasconcelos, José, 60–61
Villoro, Luis, 8, 25, 28–29, 37–40

Warman, Arturo, 61, 64
Western Institute of Technology and Higher Education (ITESO), 18, 20, 140–41, 145–48
Wixarika: academic studies of, 14, 19; activism of, 16, 18, 152, 170–181; aesthetics of, 19, 57, 67, 78; agriculture and, 57, 70; agrochemicals and, 70; Aguamilpa hydroelectric dam and, 75–76; ancestral location of, 72–73; as artesanía, 78–81; arts and crafts of, 19, 70, 78–81, 85, 107, 111–12, 143–45; authenticity of, 14–15, 32, 113, 154–59; autonomy of, 69, 72, 77–78; career choices of, 18; citizenship and, 76; colonialism and, 77–78; Colonia Zitakua and, 108–14; commodification of, 13, 70, 79, 110, 114, 144–45, 152, 160–61; communal landholdings of, 13, 19–20, 70–71, 74; communication with, 178; conflict and, 71; as constitutionally protected, 23; contemporary representations of, 7; conversions of, 39; corruption and, 71; cultural fluidity of, 151–52; cultural identity of, 7, 20; cultural revival of, 72; culture of, 78–80, 110; customs of, 57; destruction of sacred places of, 13; development of, 73; discrimination against, 7–8, 18, 79, 143–44, 152–53, 155, 169–170, 187; dispossession of, 145, 160; distrust of, 19–20; as domestic laborers, 81; drug trafficking and, 71; economic development of, 68; education and, 16–19, 68–69, 78, 83–84; employment of, 112; exclusion of, 13–14; as exclusively rural, 19; exploitation of, 67, 70, 80, 110, 112–13; fetish effect and, 160–61; folk art and, 78–81; folklorization of, 13; global economy and, 73; in Guadalajara, Jalisco, 54, 112, 151, 189–190; health of, 68, 70, 73, 82; heterogeneity of, 5; in higher education, 17–18, 32, 70, 83–84, 116–17, 140–41, 145–48, 151–52, 161, 166–172; higher-yielding seeds and, 70; humiliation of, 23; hypervisibility of, 32, 67, 111, 182; iconography of, 110, 144–45, 161; identity and, 188–89; imposition of images on, 23; inclusion of, 188–89; Instituto Nacional Indigenista (INI) and, 54; internal cultural differences of, 114; as *jornaleros*, 81–83; justice system of, 178; ladinos and, 115–16, 164; land

reclamations and, 70–71; land use by, 74; languages of, 4–5, 9, 69, 86, 113, 187; leadership of, 70–72; logging and, 71; marginalization of, 57, 80; as mestizo, 155; in Mexico, 76, 183–87; migration to cities by, 9, 20, 54, 78, 83, 143–44; mining and, 145, 179–180; mobility of, 76–78, 171–72; models of governance of, 71; modernity and, 68; music of, 156–57; natural resources of, 74, 145; nongovernmental organizations (NGOs) and, 76; performance and, 113, 161–62; pesticides and, 82; pilgrimages of, 9, 72, 77, 81–82, 102; political mobilization of, 161, 180–81; political organization of, 20; positive discrimination and, 116–17; pride in, 159–160; in primary school, 17, 69; as professionals, 16, 18, 32, 70, 83–84, 116–17, 151–52, 154, 161, 171–72; protests by, 102; psychedelic movement and, 67; racial stereotypes and, 161–62, 181–82; racial stereotypes of, 7–8, 14, 22–23, 112–13, 158, 178; racism and, 79, 115; radio and, 178; representations of, 151–52, 157; research on, 67; resistance to Spanish colonialism of, 10; sacred spaces of, 19, 78, 102, 145, 152, 179–180; as seasonal migratory workers, 81–83, 105–6; secondary school and, 17, 69, 152–53; social media and, 157–58; as street vendors, 107, 111–12, 143–45, 179; structural inequities faced by, 18; on television, 157–58; in Tepic, Nayarit, 54, 85, 151, 189–190; textiles of, 78; tobacco plantations and, 81–83; tourism and, 19–20, 57, 67, 102, 111–12, 145; traditional attire of, 13–14, 32, 57, 73, 86, 113, 116–17, 153, 157, 159–160, 169–170, 172; in urban geographies, 6–7; urban youth of, 7; as used in advertisements, 10, 13, 24, 114, 150–51, 161; as vendors, 81; as wage laborers, 144; working conditions of, 82; worldview of, 69. *See also* Colonia Zitakua; El Roble; Naranjito de Copal

Wixarika Research Center, 20–21

Wixaritari, Artistas y Artesanos Unidos en la Zona Metropolitana de Guadalajara (WAAU), 143–45, 148–49, 174–76, 179

Yañez, Agustín, 78–79

yarn painting, 78–80, 108

Young Indigenous University Students in the ZMG (JIU), 18, 149, 176, 179

Zapotecs, 45, 106, 120

Zapatista movement, 9, 66, 69, 72, 163–64, 185

Zapopan, 11, 89–90, 121

ABOUT THE AUTHOR

Diana Negrín is a native of Guadalajara, Jalisco, and the San Francisco Bay Area. Negrín received her doctorate from the Department of Geography at the University of California, Berkeley, and serves as the president of the board of directors for the Wixárika Research Center. She is currently a professor in Urban and Public Affairs and Migration Studies at the University of San Francisco.